ANIMOSITY: EV()LUTION ™

VOLUME

2

LEX MACHINA

MARGUERITE BENNETT

ERIC GAPSTUR

ROB SCHWAGER

MARSHALL DILLON

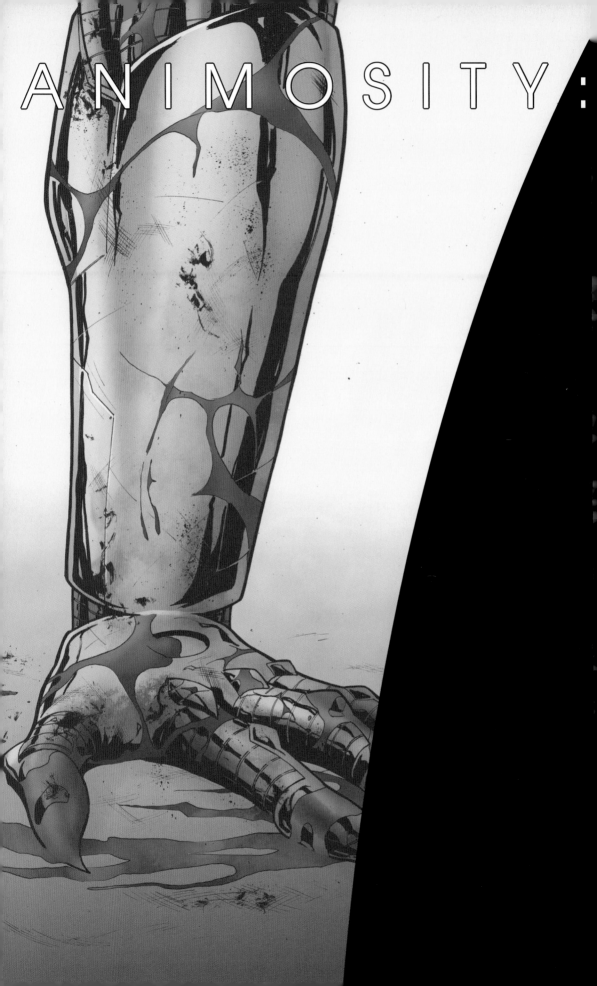

A N I M O S I T Y :

EVOLUTION

VOLUME 2

LEX MACHINA

MARGUERITE BENNETT creator & writer

ERIC GAPSTUR artist

ROB SCHWAGER colorist

MARSHALL DILLON letterer

ERIC GAPSTUR w/ GUY MAJOR front & original covers

JOHN J. HILL logo design

COREY BREEN book designer

MIKE MARTS editor

AFTERSHOCK™

MIKE MARTS - Editor-in-Chief • JOE PRUETT - Publisher/CCO • LEE KRAMER - President • JON KRAMER - Chief Executive Officer
STEVE ROTTERDAM - SVP, Sales & Marketing • LISA Y. WU - Retailer/Fan Relations Manager • CHRISTINA HARRINGTON - Managing Editor
BLAKE STOCKER - Chief Financial Officer • AARON MARION - Publicist • LISA MOODY - Finance • CHARLES PRITCHETT - Comics Production
COREY BREEN - Collections Production • TEDDY LEO - Editorial Assistant • STEPHANIE CASEBIER & SARAH PRUETT - Publishing Assistants

AfterShock Logo Design by COMICRAFT
Publicity: contact AARON MARION (aaron@publichausagency.com) & RYAN CROY (ryan@publichausagency.com) at PUBLICHAUS
Special thanks to: IRA KURGAN, MARINE KSADZHIKYAN, ANTONIA LIANOS, STEPHAN NILSON & JULIE PIFHER

ANIMOSITY: EVOLUTION VOL.2: LEX MACHINA Published by AfterShock Comics, LLC, 15300 Ventura Boulevard Suite 507, Sherman Oaks, CA 91403. Originally published as Animosity: Evolution #6-10. PRINTED IN KOREA.
First Printing: February 2019. 10 9 8 7 6 5 4 3 2 1

AFTERSHOCKCOMICS.COM Follow us on social media

I N T R O D U C T I O N

There's a phrase I love and I can't for the life of me find its true origin.

The phrase itself is "the cross is in the cradle."

I first heard it as a little girl, when one of my grandfathers mentioned it in terms of planting a vegetable garden. Certain small crops would need to be rotated according to the needs of the soil—rotten tomatoes used for fertilizer, beans to replenish the nitrogen—and so the deaths of the plants were planned before the first seed was set.

"The cross is in the cradle," he remarked, squatting over the vegetable patch.

What he meant was, "Before you begin, you need to know how and where and why it ends."

I took an art history class some years later, and the teacher was commenting on the medieval depictions of the child Christ—in this period, the infant Jesus often has the proportions of a full-grown man, simply shrunk down, instead of the large head, large eyes and short chubby limbs of a baby.

"The cross is in the cradle," the professor told us. "The purpose of his birth was for him to one day die, and so he isn't depicted as cute or innocent, but with an adult understanding and adult lineaments."

What she meant was, "The end is innate in the beginning."

A few months ago, I was in a room of people I admire, people trying to bring the world and work of ANIMOSITY to a vaster audience than I could ever imagine. They asked how it ended, gently, telling me I had the right to keep it to myself—a kindness for which I will always be grateful.

"The cross is in the cradle," I said.

And I told them.

All things end, the good and the bad.

But I'm glad you're here with us at the end of one story, and the beginning of another. The cross is in the cradle. All you have is your time, and what you choose to do with it.

Thank you for choosing to spend it, for a little while, with EVOLUTION, and with us.

MARGUERITE BENNETT
Los Angeles
January 17, 2019

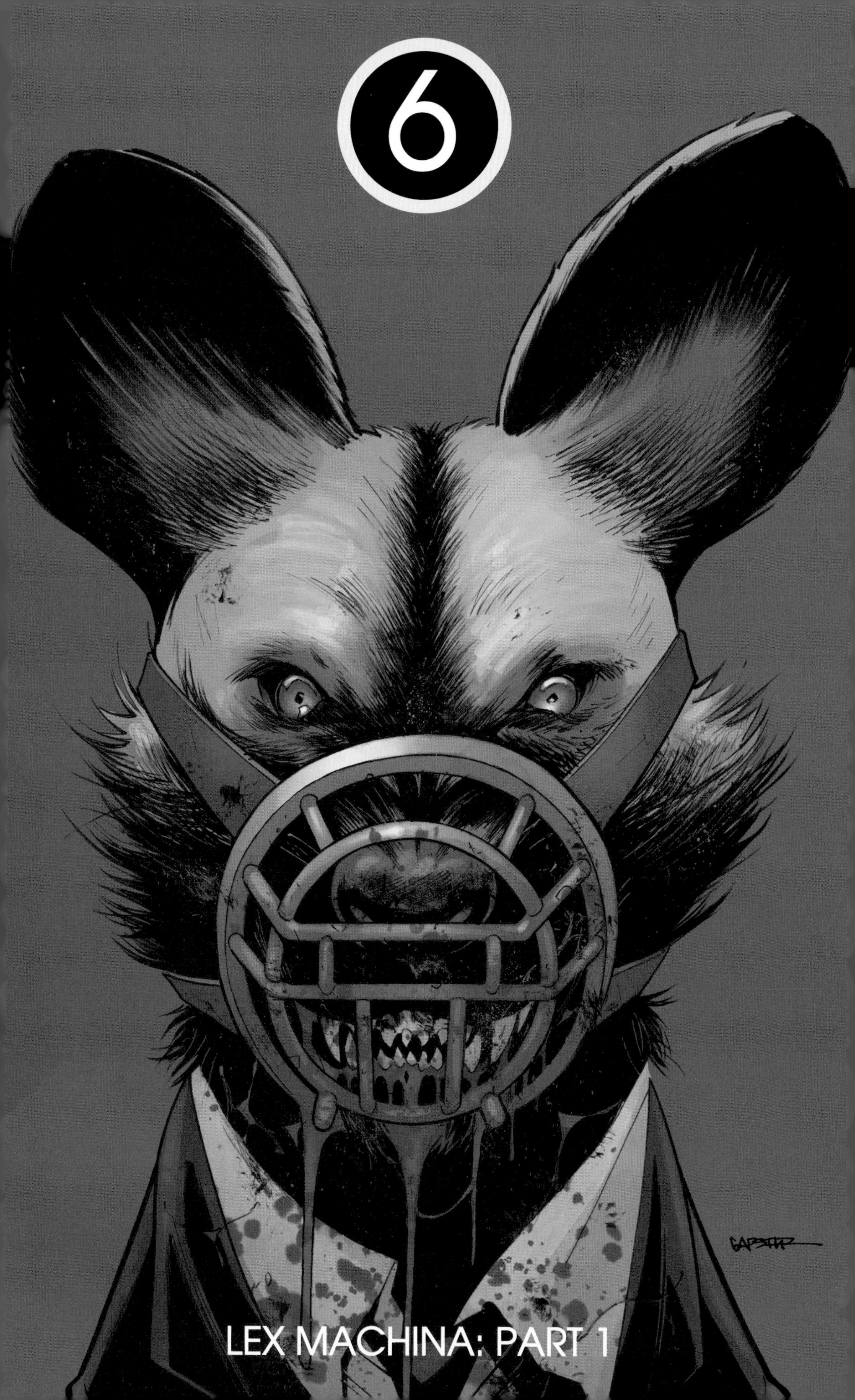
6
LEX MACHINA: PART 1

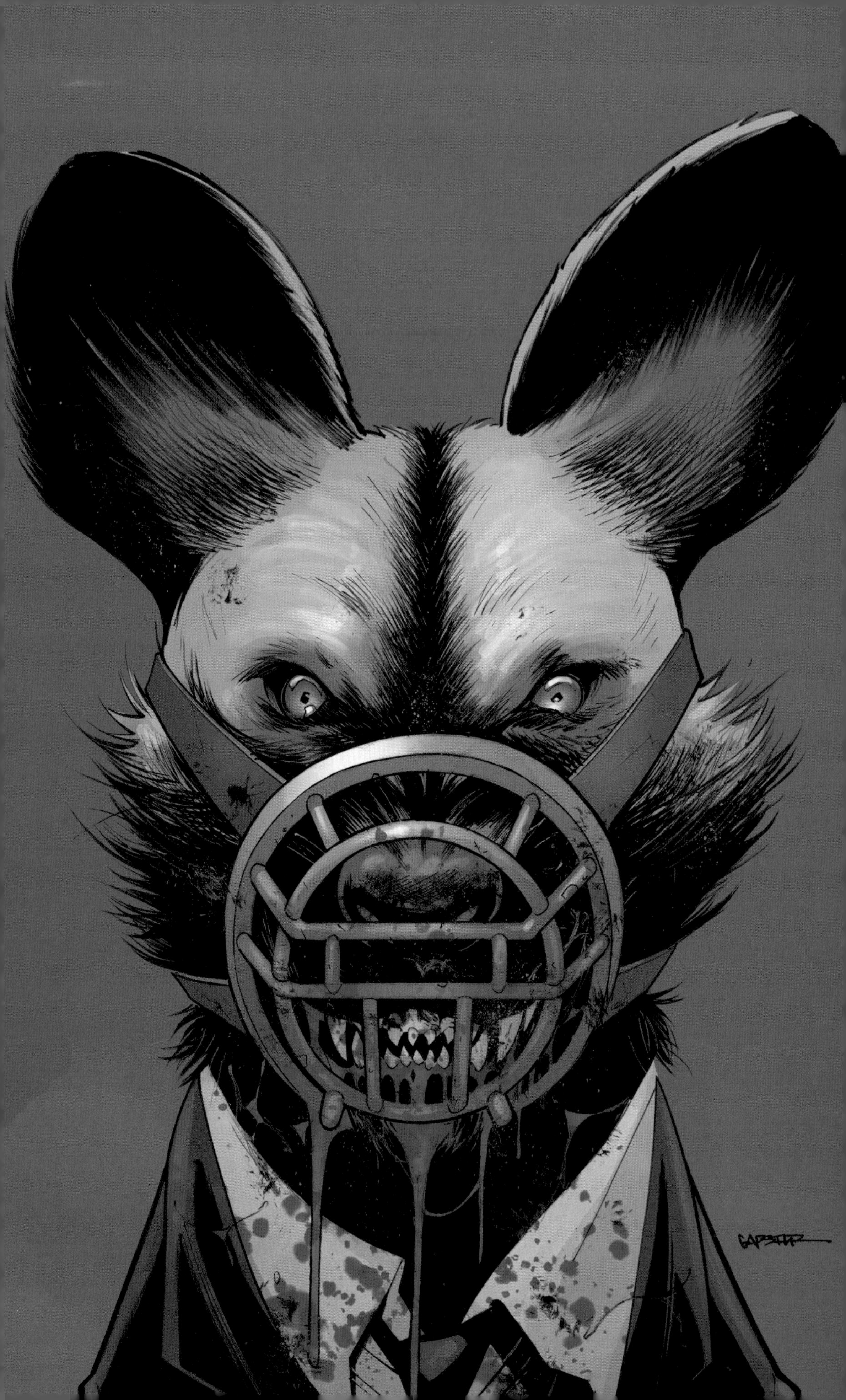

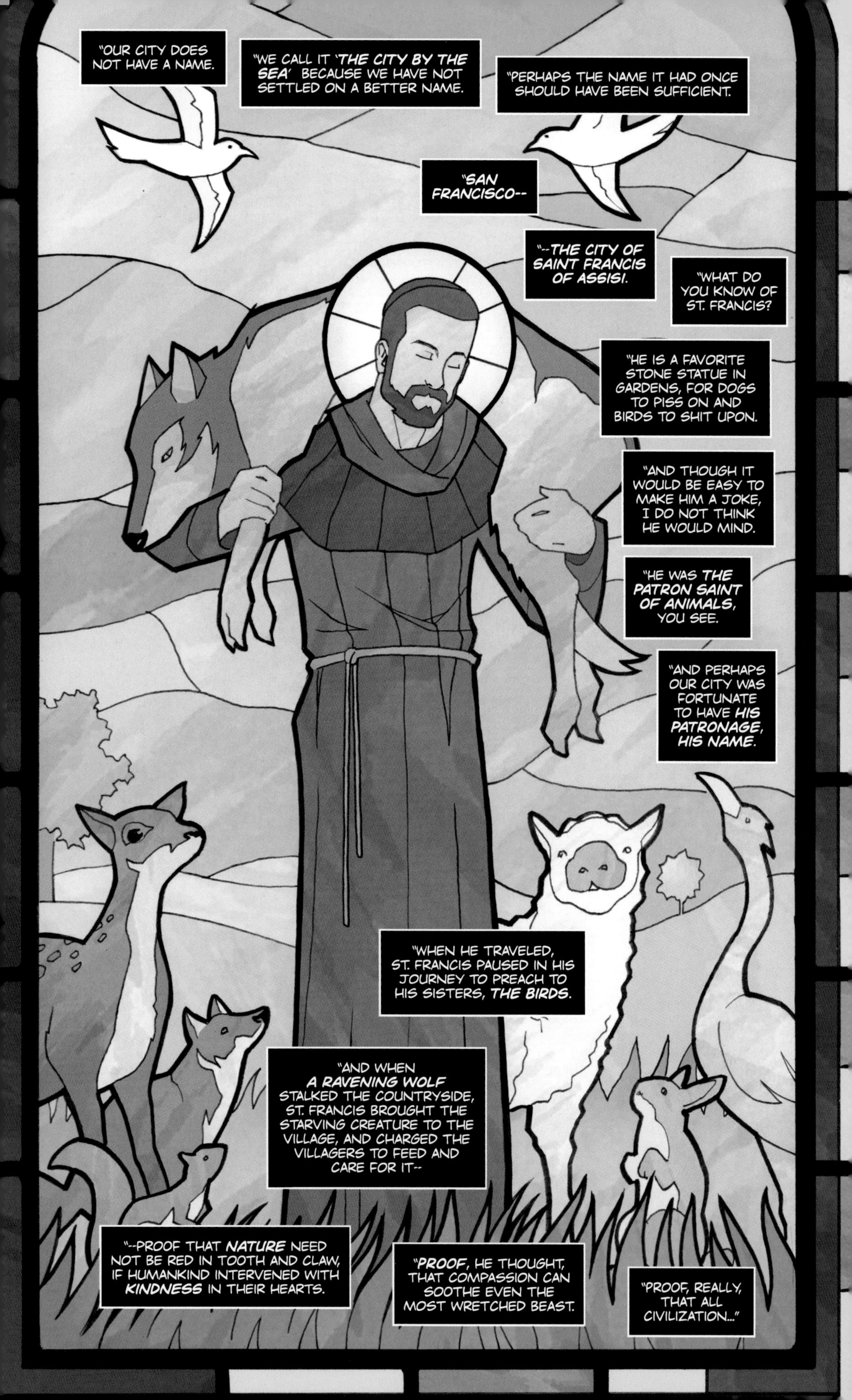
"OUR CITY DOES NOT HAVE A NAME.
"WE CALL IT '*THE CITY BY THE SEA*' BECAUSE WE HAVE NOT SETTLED ON A BETTER NAME.
"PERHAPS THE NAME IT HAD ONCE SHOULD HAVE BEEN SUFFICIENT.
"*SAN FRANCISCO*--
"--*THE CITY OF SAINT FRANCIS OF ASSISI*.
"WHAT DO YOU KNOW OF ST. FRANCIS?
"HE IS A FAVORITE STONE STATUE IN GARDENS, FOR DOGS TO PISS ON AND BIRDS TO SHIT UPON.
"AND THOUGH IT WOULD BE EASY TO MAKE HIM A JOKE, I DO NOT THINK HE WOULD MIND.
"HE WAS *THE PATRON SAINT OF ANIMALS*, YOU SEE.
"AND PERHAPS OUR CITY WAS FORTUNATE TO HAVE *HIS PATRONAGE, HIS NAME*.
"WHEN HE TRAVELED, ST. FRANCIS PAUSED IN HIS JOURNEY TO PREACH TO HIS SISTERS, *THE BIRDS*.
"AND WHEN *A RAVENING WOLF* STALKED THE COUNTRYSIDE, ST. FRANCIS BROUGHT THE STARVING CREATURE TO THE VILLAGE, AND CHARGED THE VILLAGERS TO FEED AND CARE FOR IT--
"--PROOF THAT *NATURE* NEED NOT BE RED IN TOOTH AND CLAW, IF HUMANKIND INTERVENED WITH *KINDNESS* IN THEIR HEARTS.
"*PROOF*, HE THOUGHT, THAT COMPASSION CAN SOOTHE EVEN THE MOST WRETCHED BEAST.
"PROOF, REALLY, THAT ALL CIVILIZATION..."

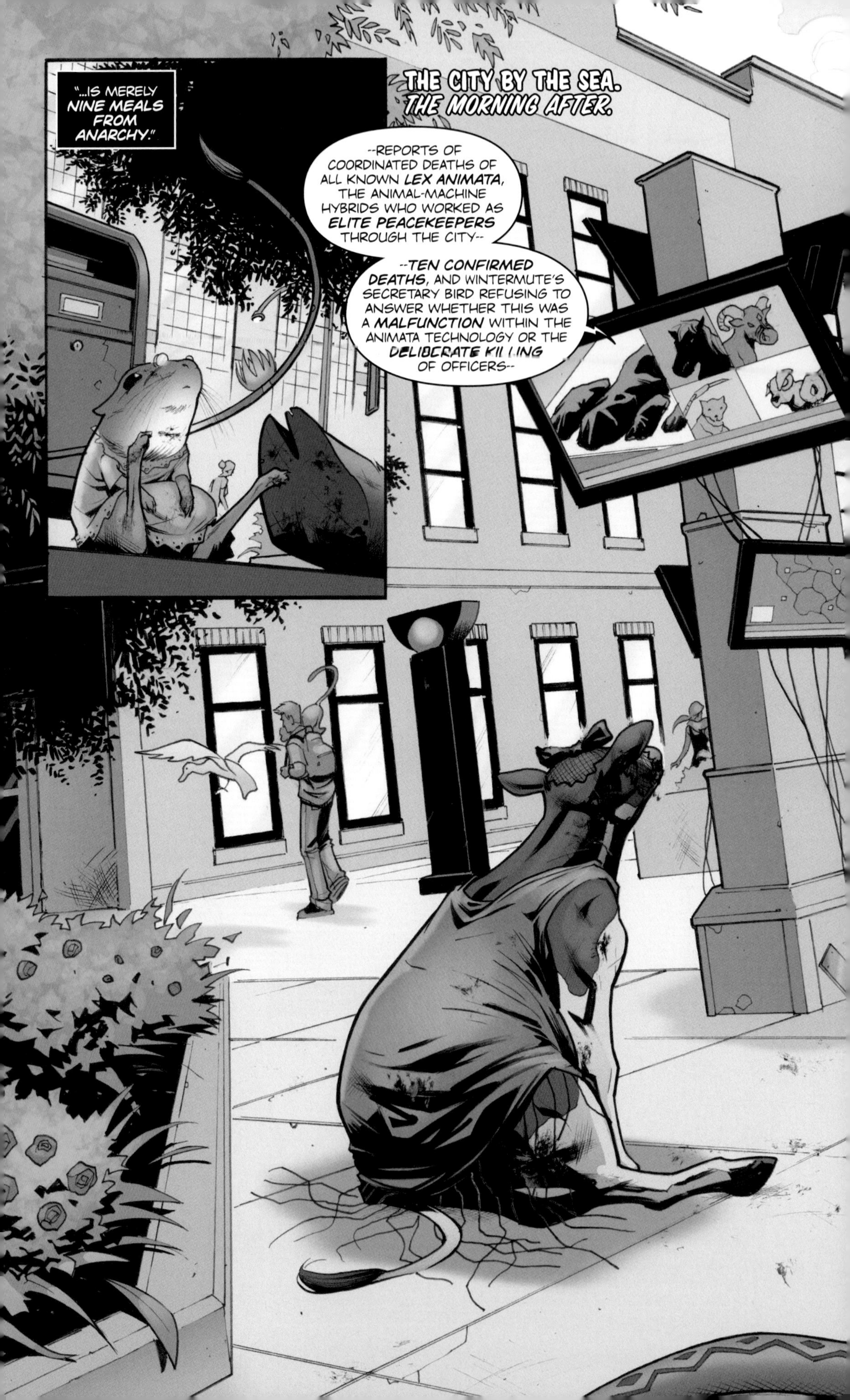
"...IS MERELY NINE MEALS FROM ANARCHY."
THE CITY BY THE SEA. THE MORNING AFTER.
--REPORTS OF COORDINATED DEATHS OF ALL KNOWN LEX ANIMATA, THE ANIMAL-MACHINE HYBRIDS WHO WORKED AS ELITE PEACEKEEPERS THROUGH THE CITY--
--TEN CONFIRMED DEATHS, AND WINTERMUTE'S SECRETARY BIRD REFUSING TO ANSWER WHETHER THIS WAS A MALFUNCTION WITHIN THE ANIMATA TECHNOLOGY OR THE DELIBERATE KILLING OF OFFICERS--

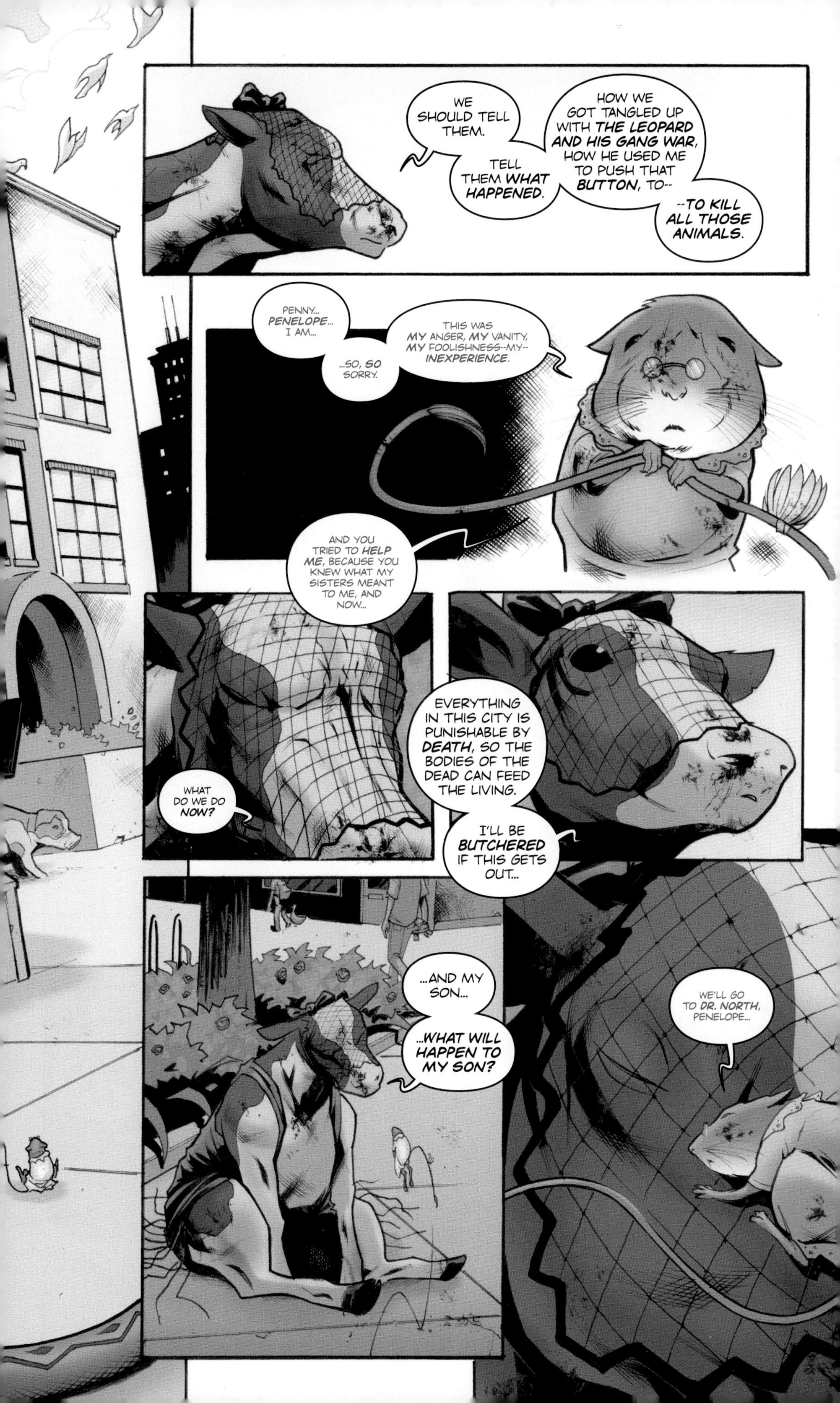
WE SHOULD TELL THEM.
TELL THEM WHAT HAPPENED.
HOW WE GOT TANGLED UP WITH THE LEOPARD AND HIS GANG WAR, HOW HE USED ME TO PUSH THAT BUTTON, TO--
--TO KILL ALL THOSE ANIMALS.
PENNY... PENELOPE... I AM...
...SO, SO SORRY.
THIS WAS MY ANGER, MY VANITY, MY FOOLISHNESS--MY--INEXPERIENCE.
AND YOU TRIED TO HELP ME, BECAUSE YOU KNEW WHAT MY SISTERS MEANT TO ME, AND NOW...
WHAT DO WE DO NOW?
EVERYTHING IN THIS CITY IS PUNISHABLE BY DEATH, SO THE BODIES OF THE DEAD CAN FEED THE LIVING.
I'LL BE BUTCHERED IF THIS GETS OUT...
...AND MY SON...
...WHAT WILL HAPPEN TO MY SON?
WE'LL GO TO DR. NORTH, PENELOPE...

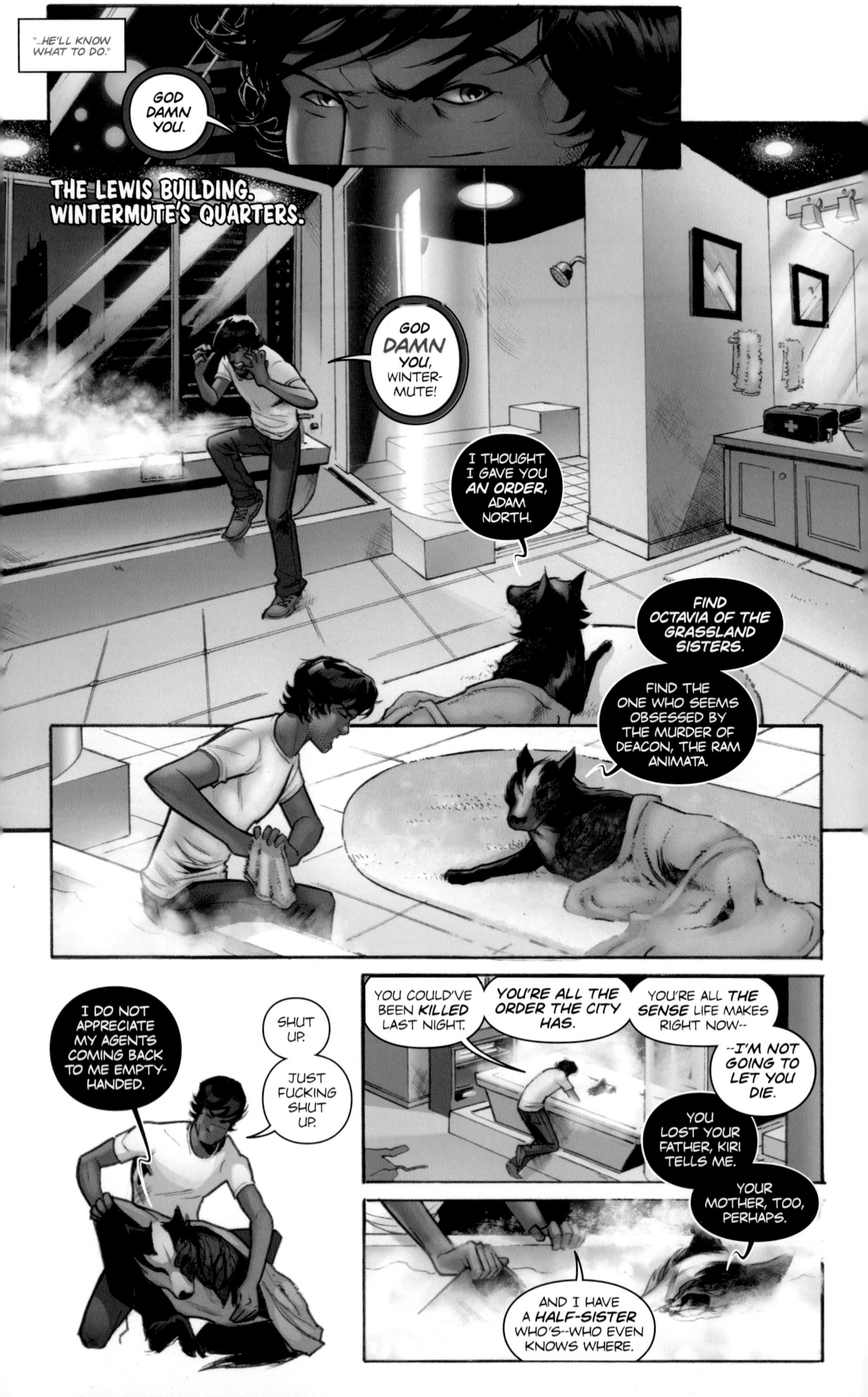
"...HE'LL KNOW WHAT TO DO."
GOD DAMN YOU.
THE LEWIS BUILDING. WINTERMUTE'S QUARTERS.
GOD DAMN YOU, WINTER-MUTE!
I THOUGHT I GAVE YOU AN ORDER, ADAM NORTH.
FIND OCTAVIA OF THE GRASSLAND SISTERS.
FIND THE ONE WHO SEEMS OBSESSED BY THE MURDER OF DEACON, THE RAM ANIMATA.
I DO NOT APPRECIATE MY AGENTS COMING BACK TO ME EMPTY-HANDED.
SHUT UP.
JUST FUCKING SHUT UP.
YOU COULD'VE BEEN KILLED LAST NIGHT.
YOU'RE ALL THE ORDER THE CITY HAS.
YOU'RE ALL THE SENSE LIFE MAKES RIGHT NOW--
--I'M NOT GOING TO LET YOU DIE.
YOU LOST YOUR FATHER, KIRI TELLS ME.
YOUR MOTHER, TOO, PERHAPS.
AND I HAVE A HALF-SISTER WHO'S--WHO EVEN KNOWS WHERE.

AND BY CARING FOR ME, YOU MAKE UP FOR THEIR DEATHS?

MAINTAIN A LITTLE ORDER IN YOUR LIFE?

IF YOU WERE A MAN, I'D HIT YOU.

NO, YOU WOULDN'T. YOU DETEST VIOLENCE IN ALL FORMS.

AT YOUR VETERINARY CLINIC, YOU PROPOSED THE SLOGAN *"BECAUSE YOUR PETS CAN'T TELL US WHERE IT HURTS."*

YOU *HATE* UNNECESSARY PAIN.

WE HAVE THAT IN COMMON.

THE PROSTHETIC SURGED, HERE ON YOUR SHOULDER. THE FLESH IS CHARRED AND NEEDS TO BE REMOVED.

"DEBRIDEMENT," IT'S CALLED--

GO ON.

I DON'T NEED ANESTHESIA.

I CAN'T FEEL IT ANYMORE.

AND IT IS EASIER TO TRY AND PREVENT THIS CITY FROM *EATING ITSELF ALIVE* WHEN I AM NOT DRIVEN MAD BY PAIN.

I COULD BE KILLED ANY MOMENT, AS WE HAVE SEEN.

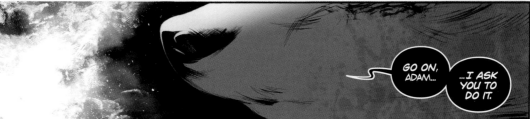

GO ON, ADAM...

...I ASK YOU TO DO IT.

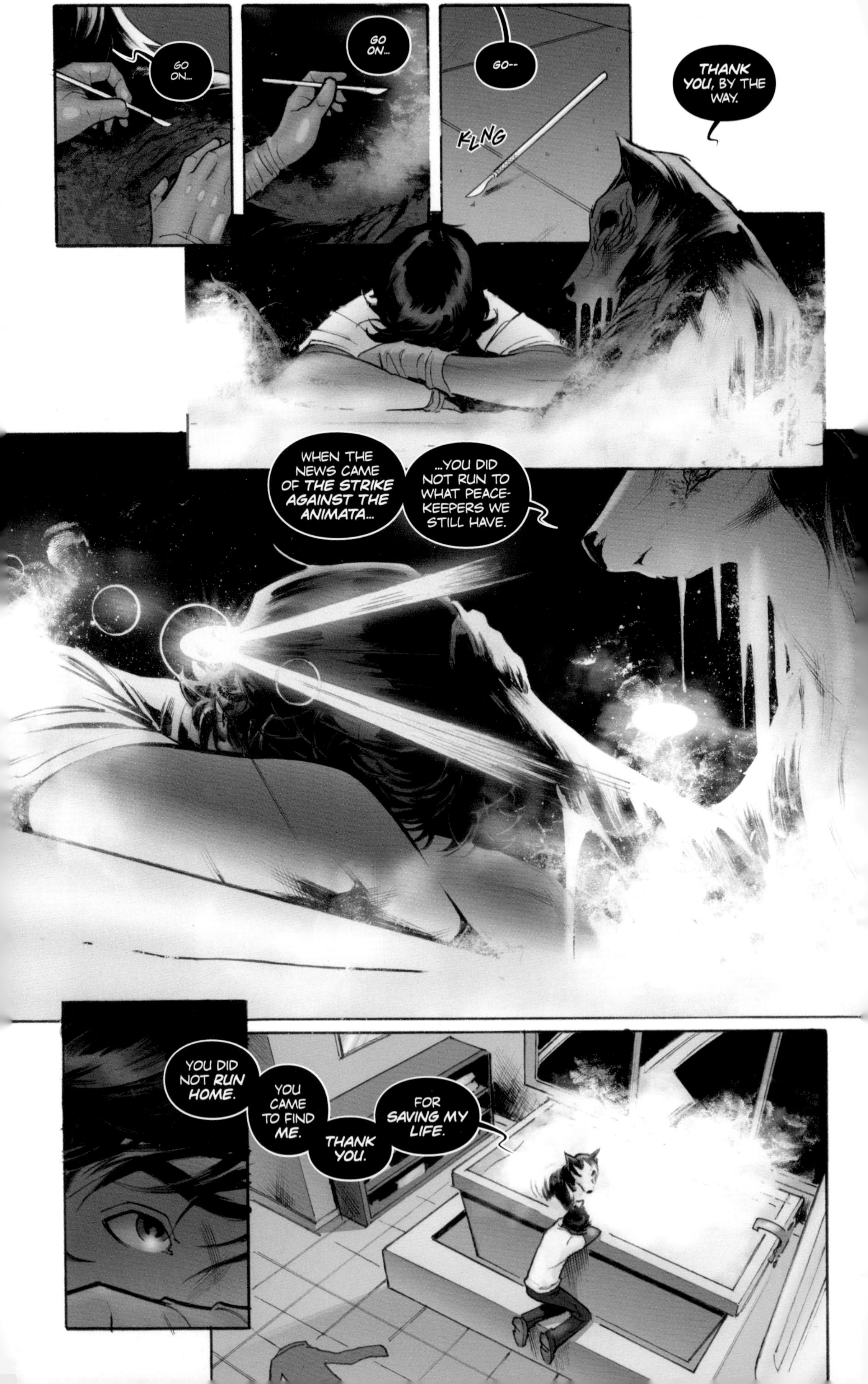
GO ON...
GO ON...
GO--
KLNG
THANK YOU, BY THE WAY.
WHEN THE NEWS CAME OF THE STRIKE AGAINST THE ANIMATA...
...YOU DID NOT RUN TO WHAT PEACE-KEEPERS WE STILL HAVE.
YOU DID NOT RUN HOME.
YOU CAME TO FIND ME.
THANK YOU.
FOR SAVING MY LIFE.

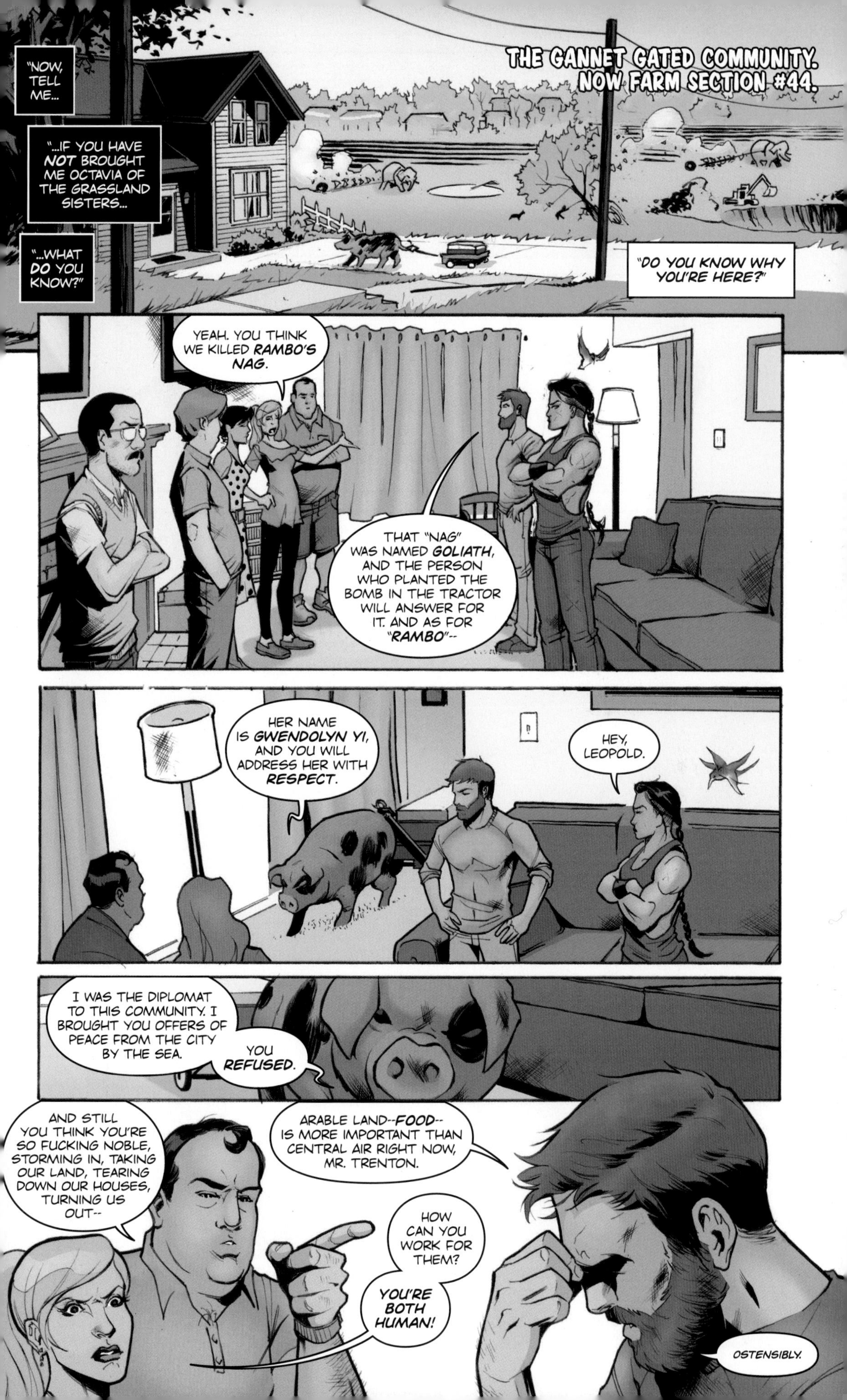

"NOW, TELL ME...
THE GANNET GATED COMMUNITY. NOW FARM SECTION #44.
"...IF YOU HAVE NOT BROUGHT ME OCTAVIA OF THE GRASSLAND SISTERS...
"...WHAT DO YOU KNOW?"
"DO YOU KNOW WHY YOU'RE HERE?"
YEAH. YOU THINK WE KILLED RAMBO'S NAG.
THAT "NAG" WAS NAMED GOLIATH, AND THE PERSON WHO PLANTED THE BOMB IN THE TRACTOR WILL ANSWER FOR IT. AND AS FOR "RAMBO"--
HER NAME IS GWENDOLYN YI, AND YOU WILL ADDRESS HER WITH RESPECT.
HEY, LEOPOLD.
I WAS THE DIPLOMAT TO THIS COMMUNITY. I BROUGHT YOU OFFERS OF PEACE FROM THE CITY BY THE SEA.
YOU REFUSED.
AND STILL YOU THINK YOU'RE SO FUCKING NOBLE, STORMING IN, TAKING OUR LAND, TEARING DOWN OUR HOUSES, TURNING US OUT--
ARABLE LAND--FOOD--IS MORE IMPORTANT THAN CENTRAL AIR RIGHT NOW, MR. TRENTON.
HOW CAN YOU WORK FOR THEM?
YOU'RE BOTH HUMAN!
OSTENSIBLY.

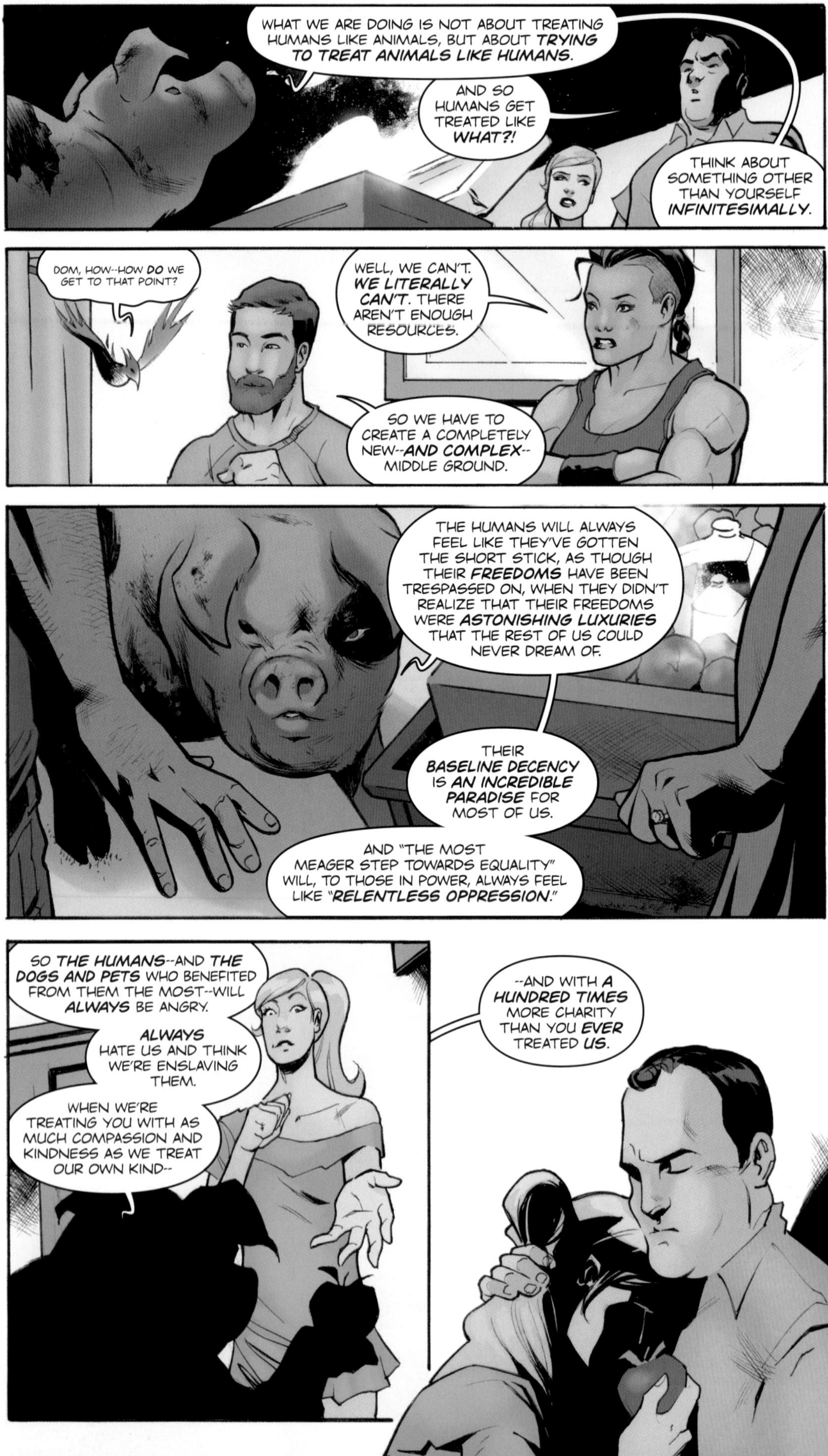
WHAT WE ARE DOING IS NOT ABOUT TREATING HUMANS LIKE ANIMALS, BUT ABOUT **TRYING TO TREAT ANIMALS LIKE HUMANS**.
AND SO HUMANS GET TREATED LIKE **WHAT?!**
THINK ABOUT SOMETHING OTHER THAN YOURSELF **INFINITESIMALLY**.
DOM, HOW--HOW **DO** WE GET TO THAT POINT?
WELL, WE CAN'T. **WE LITERALLY CAN'T**. THERE AREN'T ENOUGH RESOURCES.
SO WE HAVE TO CREATE A COMPLETELY NEW--**AND COMPLEX**-- MIDDLE GROUND.
THE HUMANS WILL ALWAYS FEEL LIKE THEY'VE GOTTEN THE SHORT STICK, AS THOUGH THEIR **FREEDOMS** HAVE BEEN TRESPASSED ON, WHEN THEY DIDN'T REALIZE THAT THEIR FREEDOMS WERE **ASTONISHING LUXURIES** THAT THE REST OF US COULD NEVER DREAM OF.
THEIR **BASELINE DECENCY** IS **AN INCREDIBLE PARADISE** FOR MOST OF US.
AND "THE MOST MEAGER STEP TOWARDS EQUALITY" WILL, TO THOSE IN POWER, ALWAYS FEEL LIKE "**RELENTLESS OPPRESSION**."
SO **THE HUMANS**--AND **THE DOGS AND PETS** WHO BENEFITED FROM THEM THE MOST--WILL **ALWAYS** BE ANGRY.
ALWAYS HATE US AND THINK WE'RE ENSLAVING THEM.
WHEN WE'RE TREATING YOU WITH AS MUCH COMPASSION AND KINDNESS AS WE TREAT OUR OWN KIND--
--AND WITH **A HUNDRED TIMES** MORE CHARITY THAN YOU **EVER** TREATED **US**.

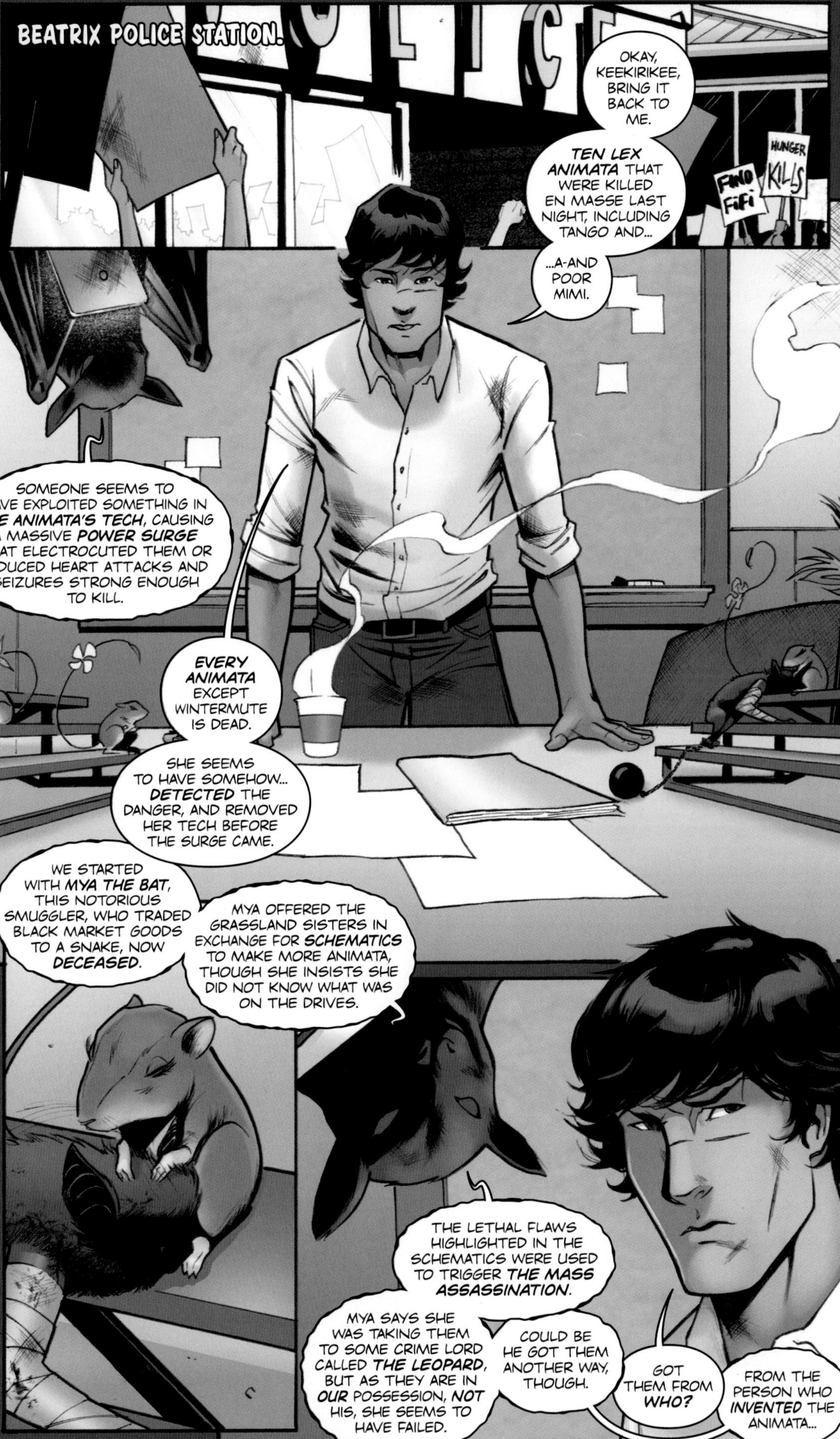
BEATRIX POLICE STATION.
HUNGER KILLS
FINO FIFI
OKAY, KEEKIRIKEE, BRING IT BACK TO ME.
TEN LEX ANIMATA THAT WERE KILLED EN MASSE LAST NIGHT, INCLUDING TANGO AND...
...A-AND POOR MIMI.
SOMEONE SEEMS TO HAVE EXPLOITED SOMETHING IN THE ANIMATA'S TECH, CAUSING A MASSIVE POWER SURGE THAT ELECTROCUTED THEM OR INDUCED HEART ATTACKS AND SEIZURES STRONG ENOUGH TO KILL.
EVERY ANIMATA EXCEPT WINTERMUTE IS DEAD.
SHE SEEMS TO HAVE SOMEHOW... DETECTED THE DANGER, AND REMOVED HER TECH BEFORE THE SURGE CAME.
WE STARTED WITH MYA THE BAT, THIS NOTORIOUS SMUGGLER, WHO TRADED BLACK MARKET GOODS TO A SNAKE, NOW DECEASED.
MYA OFFERED THE GRASSLAND SISTERS IN EXCHANGE FOR SCHEMATICS TO MAKE MORE ANIMATA, THOUGH SHE INSISTS SHE DID NOT KNOW WHAT WAS ON THE DRIVES.
THE LETHAL FLAWS HIGHLIGHTED IN THE SCHEMATICS WERE USED TO TRIGGER THE MASS ASSASSINATION.
MYA SAYS SHE WAS TAKING THEM TO SOME CRIME LORD CALLED THE LEOPARD, BUT AS THEY ARE IN OUR POSSESSION, NOT HIS, SHE SEEMS TO HAVE FAILED.
COULD BE HE GOT THEM ANOTHER WAY, THOUGH.
GOT THEM FROM WHO?
FROM THE PERSON WHO INVENTED THE ANIMATA...

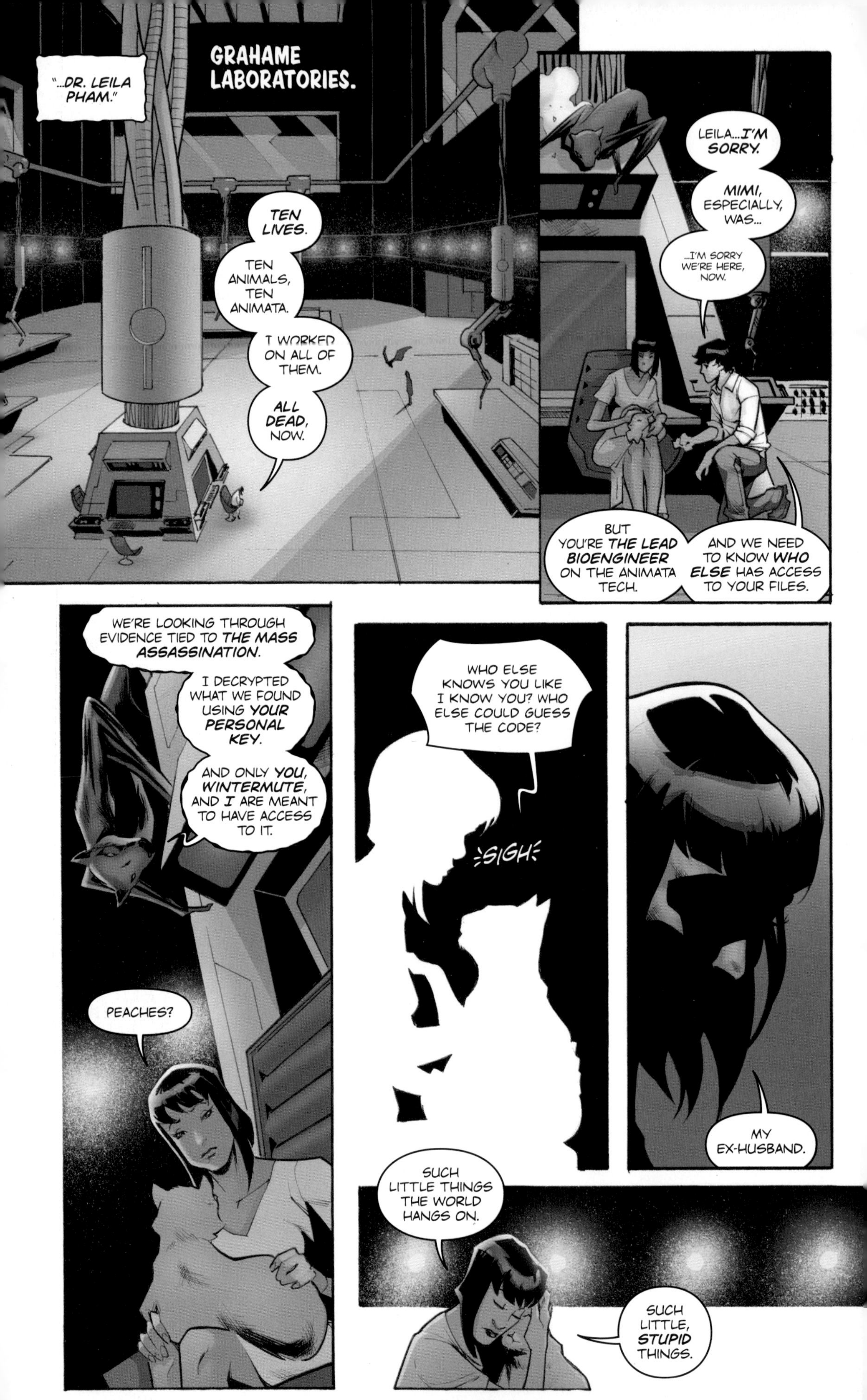
"...DR. LEILA PHAM."
GRAHAME LABORATORIES.
TEN LIVES.
TEN ANIMALS, TEN ANIMATA.
I WORKED ON ALL OF THEM.
ALL DEAD, NOW.
LEILA...I'M SORRY.
MIMI, ESPECIALLY, WAS...
...I'M SORRY WE'RE HERE, NOW.
BUT YOU'RE THE LEAD BIOENGINEER ON THE ANIMATA TECH.
AND WE NEED TO KNOW WHO ELSE HAS ACCESS TO YOUR FILES.
WE'RE LOOKING THROUGH EVIDENCE TIED TO THE MASS ASSASSINATION.
I DECRYPTED WHAT WE FOUND USING YOUR PERSONAL KEY.
AND ONLY YOU, WINTERMUTE, AND I ARE MEANT TO HAVE ACCESS TO IT.
PEACHES?
WHO ELSE KNOWS YOU LIKE I KNOW YOU? WHO ELSE COULD GUESS THE CODE?
SIGH
MY EX-HUSBAND.
SUCH LITTLE THINGS THE WORLD HANGS ON.
SUCH LITTLE, STUPID THINGS.

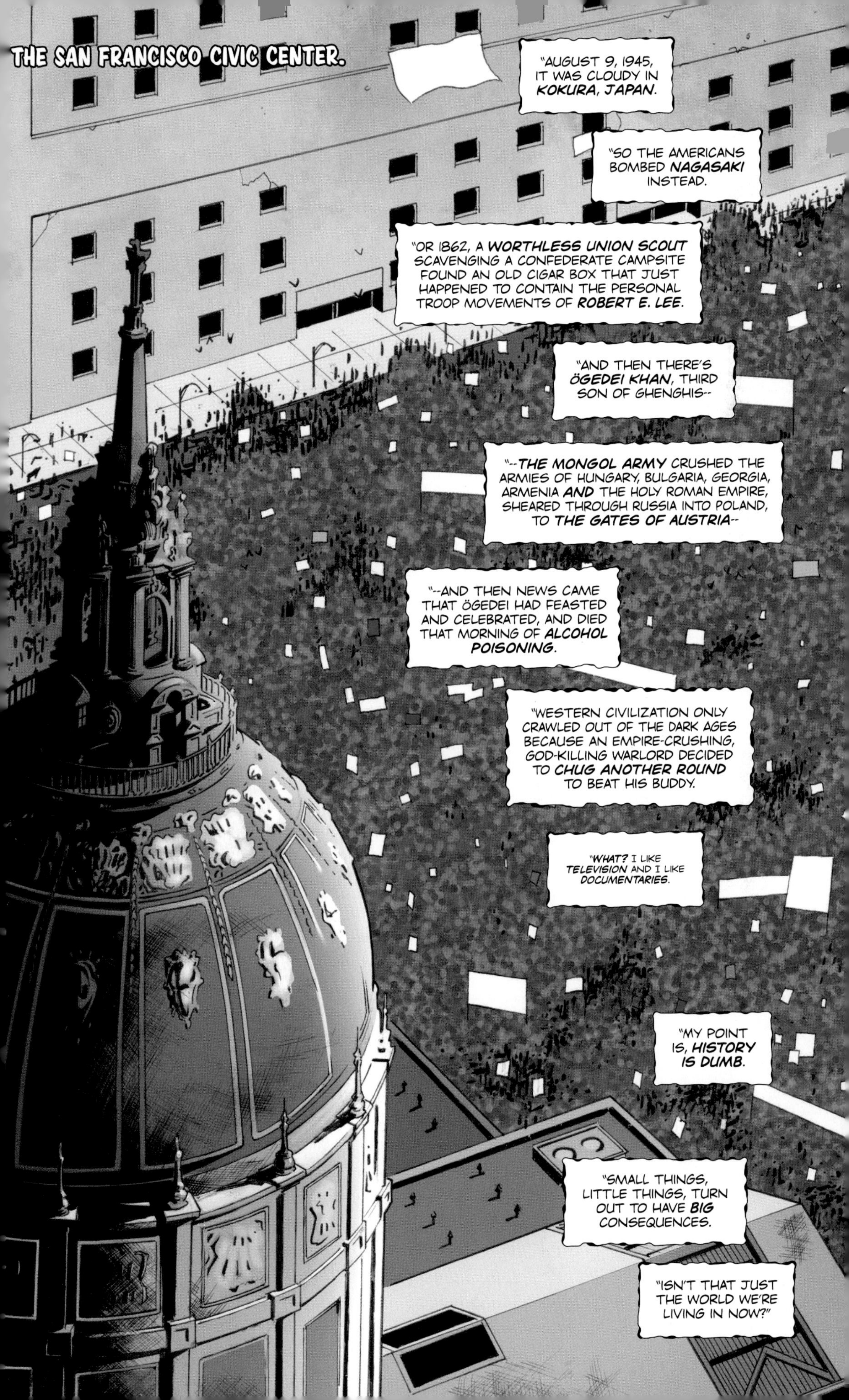
THE SAN FRANCISCO CIVIC CENTER.
"AUGUST 9, 1945, IT WAS CLOUDY IN KOKURA, JAPAN.
"SO THE AMERICANS BOMBED NAGASAKI INSTEAD.
"OR 1862, A WORTHLESS UNION SCOUT SCAVENGING A CONFEDERATE CAMPSITE FOUND AN OLD CIGAR BOX THAT JUST HAPPENED TO CONTAIN THE PERSONAL TROOP MOVEMENTS OF ROBERT E. LEE.
"AND THEN THERE'S ÖGEDEI KHAN, THIRD SON OF GHENGHIS--
"--THE MONGOL ARMY CRUSHED THE ARMIES OF HUNGARY, BULGARIA, GEORGIA, ARMENIA AND THE HOLY ROMAN EMPIRE, SHEARED THROUGH RUSSIA INTO POLAND, TO THE GATES OF AUSTRIA--
"--AND THEN NEWS CAME THAT ÖGEDEI HAD FEASTED AND CELEBRATED, AND DIED THAT MORNING OF ALCOHOL POISONING.
"WESTERN CIVILIZATION ONLY CRAWLED OUT OF THE DARK AGES BECAUSE AN EMPIRE-CRUSHING, GOD-KILLING WARLORD DECIDED TO CHUG ANOTHER ROUND TO BEAT HIS BUDDY.
"WHAT? I LIKE TELEVISION AND I LIKE DOCUMENTARIES.
"MY POINT IS, HISTORY IS DUMB.
"SMALL THINGS, LITTLE THINGS, TURN OUT TO HAVE BIG CONSEQUENCES.
"ISN'T THAT JUST THE WORLD WE'RE LIVING IN NOW?"

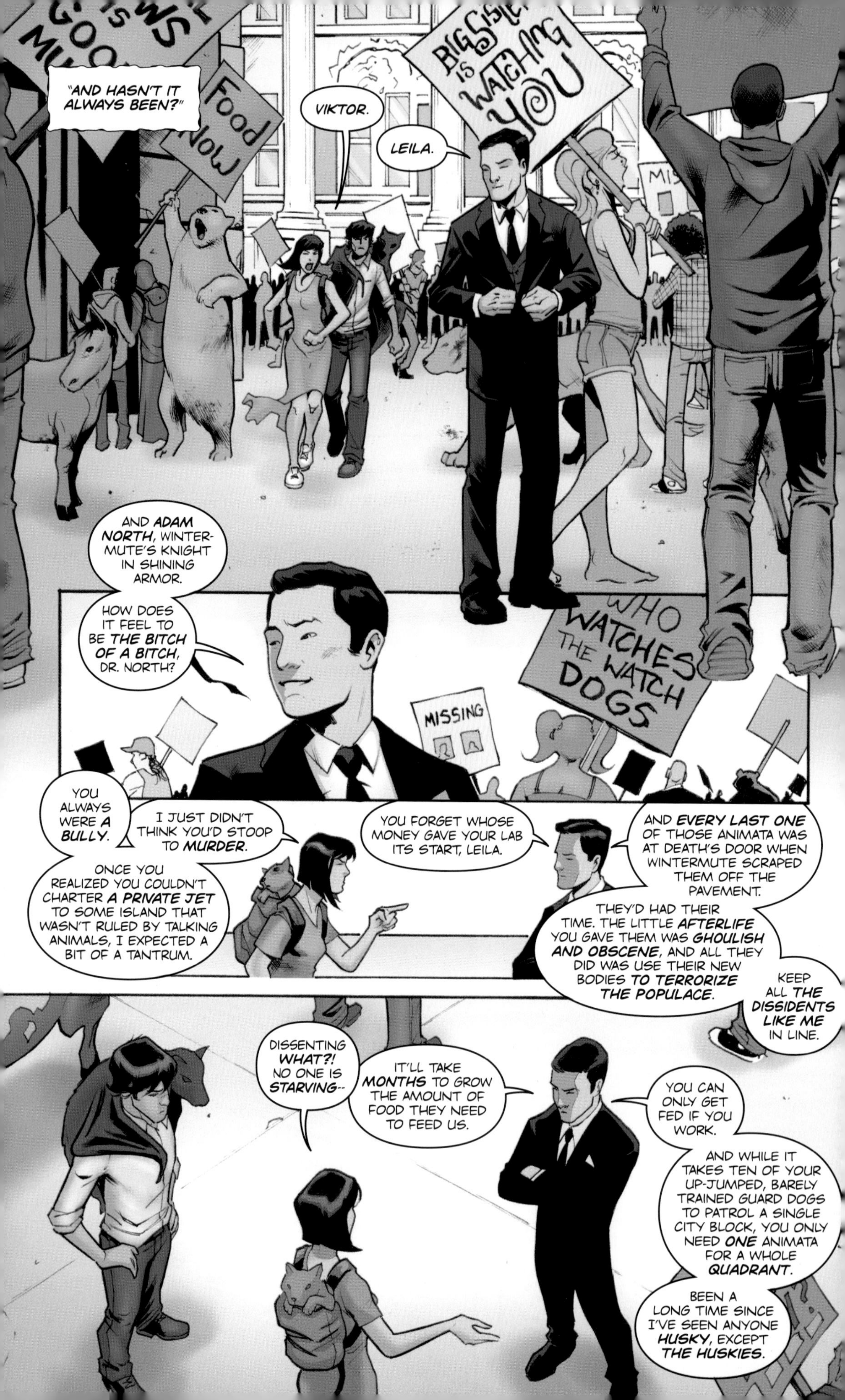

"AND HASN'T IT ALWAYS BEEN?"
Food Now
IS WATCHING YOU
VIKTOR.
LEILA.
AND **ADAM NORTH**, WINTERMUTE'S KNIGHT IN SHINING ARMOR.
HOW DOES IT FEEL TO BE **THE BITCH OF A BITCH**, DR. NORTH?
WHO WATCHES THE WATCH DOGS
MISSING
YOU ALWAYS WERE **A BULLY**.
I JUST DIDN'T THINK YOU'D STOOP TO **MURDER**.
ONCE YOU REALIZED YOU COULDN'T CHARTER **A PRIVATE JET** TO SOME ISLAND THAT WASN'T RULED BY TALKING ANIMALS, I EXPECTED A BIT OF A TANTRUM.
YOU FORGET WHOSE MONEY GAVE YOUR LAB ITS START, LEILA.
AND **EVERY LAST ONE** OF THOSE ANIMATA WAS AT DEATH'S DOOR WHEN WINTERMUTE SCRAPED THEM OFF THE PAVEMENT.
THEY'D HAD THEIR TIME. THE LITTLE **AFTERLIFE** YOU GAVE THEM WAS **GHOULISH AND OBSCENE**, AND ALL THEY DID WAS USE THEIR NEW BODIES **TO TERRORIZE THE POPULACE**.
KEEP ALL **THE DISSIDENTS LIKE ME** IN LINE.
DISSENTING **WHAT?!** NO ONE IS **STARVING**--
IT'LL TAKE **MONTHS** TO GROW THE AMOUNT OF FOOD THEY NEED TO FEED US.
YOU CAN ONLY GET FED IF YOU WORK.
AND WHILE IT TAKES TEN OF YOUR UP-JUMPED, BARELY TRAINED GUARD DOGS TO PATROL A SINGLE CITY BLOCK, YOU ONLY NEED **ONE** ANIMATA FOR A WHOLE **QUADRANT**.
BEEN A LONG TIME SINCE I'VE SEEN ANYONE **HUSKY**, EXCEPT **THE HUSKIES**.

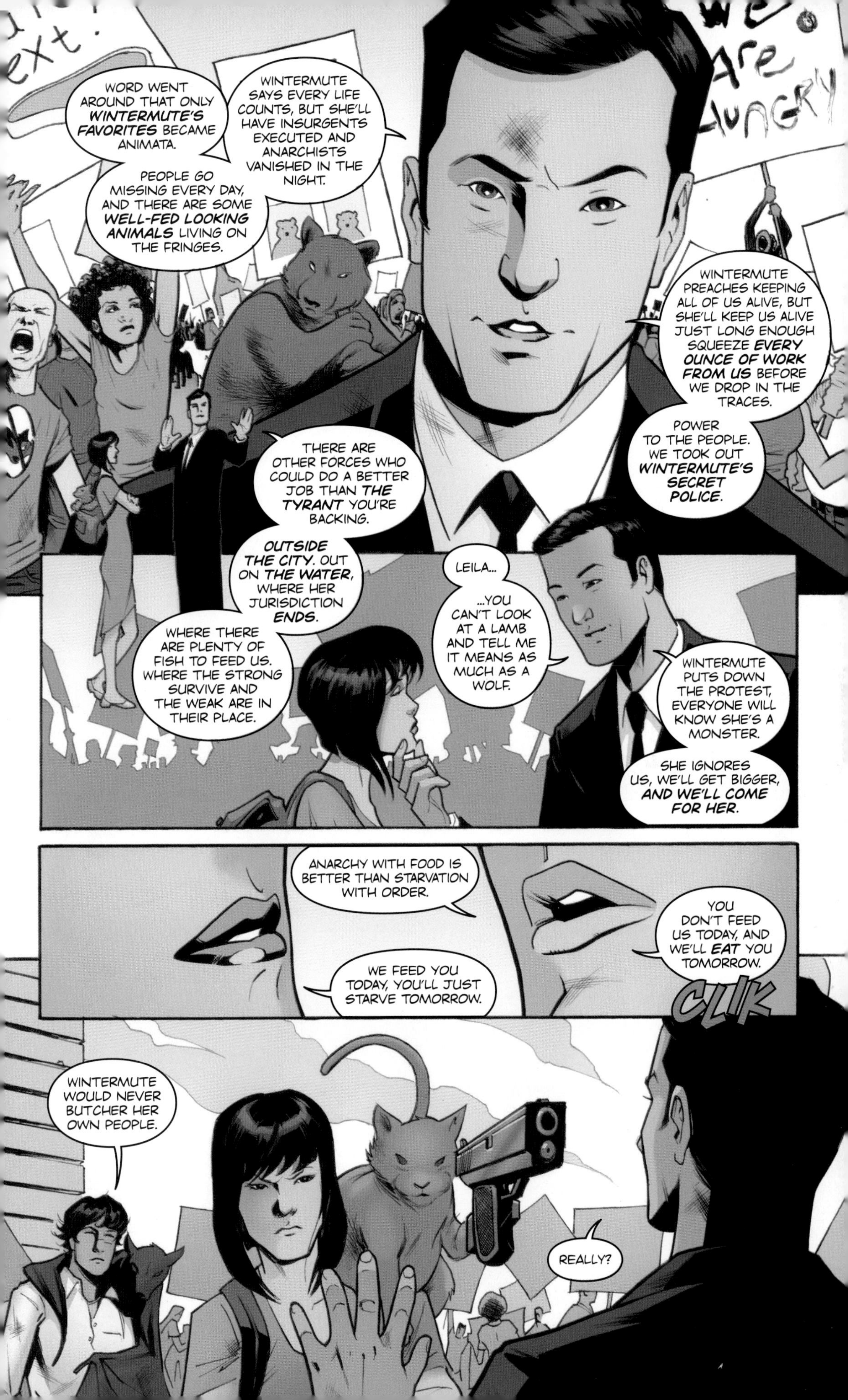
WORD WENT AROUND THAT ONLY WINTERMUTE'S FAVORITES BECAME ANIMATA.
WINTERMUTE SAYS EVERY LIFE COUNTS, BUT SHE'LL HAVE INSURGENTS EXECUTED AND ANARCHISTS VANISHED IN THE NIGHT.
PEOPLE GO MISSING EVERY DAY, AND THERE ARE SOME WELL-FED LOOKING ANIMALS LIVING ON THE FRINGES.
WINTERMUTE PREACHES KEEPING ALL OF US ALIVE, BUT SHE'LL KEEP US ALIVE JUST LONG ENOUGH SQUEEZE EVERY OUNCE OF WORK FROM US BEFORE WE DROP IN THE TRACES.
POWER TO THE PEOPLE. WE TOOK OUT WINTERMUTE'S SECRET POLICE.
THERE ARE OTHER FORCES WHO COULD DO A BETTER JOB THAN THE TYRANT YOU'RE BACKING.
OUTSIDE THE CITY. OUT ON THE WATER, WHERE HER JURISDICTION ENDS.
WHERE THERE ARE PLENTY OF FISH TO FEED US. WHERE THE STRONG SURVIVE AND THE WEAK ARE IN THEIR PLACE.
LEILA...
...YOU CAN'T LOOK AT A LAMB AND TELL ME IT MEANS AS MUCH AS A WOLF.
WINTERMUTE PUTS DOWN THE PROTEST, EVERYONE WILL KNOW SHE'S A MONSTER.
SHE IGNORES US, WE'LL GET BIGGER, AND WE'LL COME FOR HER.
ANARCHY WITH FOOD IS BETTER THAN STARVATION WITH ORDER.
WE FEED YOU TODAY, YOU'LL JUST STARVE TOMORROW.
YOU DON'T FEED US TODAY, AND WE'LL EAT YOU TOMORROW.
CLIK
WINTERMUTE WOULD NEVER BUTCHER HER OWN PEOPLE.
REALLY?

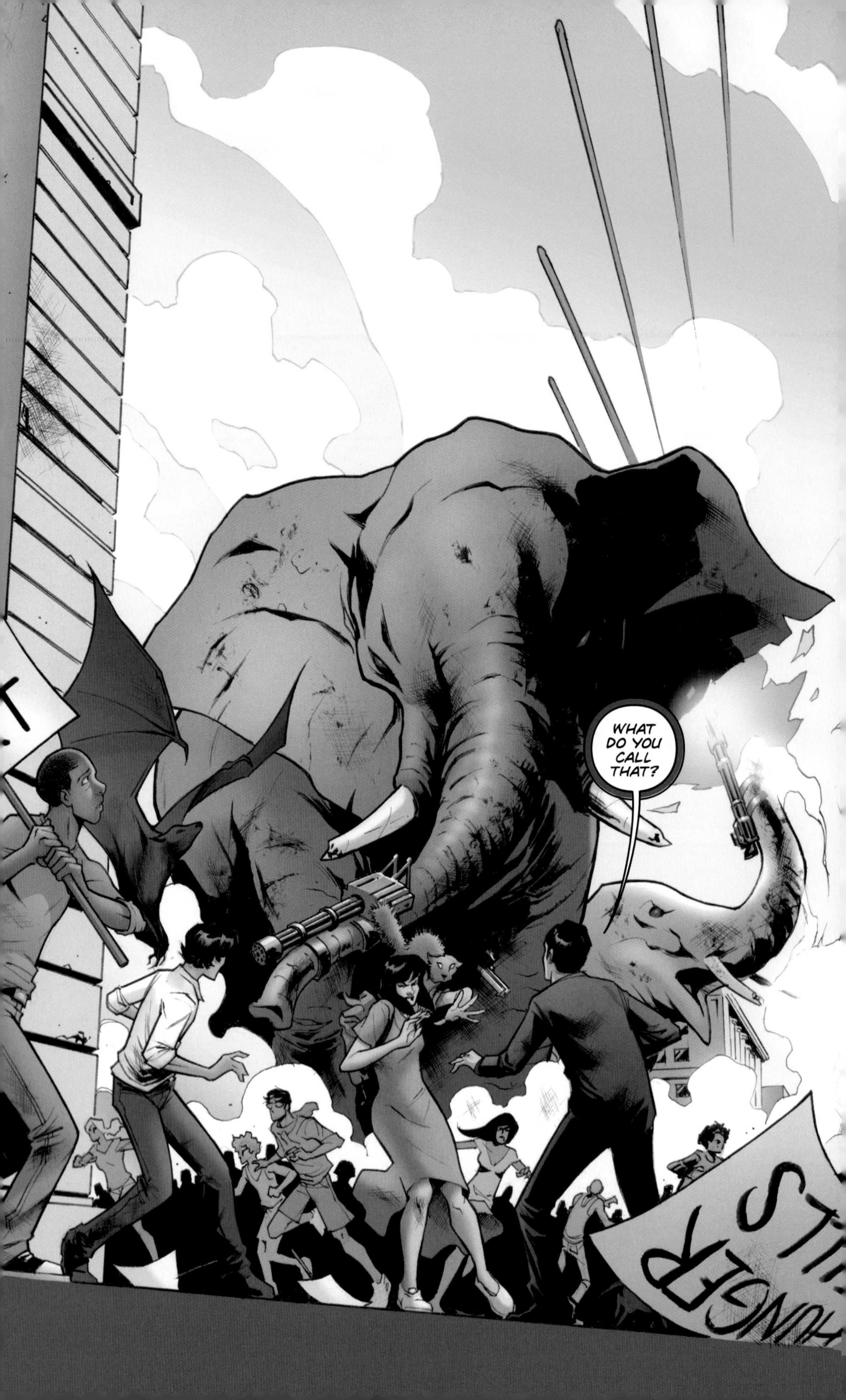
WHAT DO YOU CALL THAT?

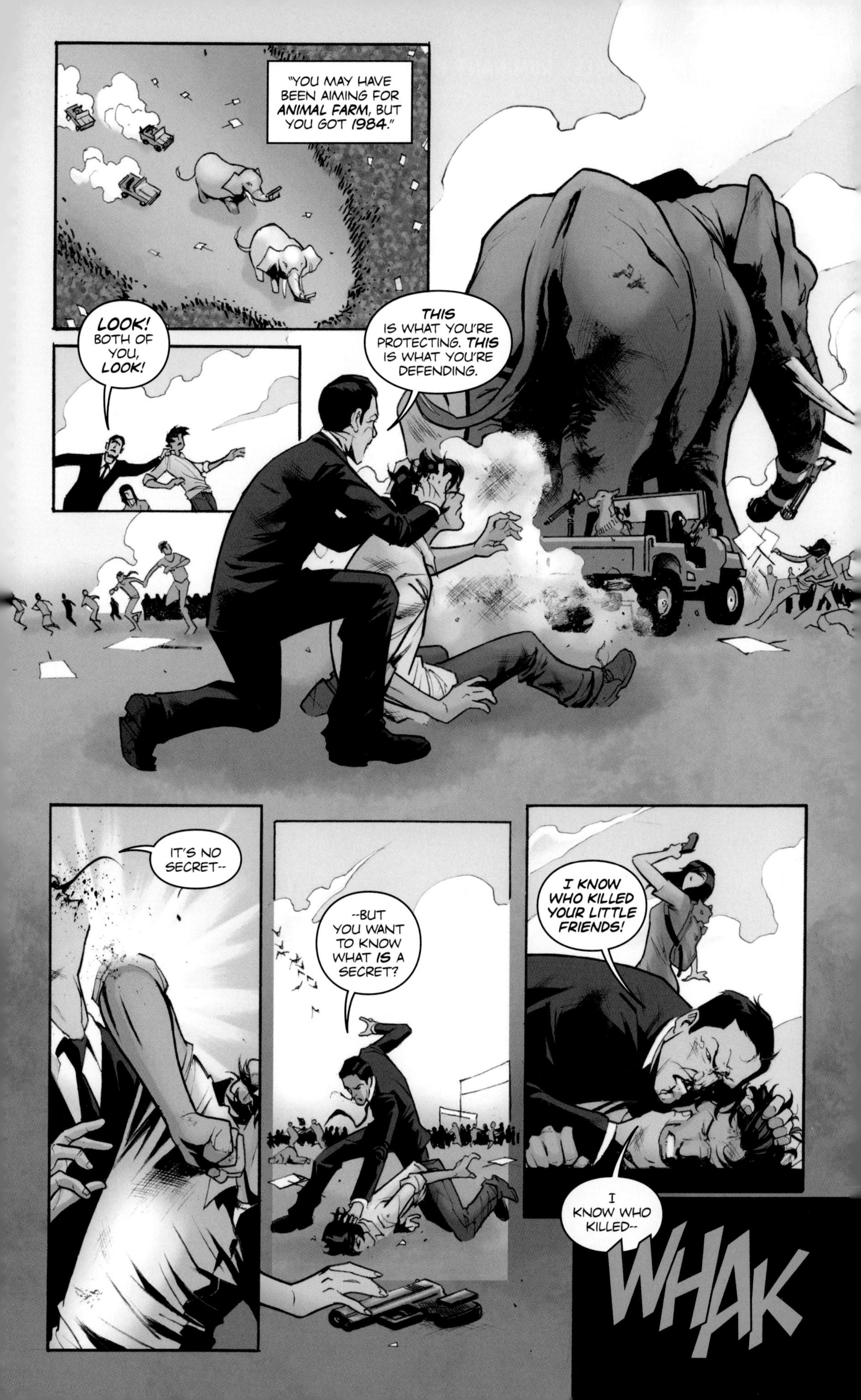
"YOU MAY HAVE BEEN AIMING FOR ANIMAL FARM, BUT YOU GOT 1984."
LOOK! BOTH OF YOU, LOOK!
THIS IS WHAT YOU'RE PROTECTING. THIS IS WHAT YOU'RE DEFENDING.
IT'S NO SECRET--
--BUT YOU WANT TO KNOW WHAT IS A SECRET?
I KNOW WHO KILLED YOUR LITTLE FRIENDS!
I KNOW WHO KILLED--
WHAK

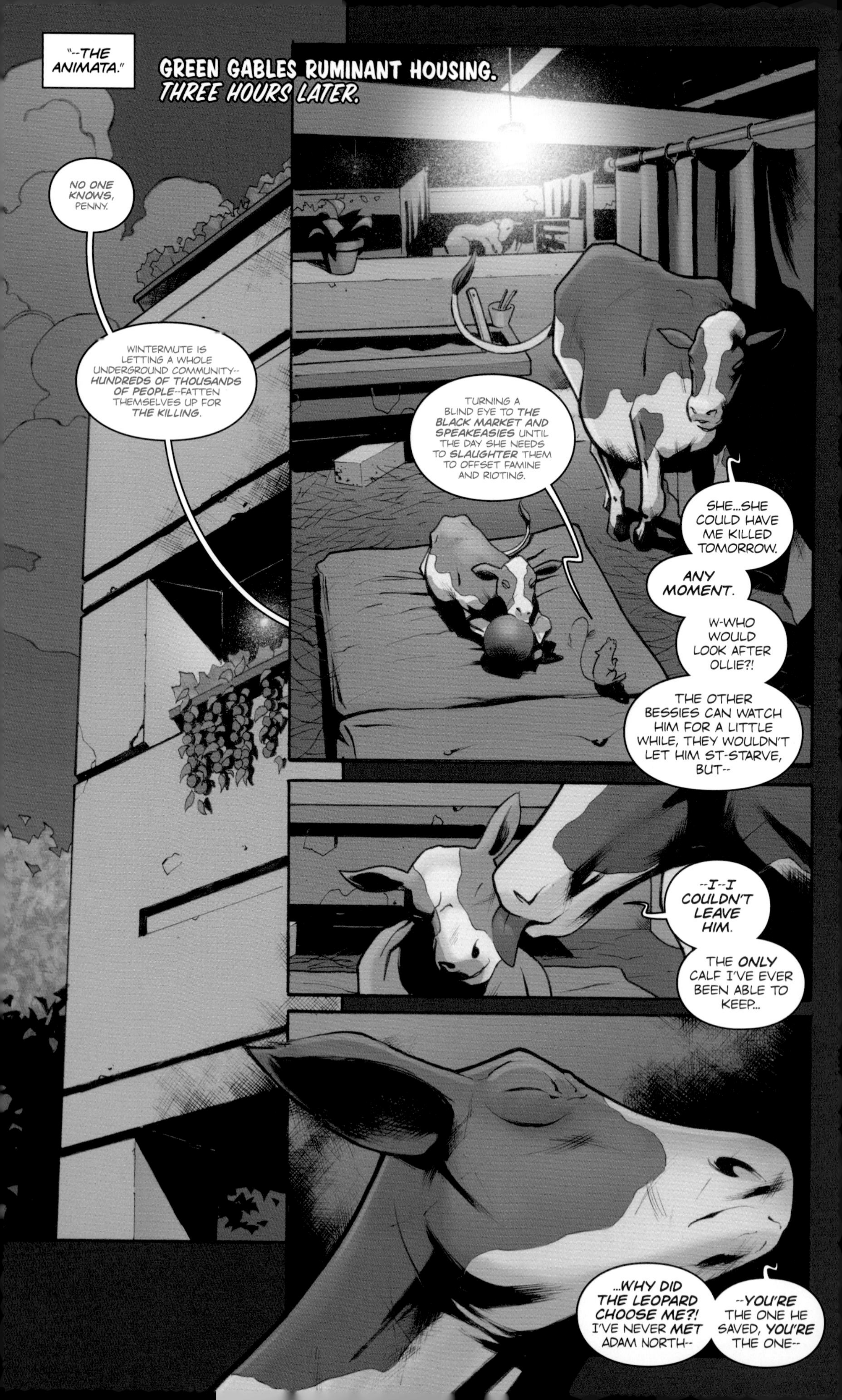
"--THE ANIMATA."
GREEN GABLES RUMINANT HOUSING. THREE HOURS LATER.
NO ONE KNOWS, PENNY.
WINTERMUTE IS LETTING A WHOLE UNDERGROUND COMMUNITY-- HUNDREDS OF THOUSANDS OF PEOPLE--FATTEN THEMSELVES UP FOR THE KILLING.
TURNING A BLIND EYE TO THE BLACK MARKET AND SPEAKEASIES UNTIL THE DAY SHE NEEDS TO SLAUGHTER THEM TO OFFSET FAMINE AND RIOTING.
SHE...SHE COULD HAVE ME KILLED TOMORROW.
ANY MOMENT.
W-WHO WOULD LOOK AFTER OLLIE?!
THE OTHER BESSIES CAN WATCH HIM FOR A LITTLE WHILE, THEY WOULDN'T LET HIM ST-STARVE, BUT--
--I--I COULDN'T LEAVE HIM.
THE ONLY CALF I'VE EVER BEEN ABLE TO KEEP...
...WHY DID THE LEOPARD CHOOSE ME?! I'VE NEVER MET ADAM NORTH--
--YOU'RE THE ONE HE SAVED, YOU'RE THE ONE--

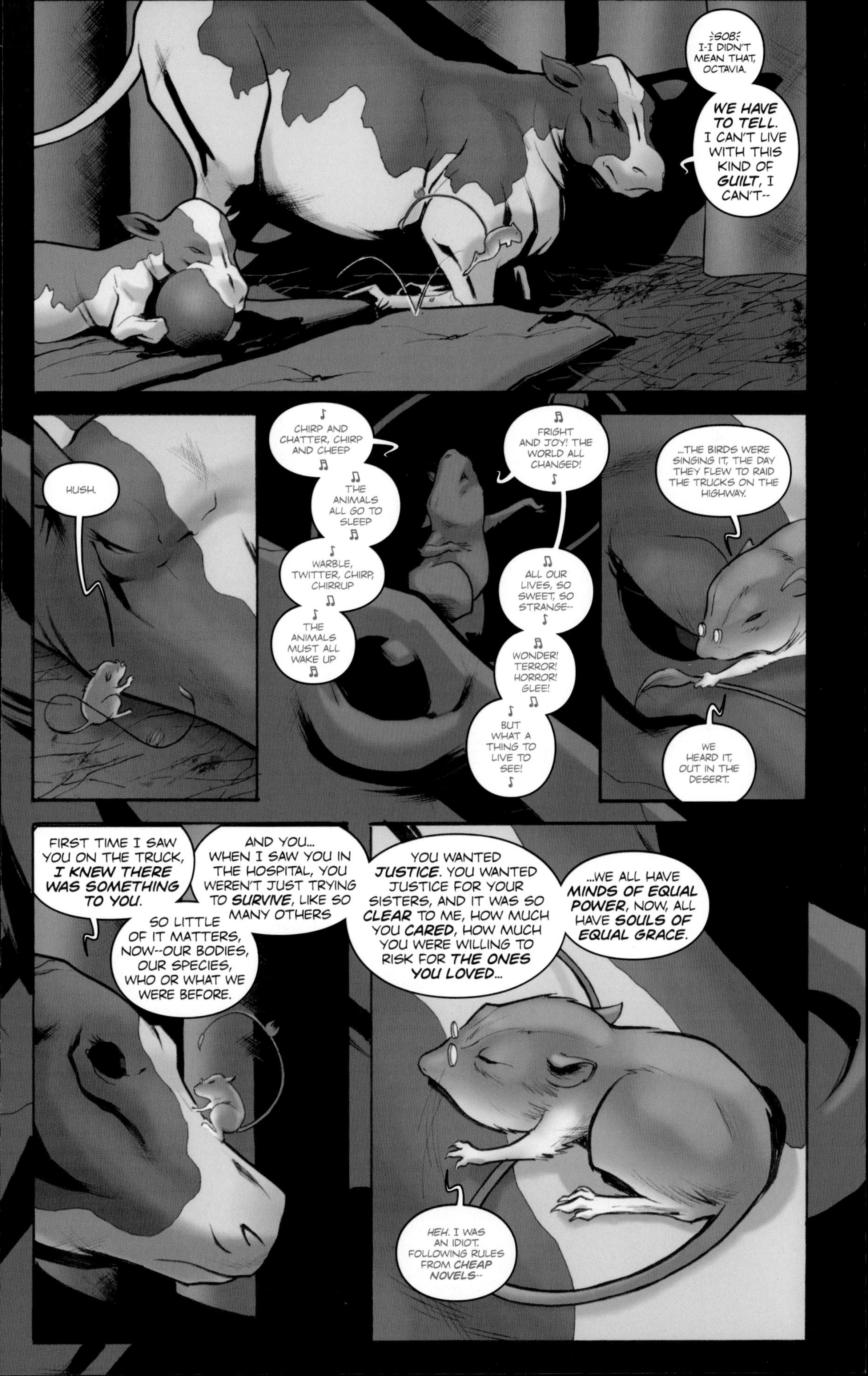

SOB I-I DIDN'T MEAN THAT, OCTAVIA.
WE HAVE TO TELL. I CAN'T LIVE WITH THIS KIND OF **GUILT**, I CAN'T--
HUSH.
♪ CHIRP AND CHATTER, CHIRP AND CHEEP ♫
♫ THE ANIMALS ALL GO TO SLEEP ♫
♪ WARBLE, TWITTER, CHIRP, CHIRRUP ♫
♪ THE ANIMALS MUST ALL WAKE UP ♫
♫ FRIGHT AND JOY! THE WORLD ALL CHANGED! ♪
♫ ALL OUR LIVES, SO SWEET, SO STRANGE-- ♪
♫ WONDER! TERROR! HORROR! GLEE! ♫
♪ BUT WHAT A THING TO LIVE TO SEE! ♪
...THE BIRDS WERE SINGING IT, THE DAY THEY FLEW TO RAID THE TRUCKS ON THE HIGHWAY.
WE HEARD IT, OUT IN THE DESERT.
FIRST TIME I SAW YOU ON THE TRUCK, **I KNEW THERE WAS SOMETHING TO YOU.**
SO LITTLE OF IT MATTERS, NOW--OUR BODIES, OUR SPECIES, WHO OR WHAT WE WERE BEFORE.
AND YOU... WHEN I SAW YOU IN THE HOSPITAL, YOU WEREN'T JUST TRYING TO **SURVIVE**, LIKE SO MANY OTHERS
YOU WANTED **JUSTICE**. YOU WANTED JUSTICE FOR YOUR SISTERS, AND IT WAS SO **CLEAR** TO ME, HOW MUCH YOU **CARED**, HOW MUCH YOU WERE WILLING TO RISK FOR **THE ONES YOU LOVED...**
...WE ALL HAVE **MINDS OF EQUAL POWER**, NOW, ALL HAVE **SOULS OF EQUAL GRACE.**
HEH. I WAS AN IDIOT. FOLLOWING RULES FROM **CHEAP NOVELS**--

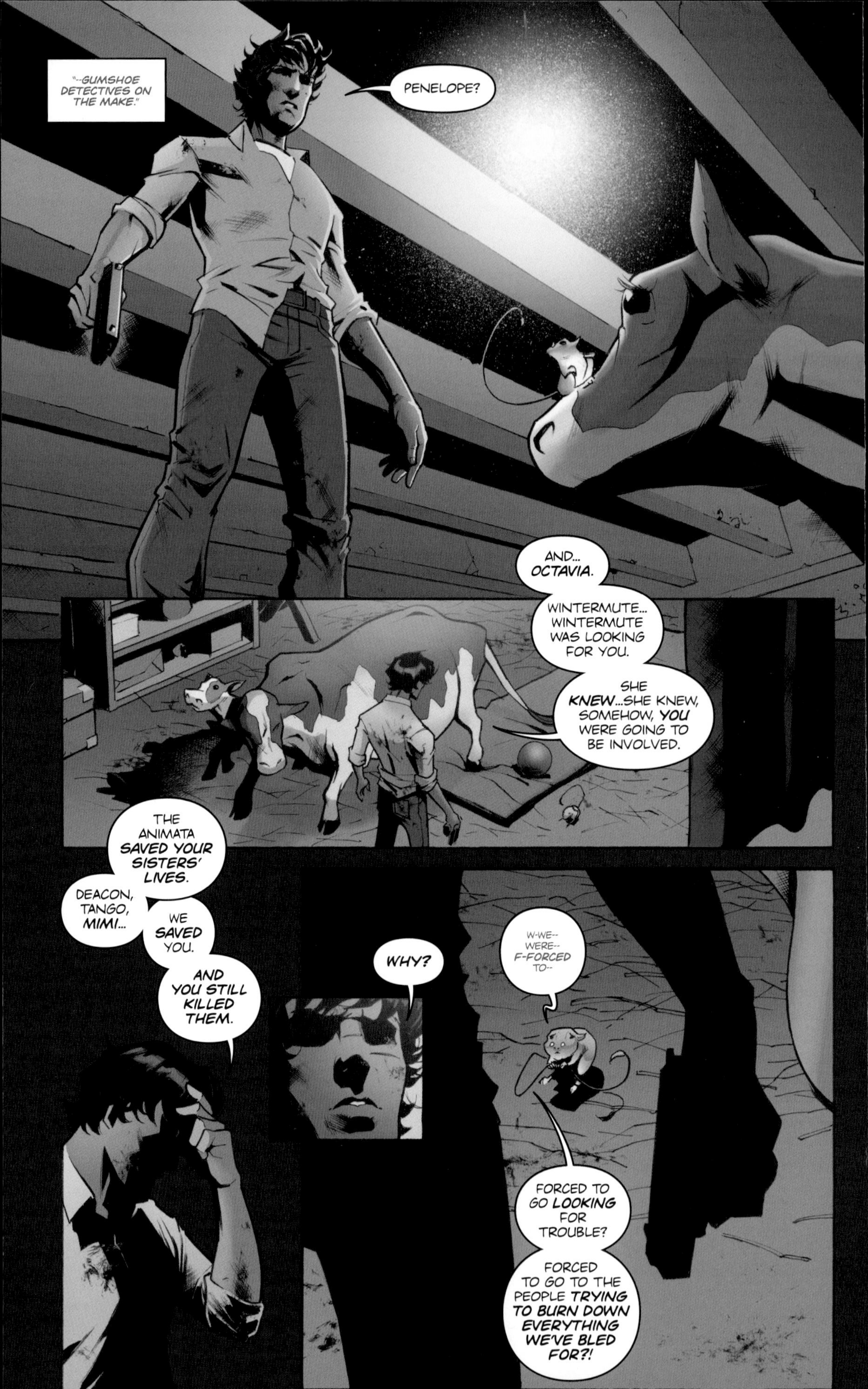
"--GUMSHOE DETECTIVES ON THE MAKE."
PENELOPE?
AND... OCTAVIA.
WINTERMUTE... WINTERMUTE WAS LOOKING FOR YOU.
SHE KNEW...SHE KNEW, SOMEHOW, YOU WERE GOING TO BE INVOLVED.
THE ANIMATA SAVED YOUR SISTERS' LIVES.
DEACON, TANGO, MIMI...
WE SAVED YOU.
AND YOU STILL KILLED THEM.
WHY?
W-WE-- WERE-- F-FORCED TO--
FORCED TO GO LOOKING FOR TROUBLE?
FORCED TO GO TO THE PEOPLE TRYING TO BURN DOWN EVERYTHING WE'VE BLED FOR?!

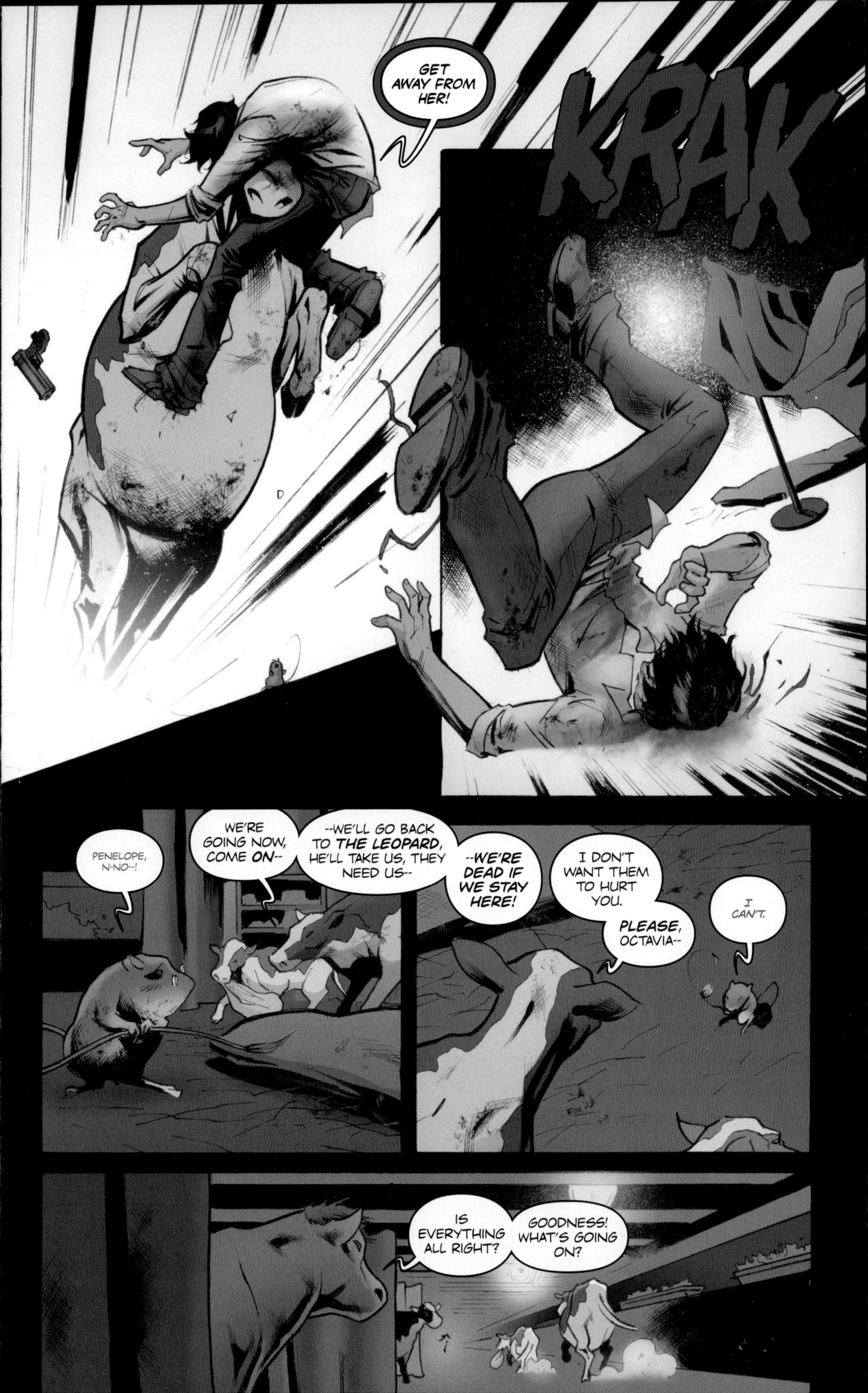
GET AWAY FROM HER!
KRAK
PENELOPE, N-NO--!
WE'RE GOING NOW, COME ON--
--WE'LL GO BACK TO THE LEOPARD, HE'LL TAKE US, THEY NEED US--
--WE'RE DEAD IF WE STAY HERE!
I DON'T WANT THEM TO HURT YOU.
PLEASE, OCTAVIA--
I CAN'T.
IS EVERYTHING ALL RIGHT?
GOODNESS! WHAT'S GOING ON?

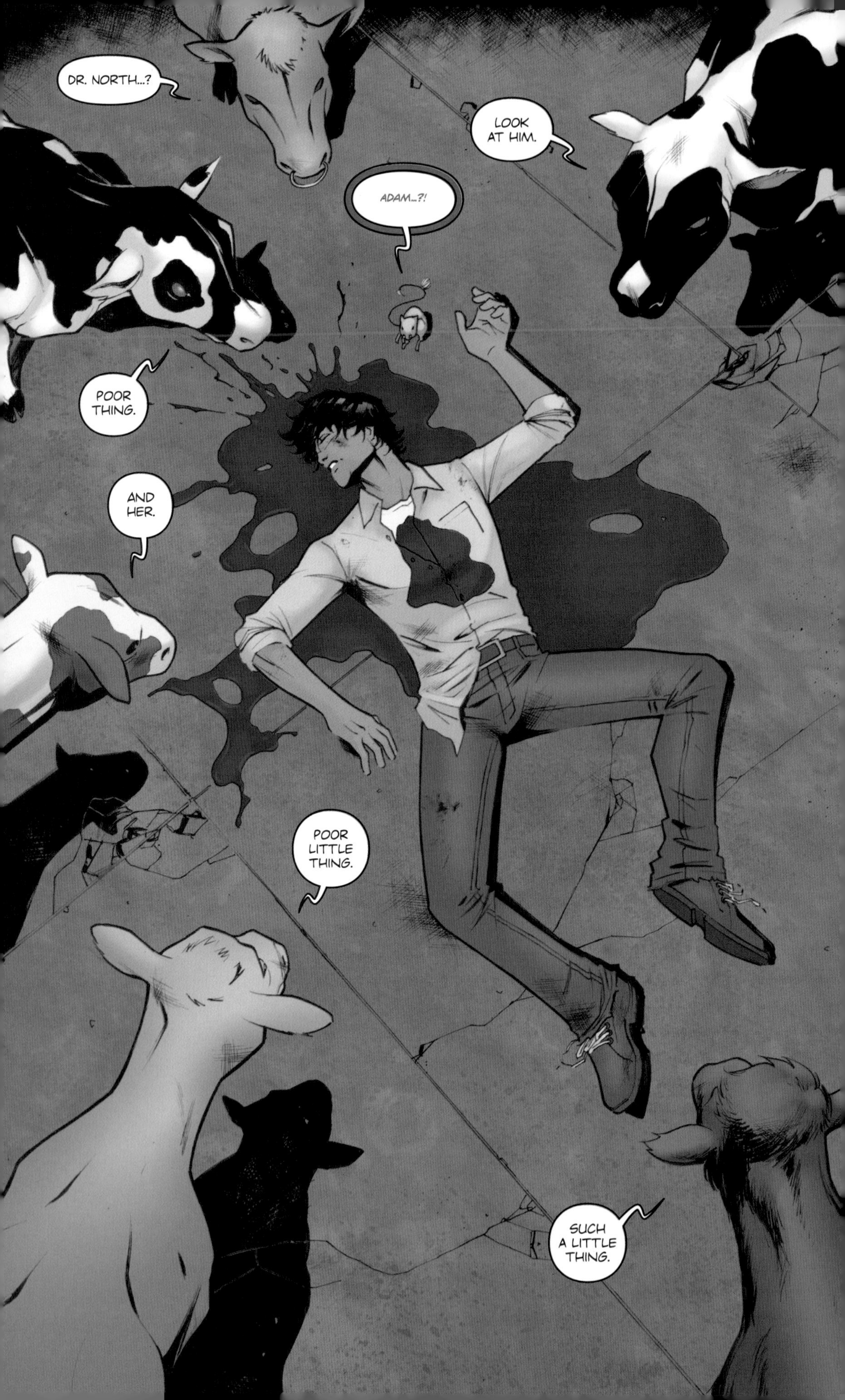
DR. NORTH...?
LOOK AT HIM.
ADAM...?!
POOR THING.
AND HER.
POOR LITTLE THING.
SUCH A LITTLE THING.

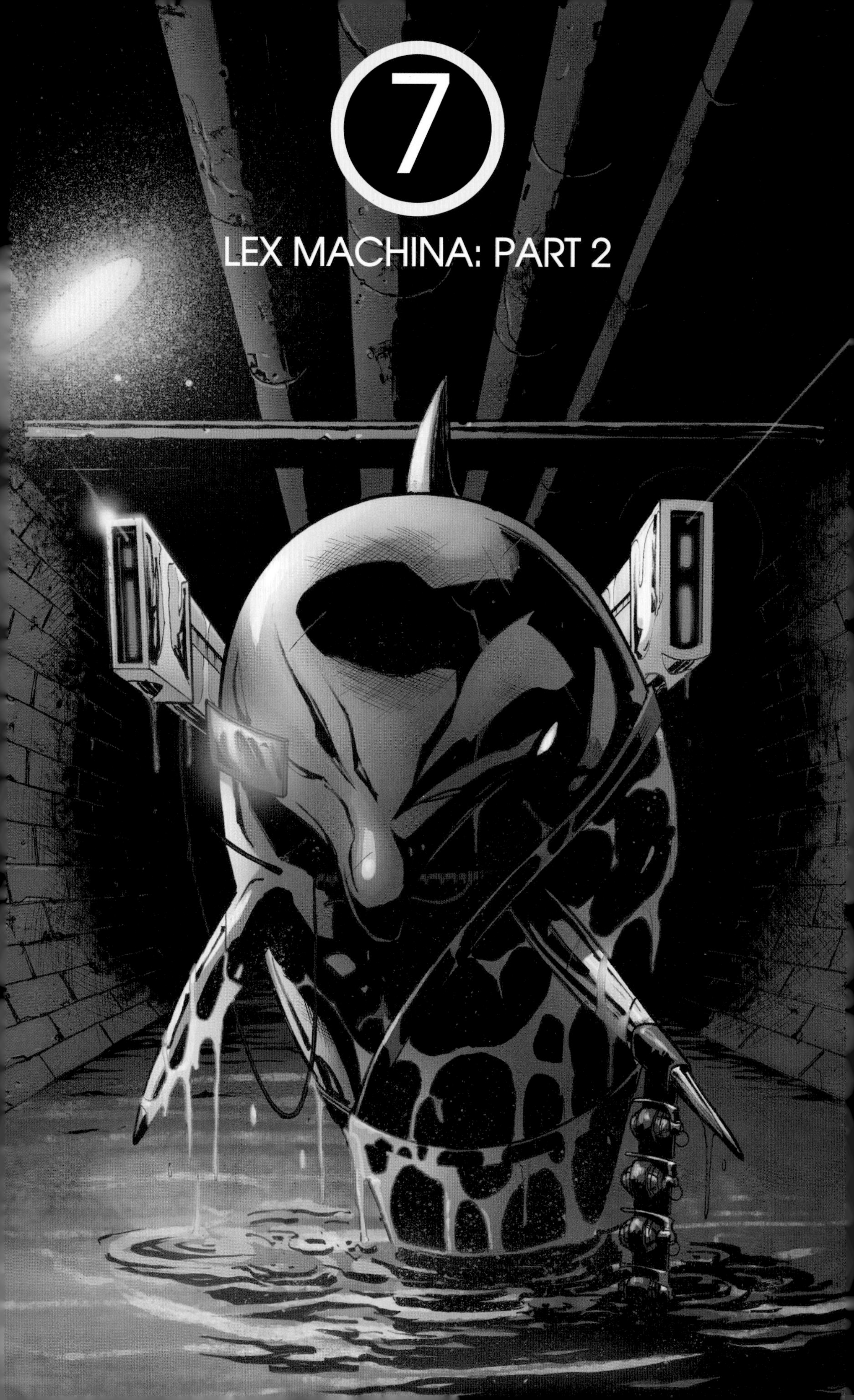
7
LEX MACHINA: PART 2

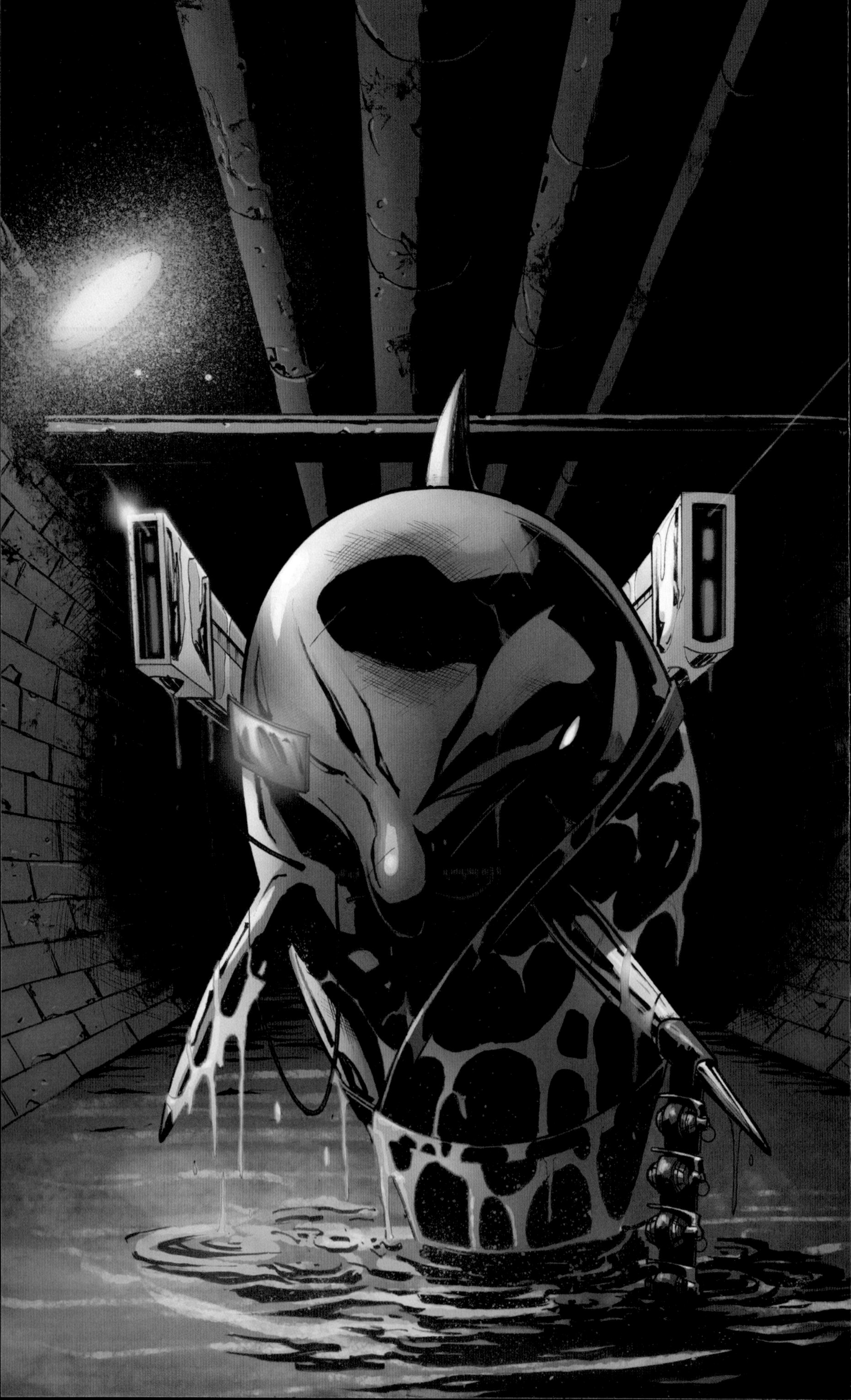

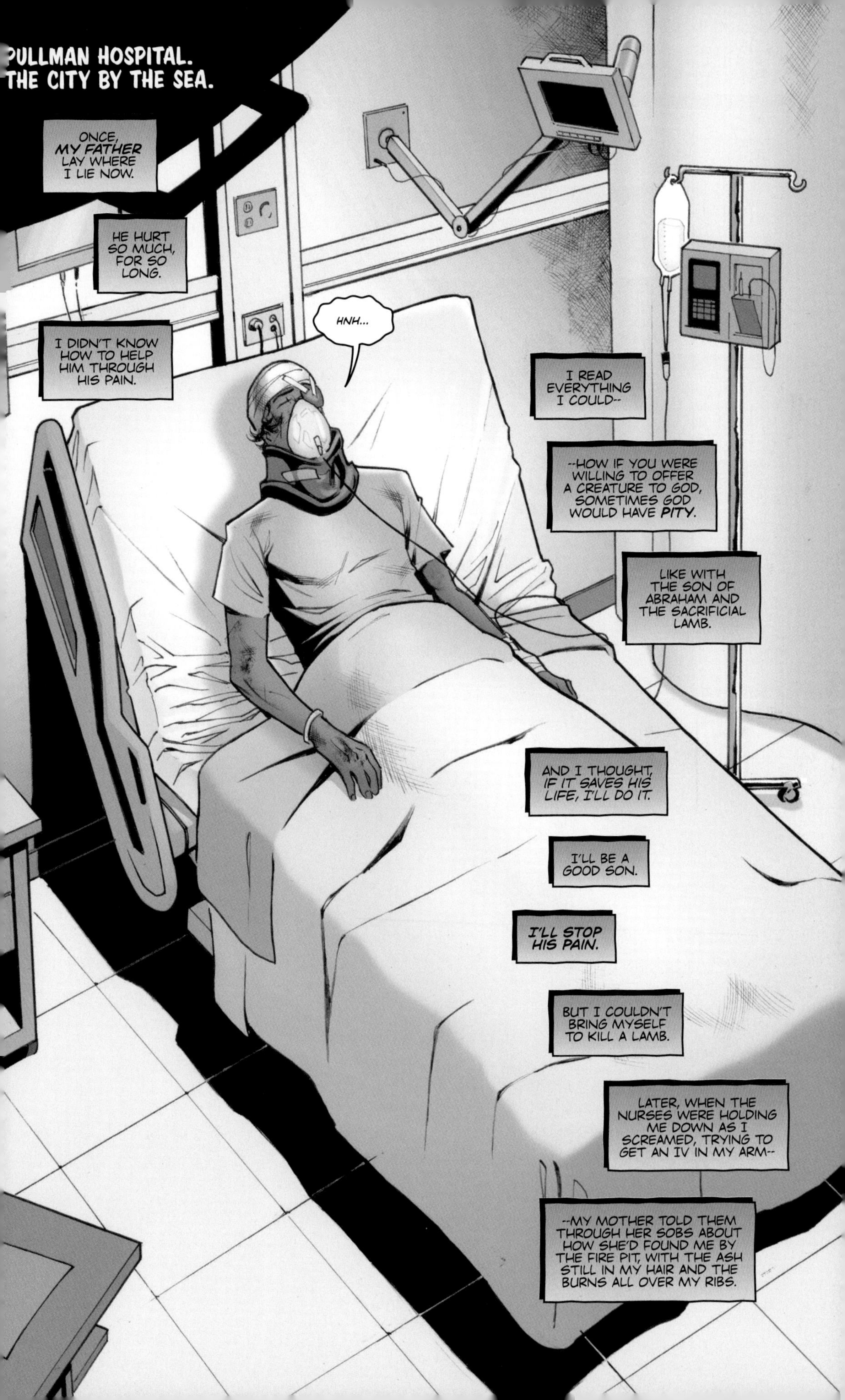
PULLMAN HOSPITAL.
THE CITY BY THE SEA.
ONCE, MY FATHER LAY WHERE I LIE NOW.
HE HURT SO MUCH, FOR SO LONG.
I DIDN'T KNOW HOW TO HELP HIM THROUGH HIS PAIN.
HNH...
I READ EVERYTHING I COULD--
--HOW IF YOU WERE WILLING TO OFFER A CREATURE TO GOD, SOMETIMES GOD WOULD HAVE PITY.
LIKE WITH THE SON OF ABRAHAM AND THE SACRIFICIAL LAMB.
AND I THOUGHT, IF IT SAVES HIS LIFE, I'LL DO IT.
I'LL BE A GOOD SON.
I'LL STOP HIS PAIN.
BUT I COULDN'T BRING MYSELF TO KILL A LAMB.
LATER, WHEN THE NURSES WERE HOLDING ME DOWN AS I SCREAMED, TRYING TO GET AN IV IN MY ARM--
--MY MOTHER TOLD THEM THROUGH HER SOBS ABOUT HOW SHE'D FOUND ME BY THE FIRE PIT, WITH THE ASH STILL IN MY HAIR AND THE BURNS ALL OVER MY RIBS.

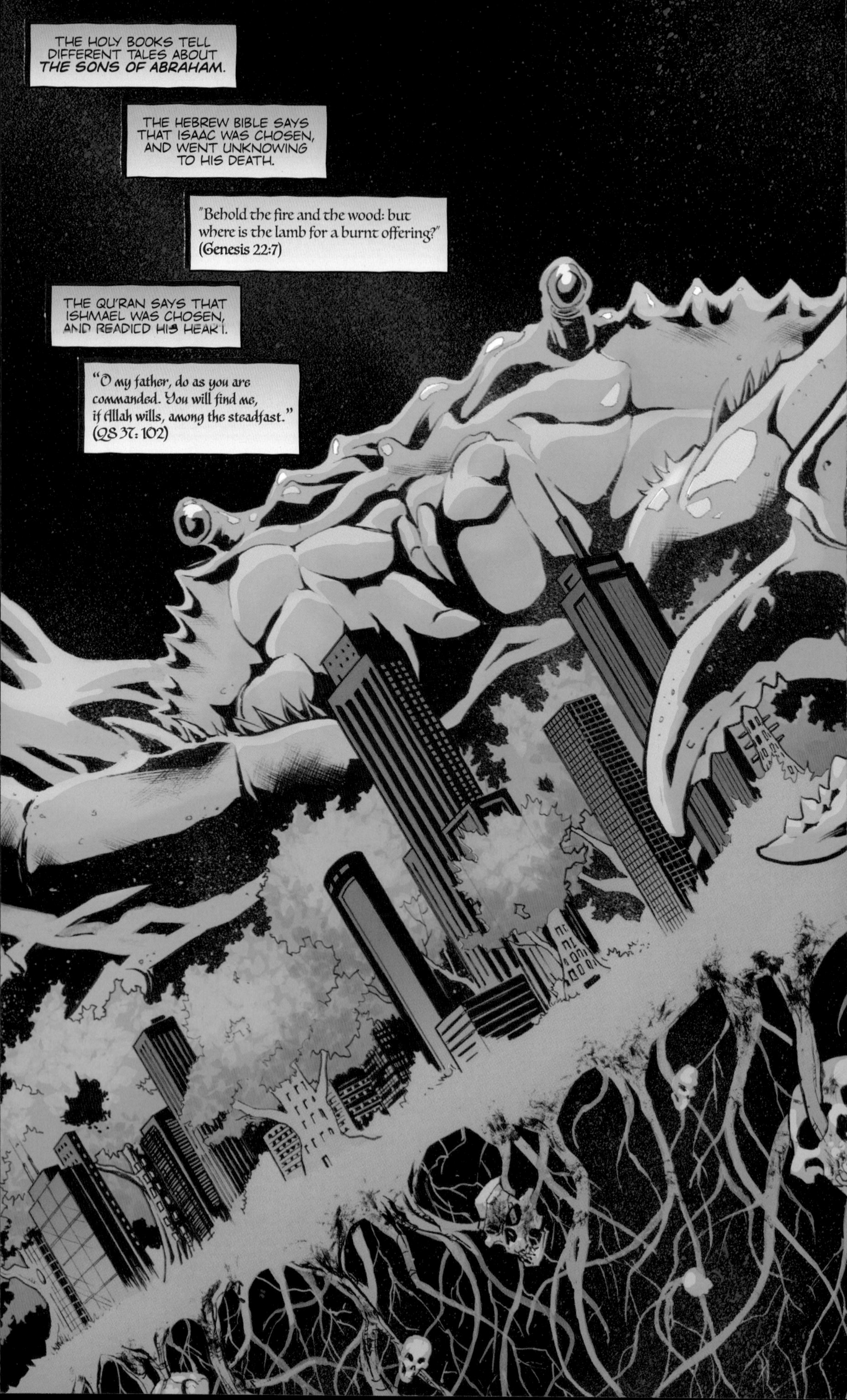
THE HOLY BOOKS TELL DIFFERENT TALES ABOUT THE SONS OF ABRAHAM.
THE HEBREW BIBLE SAYS THAT ISAAC WAS CHOSEN, AND WENT UNKNOWING TO HIS DEATH.
"Behold the fire and the wood: but where is the lamb for a burnt offering?" (Genesis 22:7)
THE QU'RAN SAYS THAT ISHMAEL WAS CHOSEN, AND READIED HIS HEART.
"O my father, do as you are commanded. You will find me, if Allah wills, among the steadfast." (QS 37: 102)

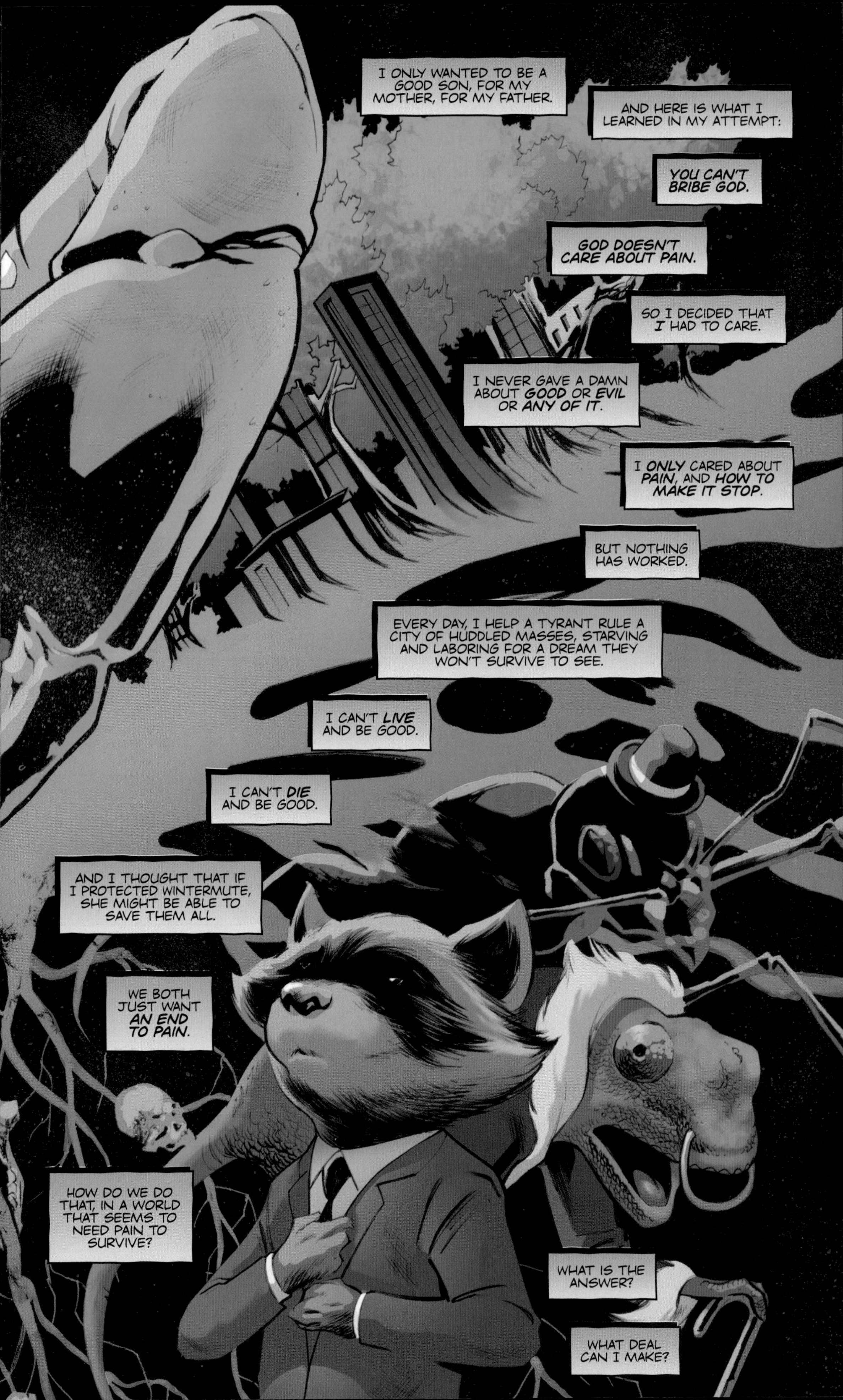
I ONLY WANTED TO BE A GOOD SON, FOR MY MOTHER, FOR MY FATHER.
AND HERE IS WHAT I LEARNED IN MY ATTEMPT:
YOU CAN'T BRIBE GOD.
GOD DOESN'T CARE ABOUT PAIN.
SO I DECIDED THAT I HAD TO CARE.
I NEVER GAVE A DAMN ABOUT GOOD OR EVIL OR ANY OF IT.
I ONLY CARED ABOUT PAIN, AND HOW TO MAKE IT STOP.
BUT NOTHING HAS WORKED.
EVERY DAY, I HELP A TYRANT RULE A CITY OF HUDDLED MASSES, STARVING AND LABORING FOR A DREAM THEY WON'T SURVIVE TO SEE.
I CAN'T LIVE AND BE GOOD.
I CAN'T DIE AND BE GOOD.
AND I THOUGHT THAT IF I PROTECTED WINTERMUTE, SHE MIGHT BE ABLE TO SAVE THEM ALL.
WE BOTH JUST WANT AN END TO PAIN.
HOW DO WE DO THAT, IN A WORLD THAT SEEMS TO NEED PAIN TO SURVIVE?
WHAT IS THE ANSWER?
WHAT DEAL CAN I MAKE?

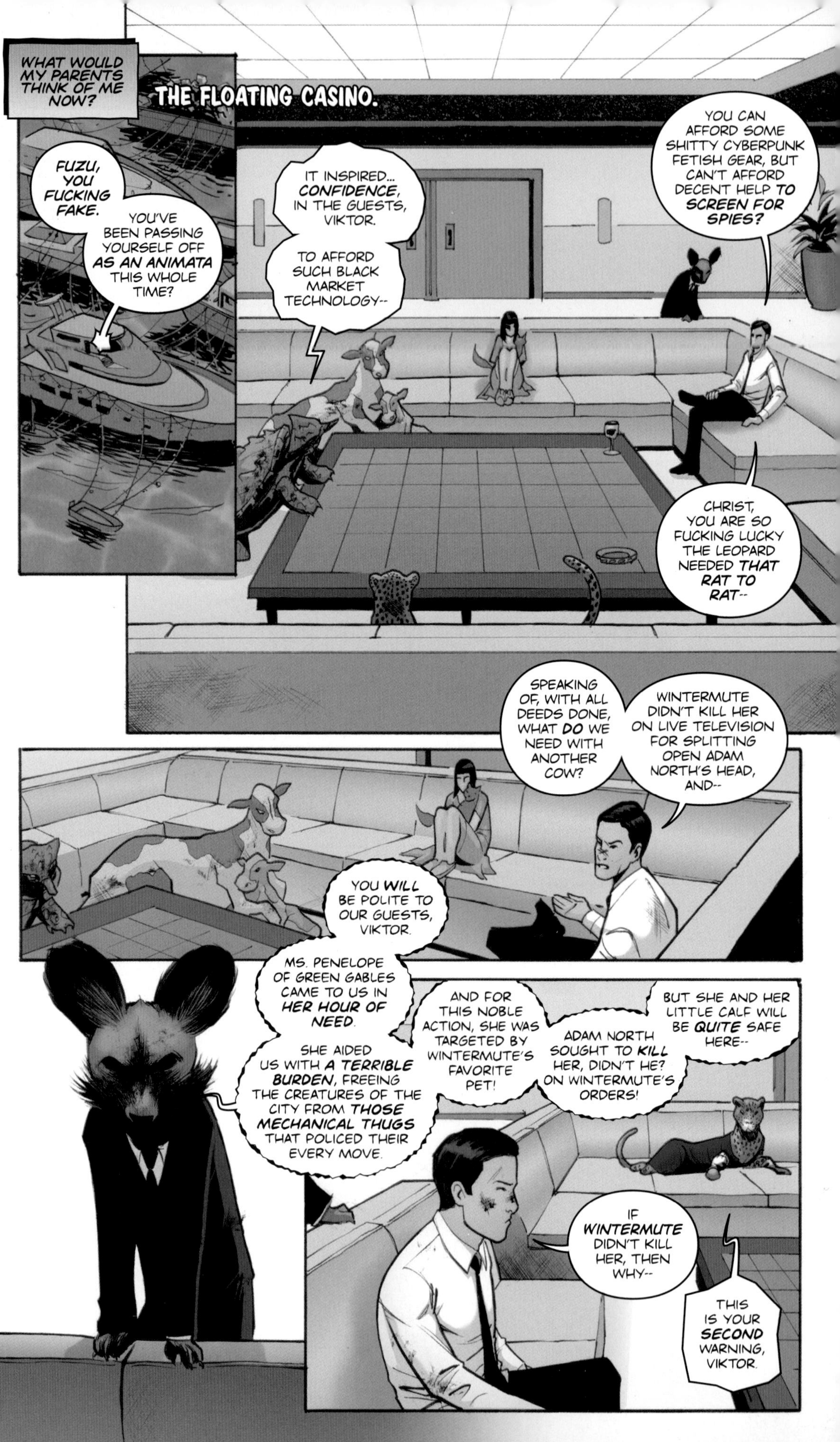
WHAT WOULD MY PARENTS THINK OF ME NOW?
THE FLOATING CASINO.
FUZU, YOU FUCKING FAKE.
YOU'VE BEEN PASSING YOURSELF OFF AS AN ANIMATA THIS WHOLE TIME?
IT INSPIRED... CONFIDENCE, IN THE GUESTS, VIKTOR.
TO AFFORD SUCH BLACK MARKET TECHNOLOGY--
YOU CAN AFFORD SOME SHITTY CYBERPUNK FETISH GEAR, BUT CAN'T AFFORD DECENT HELP TO SCREEN FOR SPIES?
CHRIST, YOU ARE SO FUCKING LUCKY THE LEOPARD NEEDED THAT RAT TO RAT--
SPEAKING OF, WITH ALL DEEDS DONE, WHAT DO WE NEED WITH ANOTHER COW?
WINTERMUTE DIDN'T KILL HER ON LIVE TELEVISION FOR SPLITTING OPEN ADAM NORTH'S HEAD, AND--
YOU WILL BE POLITE TO OUR GUESTS, VIKTOR.
MS. PENELOPE OF GREEN GABLES CAME TO US IN HER HOUR OF NEED.
SHE AIDED US WITH A TERRIBLE BURDEN, FREEING THE CREATURES OF THE CITY FROM THOSE MECHANICAL THUGS THAT POLICED THEIR EVERY MOVE.
AND FOR THIS NOBLE ACTION, SHE WAS TARGETED BY WINTERMUTE'S FAVORITE PET!
ADAM NORTH SOUGHT TO KILL HER, DIDN'T HE? ON WINTERMUTE'S ORDERS!
BUT SHE AND HER LITTLE CALF WILL BE QUITE SAFE HERE--
IF WINTERMUTE DIDN'T KILL HER, THEN WHY--
THIS IS YOUR SECOND WARNING, VIKTOR.

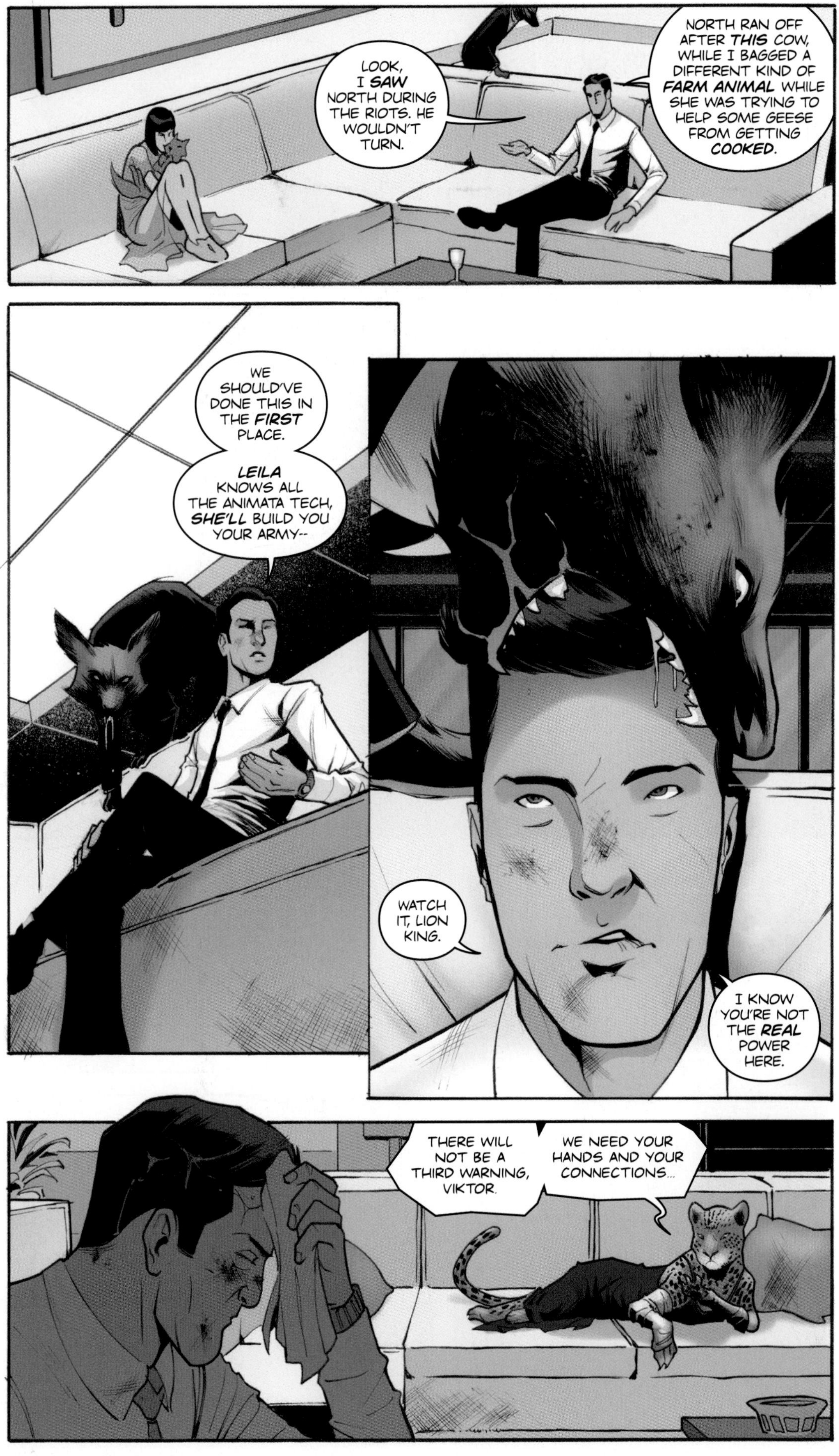
LOOK, I SAW NORTH DURING THE RIOTS. HE WOULDN'T TURN.
NORTH RAN OFF AFTER THIS COW, WHILE I BAGGED A DIFFERENT KIND OF FARM ANIMAL WHILE SHE WAS TRYING TO HELP SOME GEESE FROM GETTING COOKED.
WE SHOULD'VE DONE THIS IN THE FIRST PLACE.
LEILA KNOWS ALL THE ANIMATA TECH, SHE'LL BUILD YOU YOUR ARMY--
WATCH IT, LION KING.
I KNOW YOU'RE NOT THE REAL POWER HERE.
WE NEED YOUR HANDS AND YOUR CONNECTIONS...
THERE WILL NOT BE A THIRD WARNING, VIKTOR.

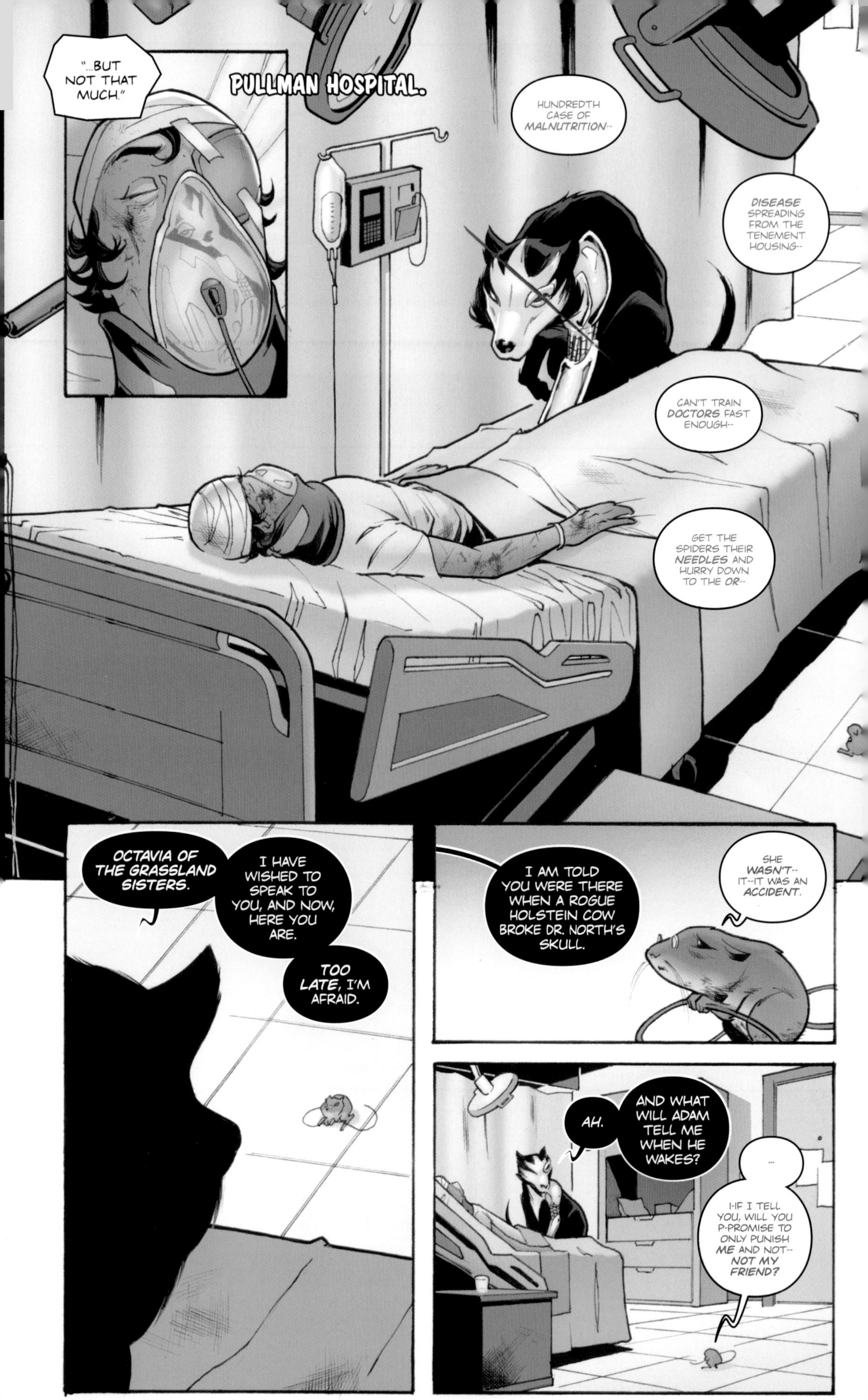
"...BUT NOT THAT MUCH."
PULLMAN HOSPITAL.
HUNDREDTH CASE OF MALNUTRITION--
DISEASE SPREADING FROM THE TENEMENT HOUSING--
CAN'T TRAIN DOCTORS FAST ENOUGH--
GET THE SPIDERS THEIR NEEDLES AND HURRY DOWN TO THE OR--
OCTAVIA OF THE GRASSLAND SISTERS.
I HAVE WISHED TO SPEAK TO YOU, AND NOW, HERE YOU ARE.
TOO LATE, I'M AFRAID.
I AM TOLD YOU WERE THERE WHEN A ROGUE HOLSTEIN COW BROKE DR. NORTH'S SKULL.
SHE WASN'T-- IT--IT WAS AN ACCIDENT.
AH.
AND WHAT WILL ADAM TELL ME WHEN HE WAKES?
...
I-IF I TELL YOU, WILL YOU P-PROMISE TO ONLY PUNISH ME AND NOT-- NOT MY FRIEND?

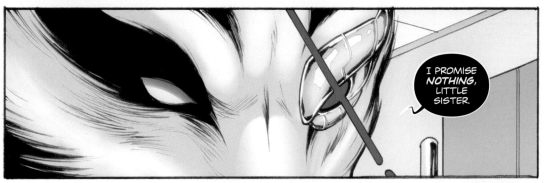

I PROMISE *NOTHING,* LITTLE SISTER.

...THE LEOPARD BAITED ME, CHOOSING A GENTLE, NURSING COW FOR THEIR WEAPON.

THEY WISHED TO TRAP ME INTO *EXECUTING A MOTHER* IN FRONT OF HER NEWBORN CHILD.

THEY WISH TO MAKE ME *A MONSTER.*

BUT I NEED NO ONE'S HELP TO BE *THAT.*

...

I...

I HELPED THE CREATURES WHO KILLED THE ANIMATA.

THEY *THREATENED* US, AND...I KNOW THAT'S WHERE MY FRIEND... *PENELOPE*...THAT'S WHERE SHE RAN, WHEN ADAM CAME...

THOSE PEOPLE...ON *THE BOATS*...THEY WERE *AWFUL* TO US. BUT THEY *HATE* YOU. AND THEY COULD *PROTECT* HER.

SHE JUST...

SHE HAD NOWHERE ELSE TO GO.

TELL ME--IF TOMORROW THERE WERE A VAST, UNTAPPED RESOURCE OF FOOD, AND THAT ALL WE HAD TO DO WAS DRAG THE YOUNG AWAY FROM THEIR PARENTS, AND THE PARENTS AWAY FROM THEIR YOUNG--

--WOULD *YOU* PARTAKE?

THE... THE *BLACK MARKET*--?

NO.

YOU *MISTAKE* ME.

I DO NOT MEAN THOSE EATEN FOR *WHAT THEY HAVE DONE.*

I MEAN THOSE EATEN FOR *WHO THEY ARE.*

TO SAVE YOUR SISTERS. TO SAVE YOUR *FAMILY*...

HNH...

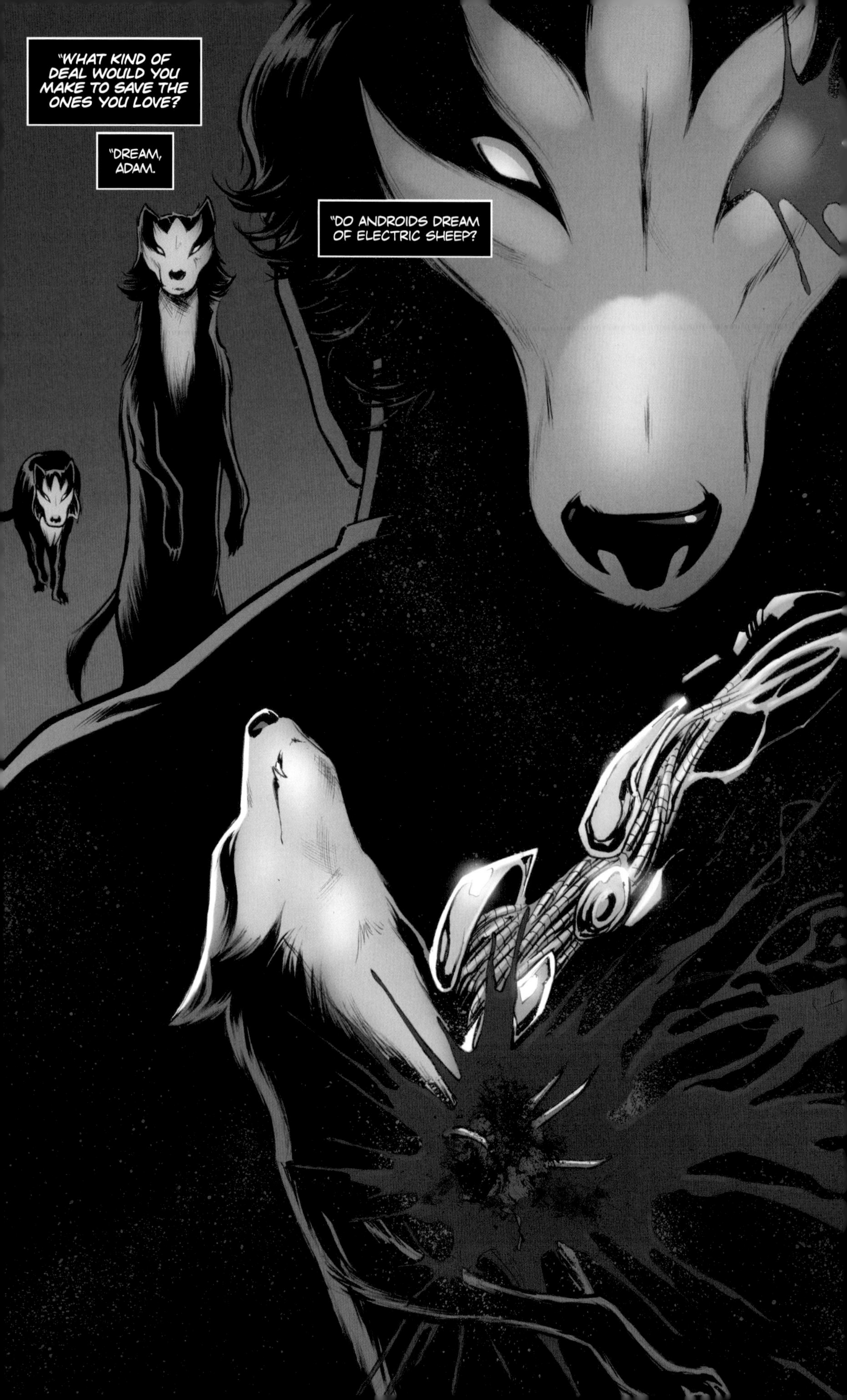
"WHAT KIND OF DEAL WOULD YOU MAKE TO SAVE THE ONES YOU LOVE?
"DREAM, ADAM.
"DO ANDROIDS DREAM OF ELECTRIC SHEEP?

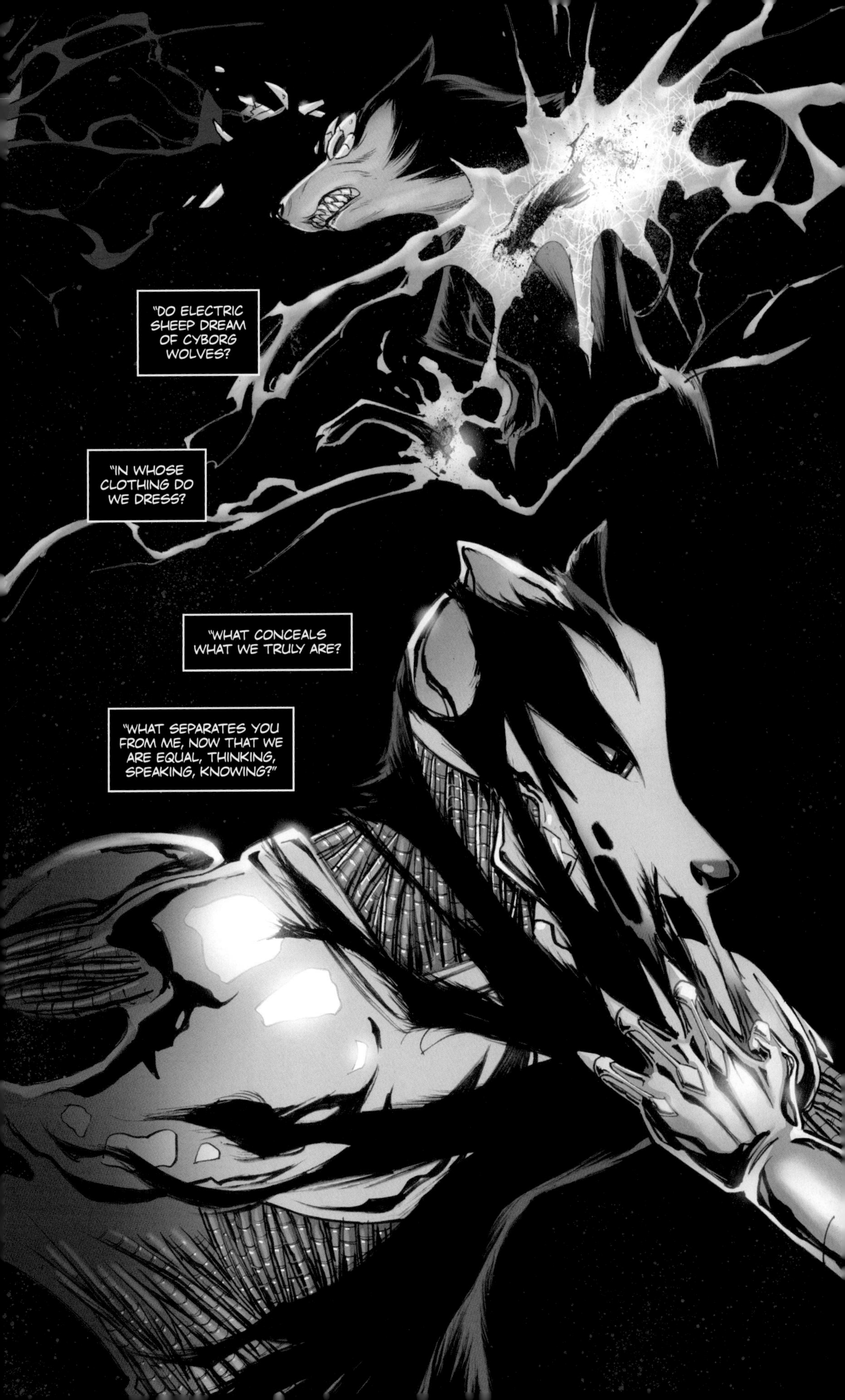
"DO ELECTRIC SHEEP DREAM OF CYBORG WOLVES?
"IN WHOSE CLOTHING DO WE DRESS?
"WHAT CONCEALS WHAT WE TRULY ARE?
"WHAT SEPARATES YOU FROM ME, NOW THAT WE ARE EQUAL, THINKING, SPEAKING, KNOWING?"

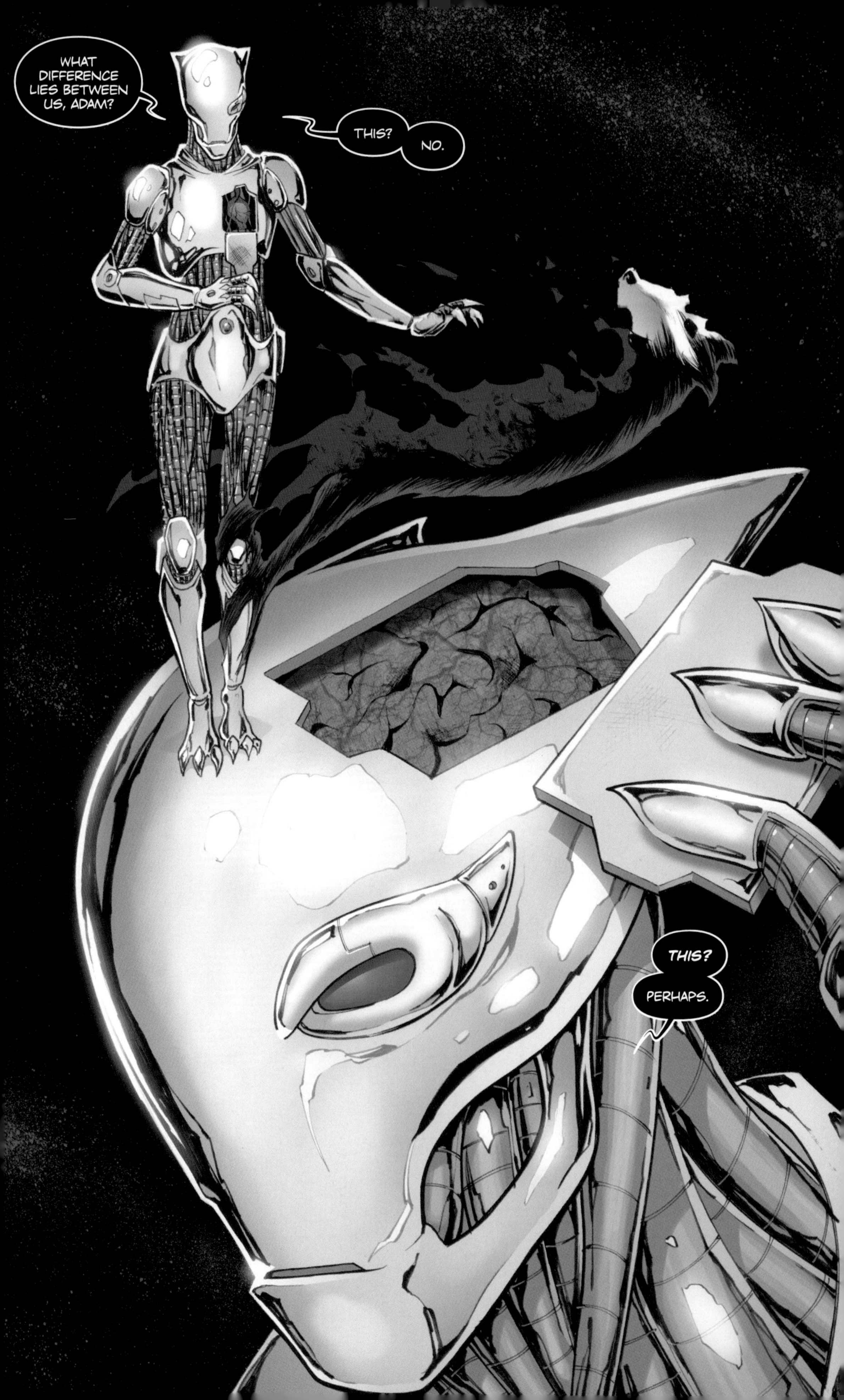
WHAT DIFFERENCE LIES BETWEEN US, ADAM?
THIS?
NO.
THIS?
PERHAPS.

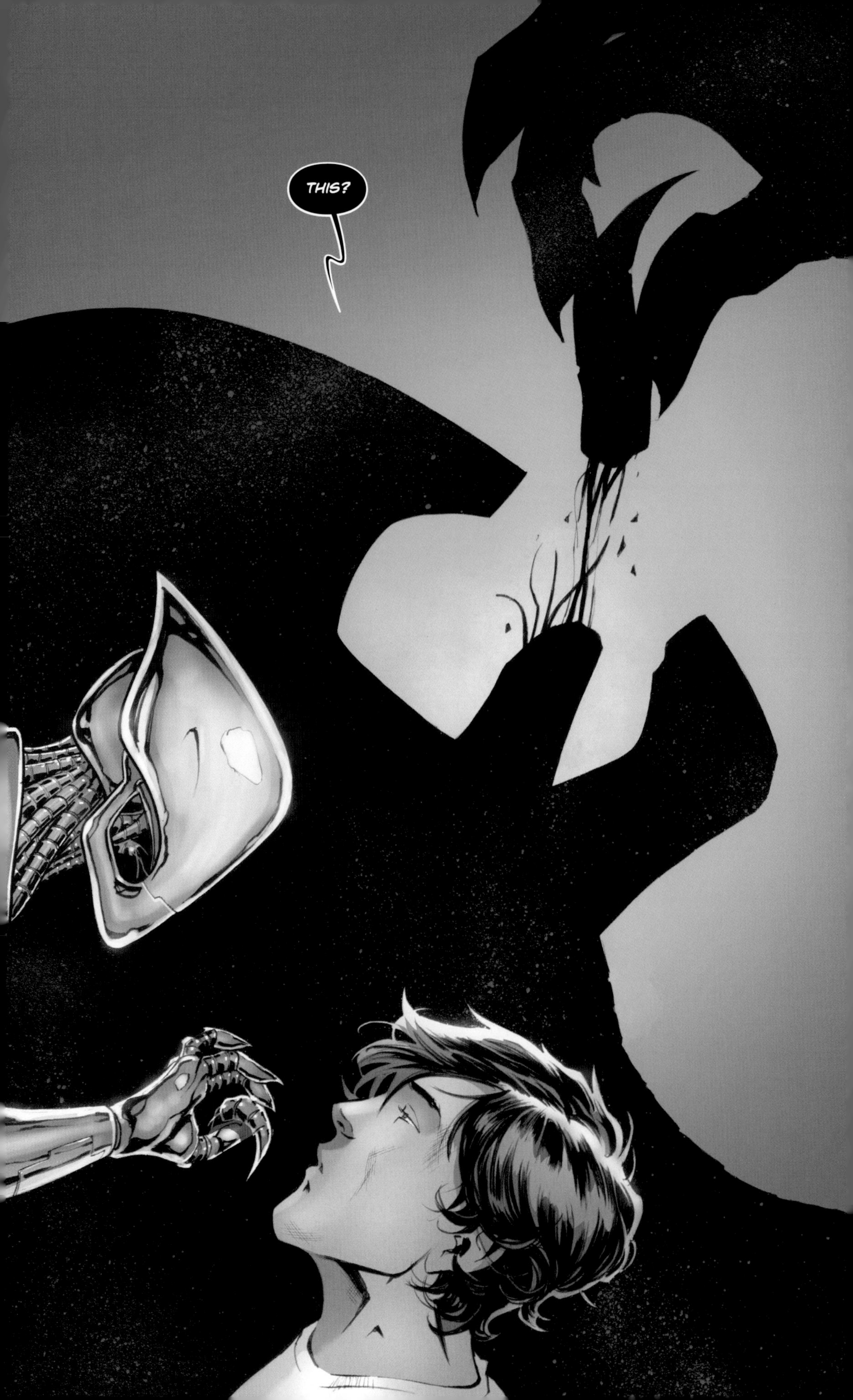
THIS?

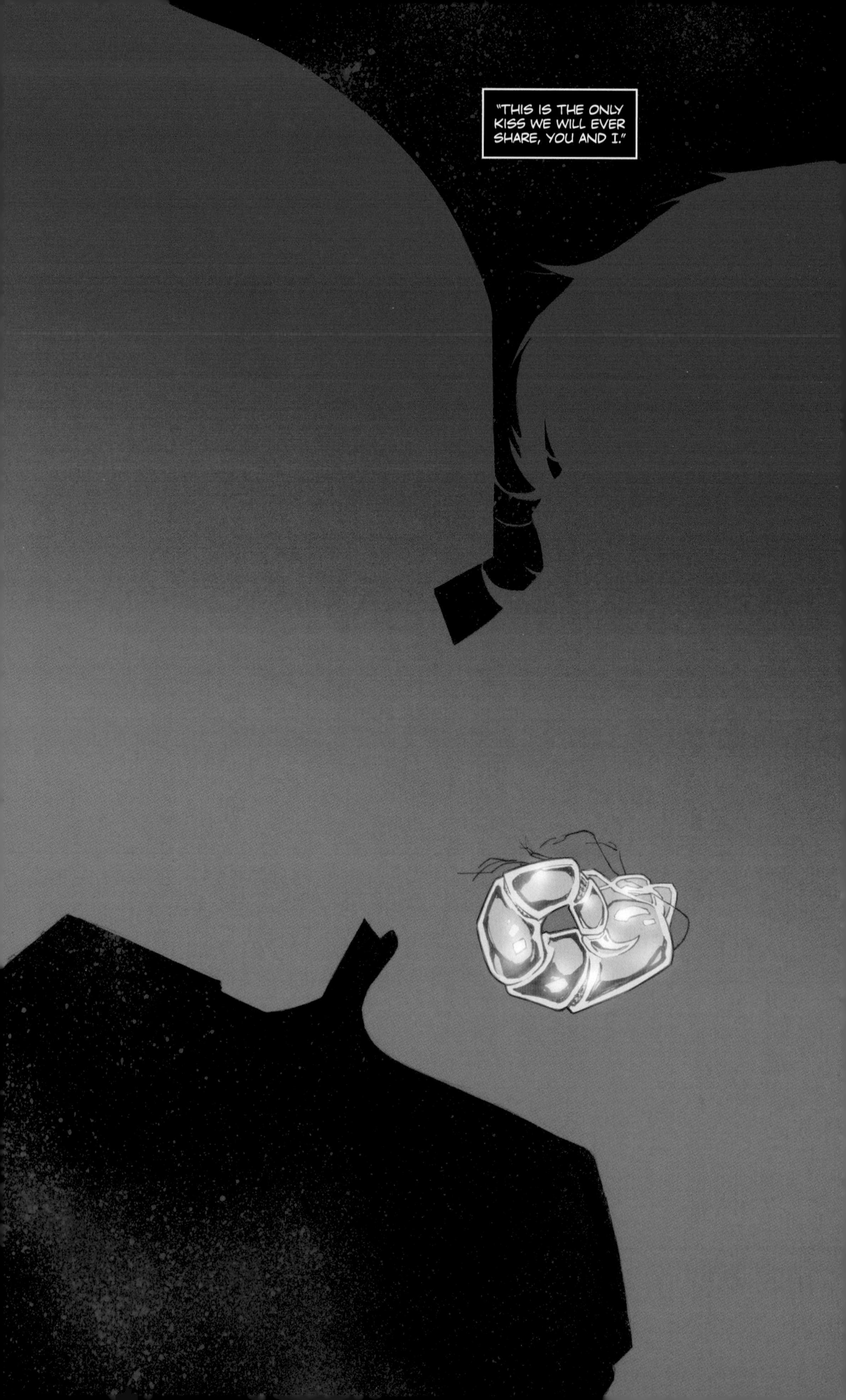
"THIS IS THE ONLY KISS WE WILL EVER SHARE, YOU AND I."

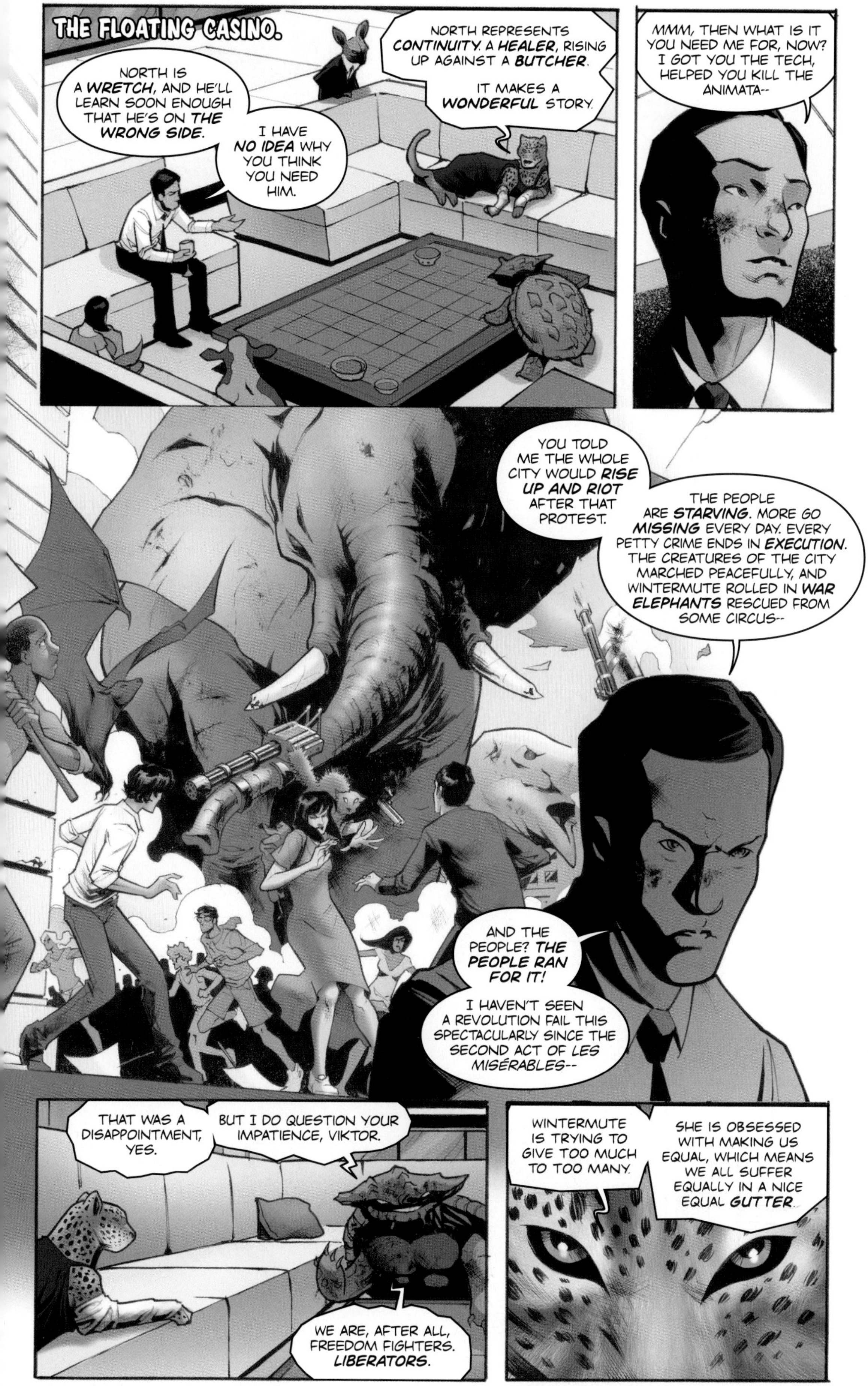
THE FLOATING CASINO.
NORTH IS A WRETCH, AND HE'LL LEARN SOON ENOUGH THAT HE'S ON THE WRONG SIDE.
I HAVE NO IDEA WHY YOU THINK YOU NEED HIM.
NORTH REPRESENTS CONTINUITY. A HEALER, RISING UP AGAINST A BUTCHER.
IT MAKES A WONDERFUL STORY.
MMM, THEN WHAT IS IT YOU NEED ME FOR, NOW? I GOT YOU THE TECH, HELPED YOU KILL THE ANIMATA--
YOU TOLD ME THE WHOLE CITY WOULD RISE UP AND RIOT AFTER THAT PROTEST.
THE PEOPLE ARE STARVING. MORE GO MISSING EVERY DAY. EVERY PETTY CRIME ENDS IN EXECUTION. THE CREATURES OF THE CITY MARCHED PEACEFULLY, AND WINTERMUTE ROLLED IN WAR ELEPHANTS RESCUED FROM SOME CIRCUS--
AND THE PEOPLE? THE PEOPLE RAN FOR IT!
I HAVEN'T SEEN A REVOLUTION FAIL THIS SPECTACULARLY SINCE THE SECOND ACT OF LES MISÉRABLES--
THAT WAS A DISAPPOINTMENT, YES.
BUT I DO QUESTION YOUR IMPATIENCE, VIKTOR.
WE ARE, AFTER ALL, FREEDOM FIGHTERS. LIBERATORS.
WINTERMUTE IS TRYING TO GIVE TOO MUCH TO TOO MANY.
SHE IS OBSESSED WITH MAKING US EQUAL, WHICH MEANS WE ALL SUFFER EQUALLY IN A NICE EQUAL GUTTER.

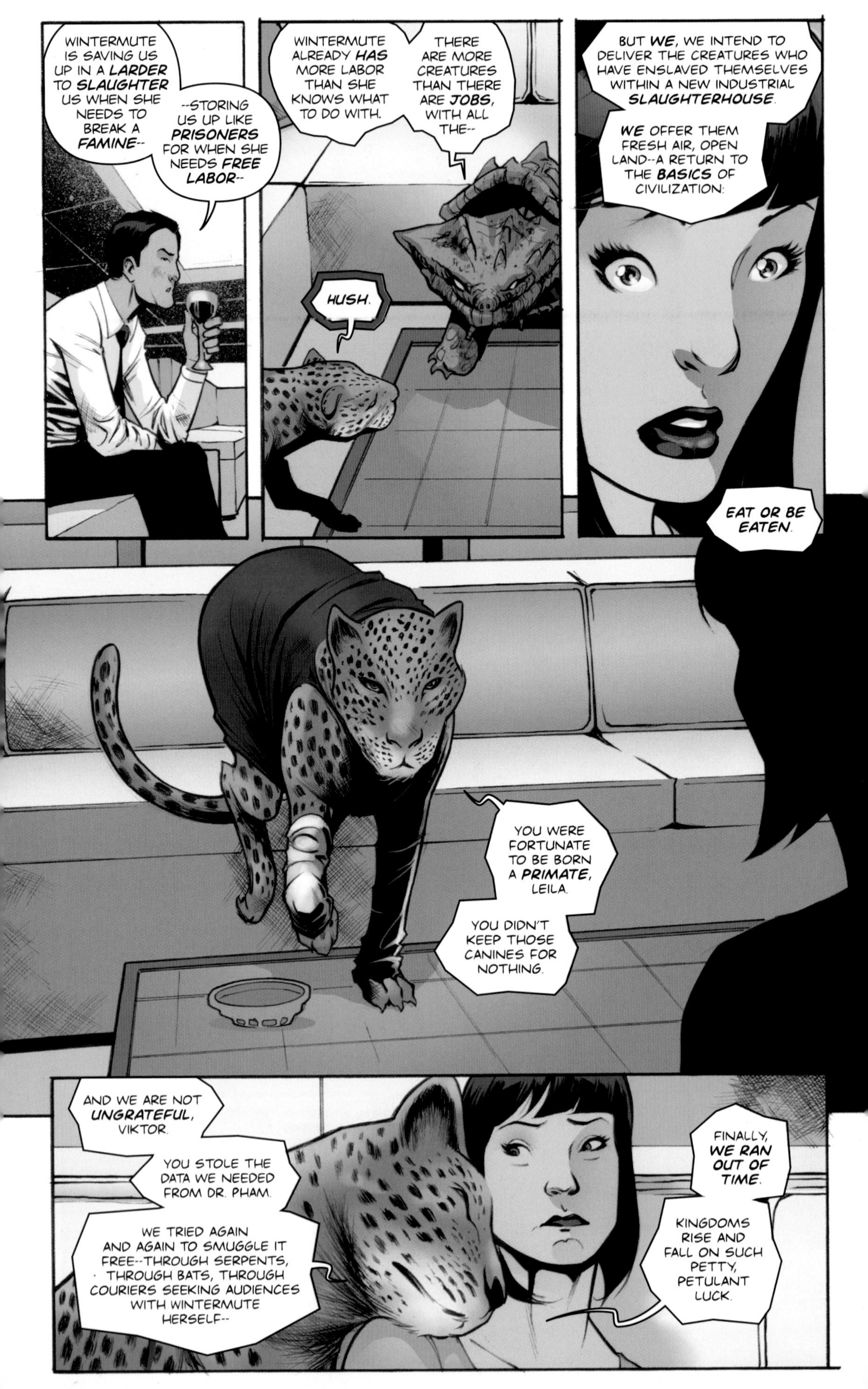
WINTERMUTE IS SAVING US UP IN A LARDER TO SLAUGHTER US WHEN SHE NEEDS TO BREAK A FAMINE--
--STORING US UP LIKE PRISONERS FOR WHEN SHE NEEDS FREE LABOR--
WINTERMUTE ALREADY HAS MORE LABOR THAN SHE KNOWS WHAT TO DO WITH.
THERE ARE MORE CREATURES THAN THERE ARE JOBS, WITH ALL THE--
HUSH.
BUT WE, WE INTEND TO DELIVER THE CREATURES WHO HAVE ENSLAVED THEMSELVES WITHIN A NEW INDUSTRIAL SLAUGHTERHOUSE.
WE OFFER THEM FRESH AIR, OPEN LAND--A RETURN TO THE BASICS OF CIVILIZATION:
EAT OR BE EATEN.
YOU WERE FORTUNATE TO BE BORN A PRIMATE, LEILA.
YOU DIDN'T KEEP THOSE CANINES FOR NOTHING.
AND WE ARE NOT UNGRATEFUL, VIKTOR.
YOU STOLE THE DATA WE NEEDED FROM DR. PHAM.
WE TRIED AGAIN AND AGAIN TO SMUGGLE IT FREE--THROUGH SERPENTS, THROUGH BATS, THROUGH COURIERS SEEKING AUDIENCES WITH WINTERMUTE HERSELF--
FINALLY, WE RAN OUT OF TIME.
KINGDOMS RISE AND FALL ON SUCH PETTY, PETULANT LUCK.

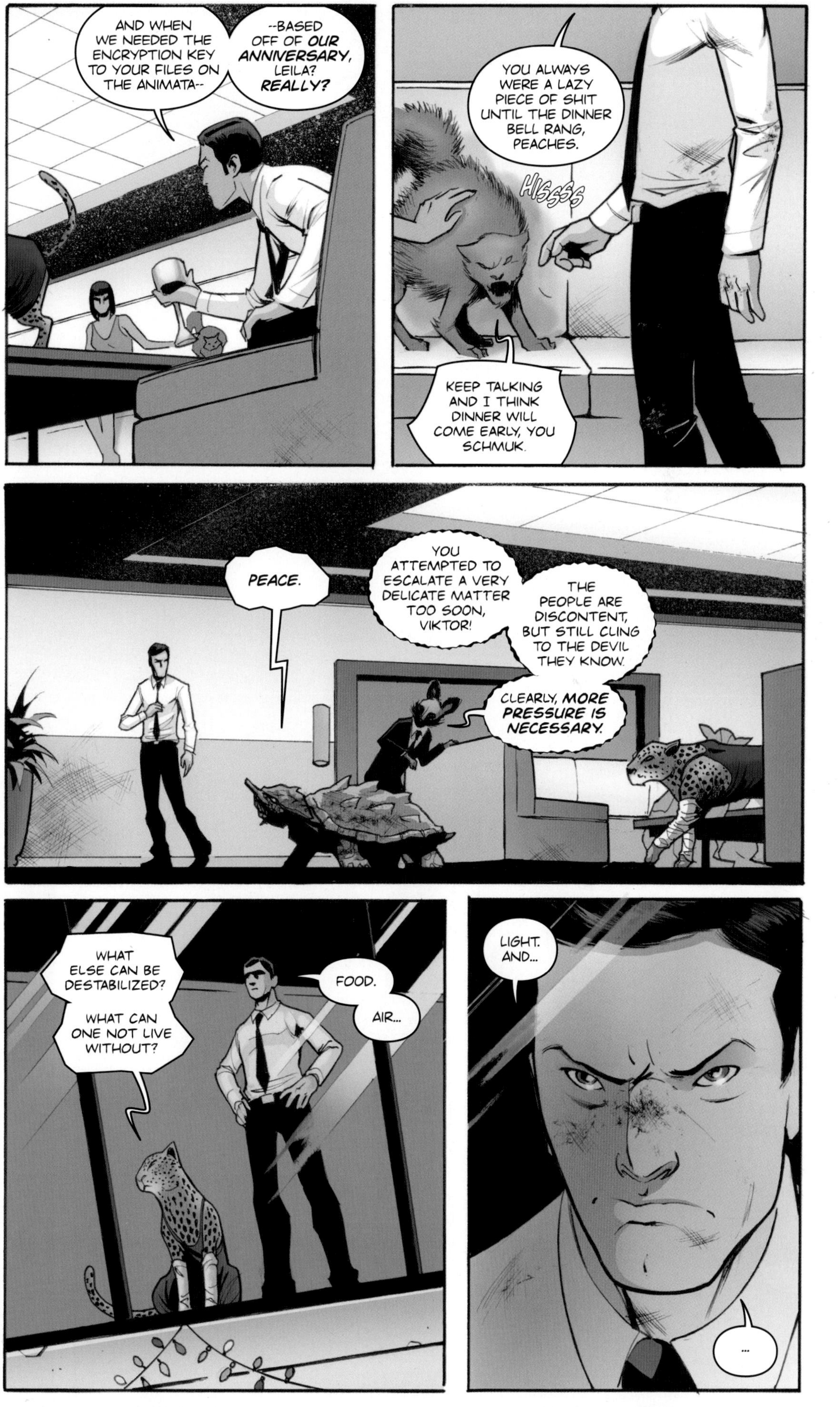
AND WHEN WE NEEDED THE ENCRYPTION KEY TO YOUR FILES ON THE ANIMATA--
--BASED OFF OF **OUR ANNIVERSARY,** LEILA? ***REALLY?***
YOU ALWAYS WERE A LAZY PIECE OF SHIT UNTIL THE DINNER BELL RANG, PEACHES.
HISSSS
KEEP TALKING AND I THINK DINNER WILL COME EARLY, YOU SCHMUK.
PEACE.
YOU ATTEMPTED TO ESCALATE A VERY DELICATE MATTER TOO SOON, VIKTOR!
THE PEOPLE ARE DISCONTENT, BUT STILL CLING TO THE DEVIL THEY KNOW.
CLEARLY, ***MORE PRESSURE IS NECESSARY.***
WHAT ELSE CAN BE DESTABILIZED?
WHAT CAN ONE NOT LIVE WITHOUT?
FOOD.
AIR...
LIGHT. AND...
...

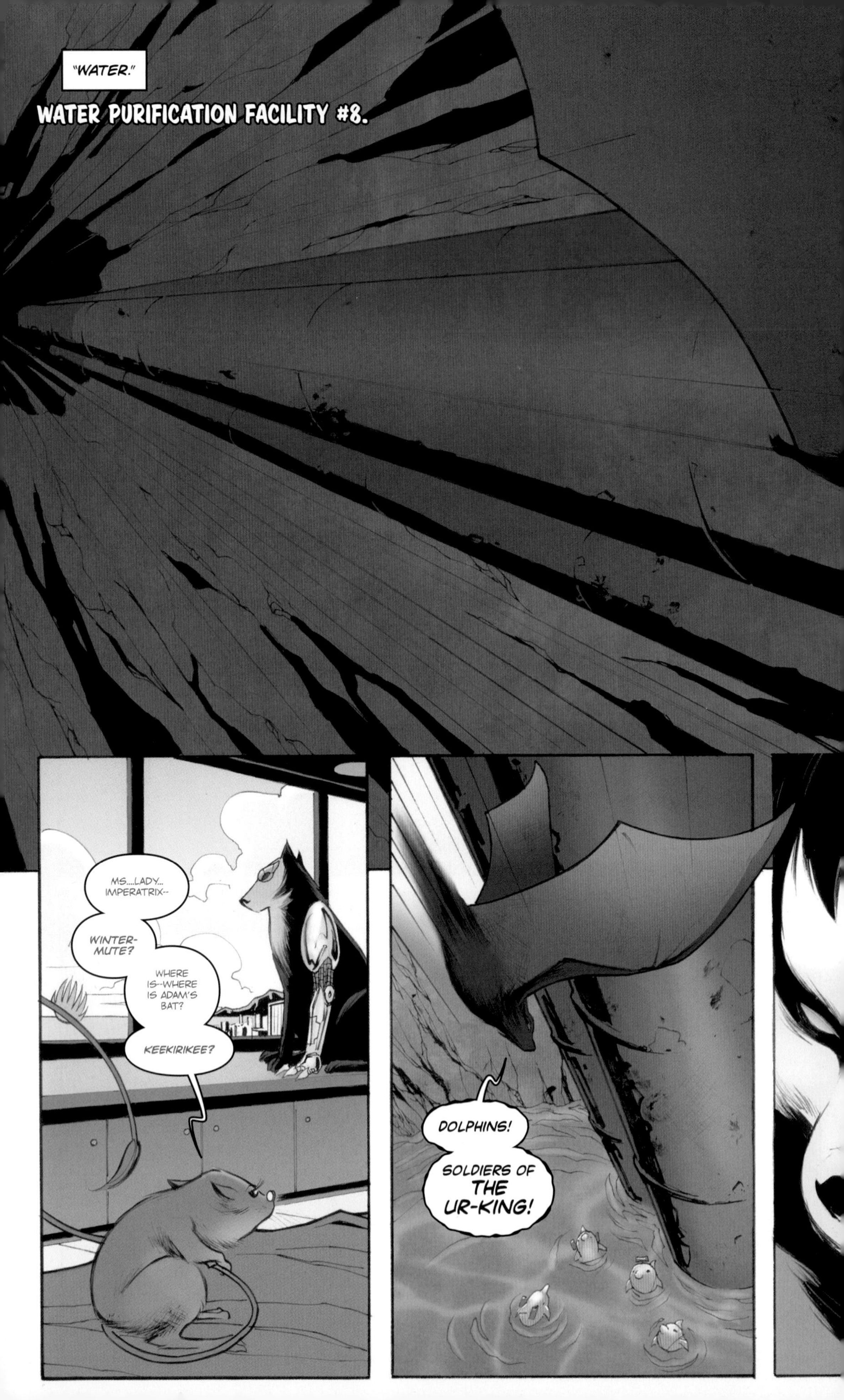
"WATER."
WATER PURIFICATION FACILITY #8.
MS....LADY... IMPERATRIX--
WINTER-MUTE?
WHERE IS--WHERE IS ADAM'S BAT?
KEEKIRIKEE?
DOLPHINS!
SOLDIERS OF THE UR-KING!

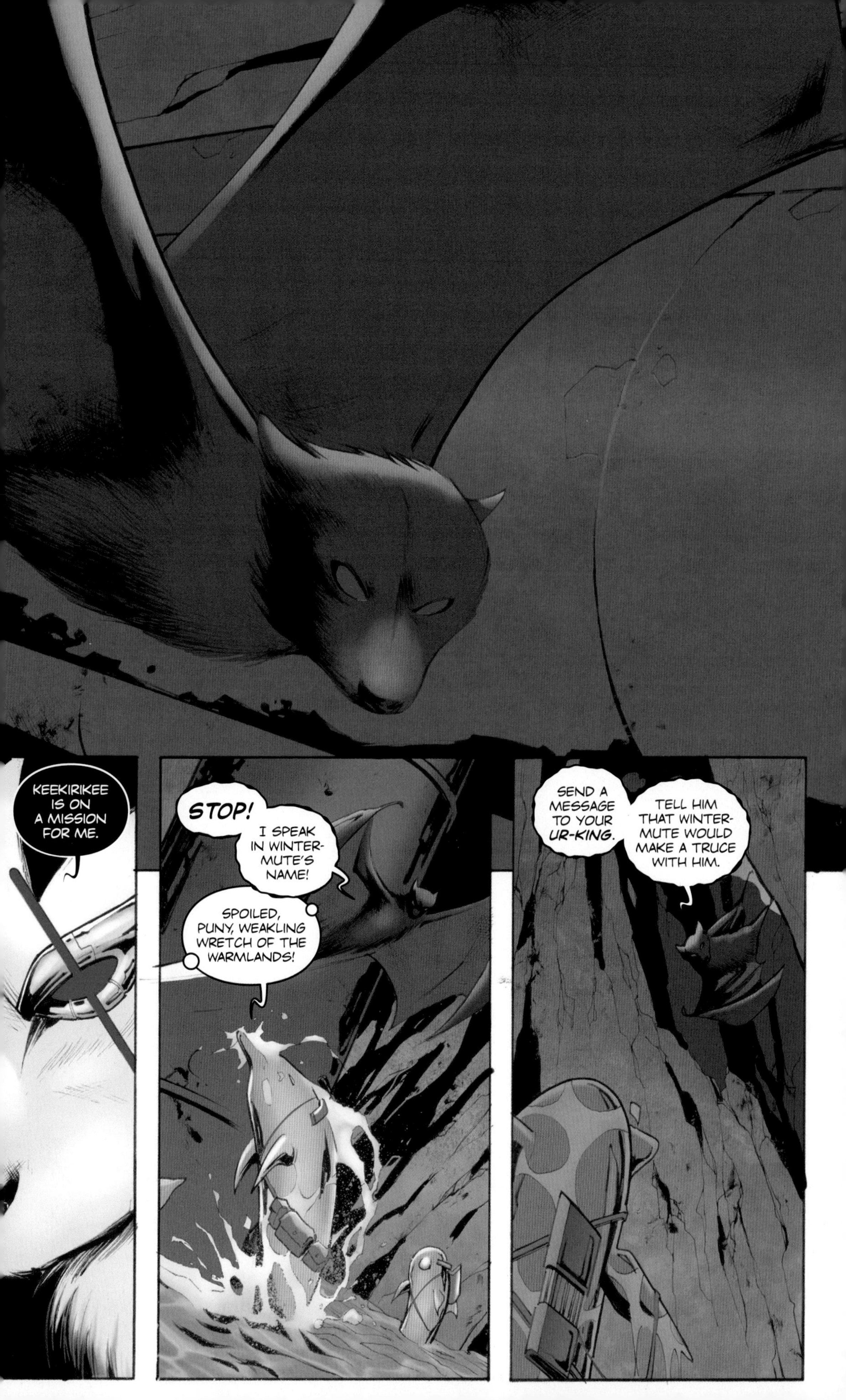
KEEKIRIKEE IS ON A MISSION FOR ME.
STOP!
I SPEAK IN WINTER-MUTE'S NAME!
SPOILED, PUNY, WEAKLING WRETCH OF THE WARMLANDS!
SEND A MESSAGE TO YOUR UR-KING.
TELL HIM THAT WINTER-MUTE WOULD MAKE A TRUCE WITH HIM.

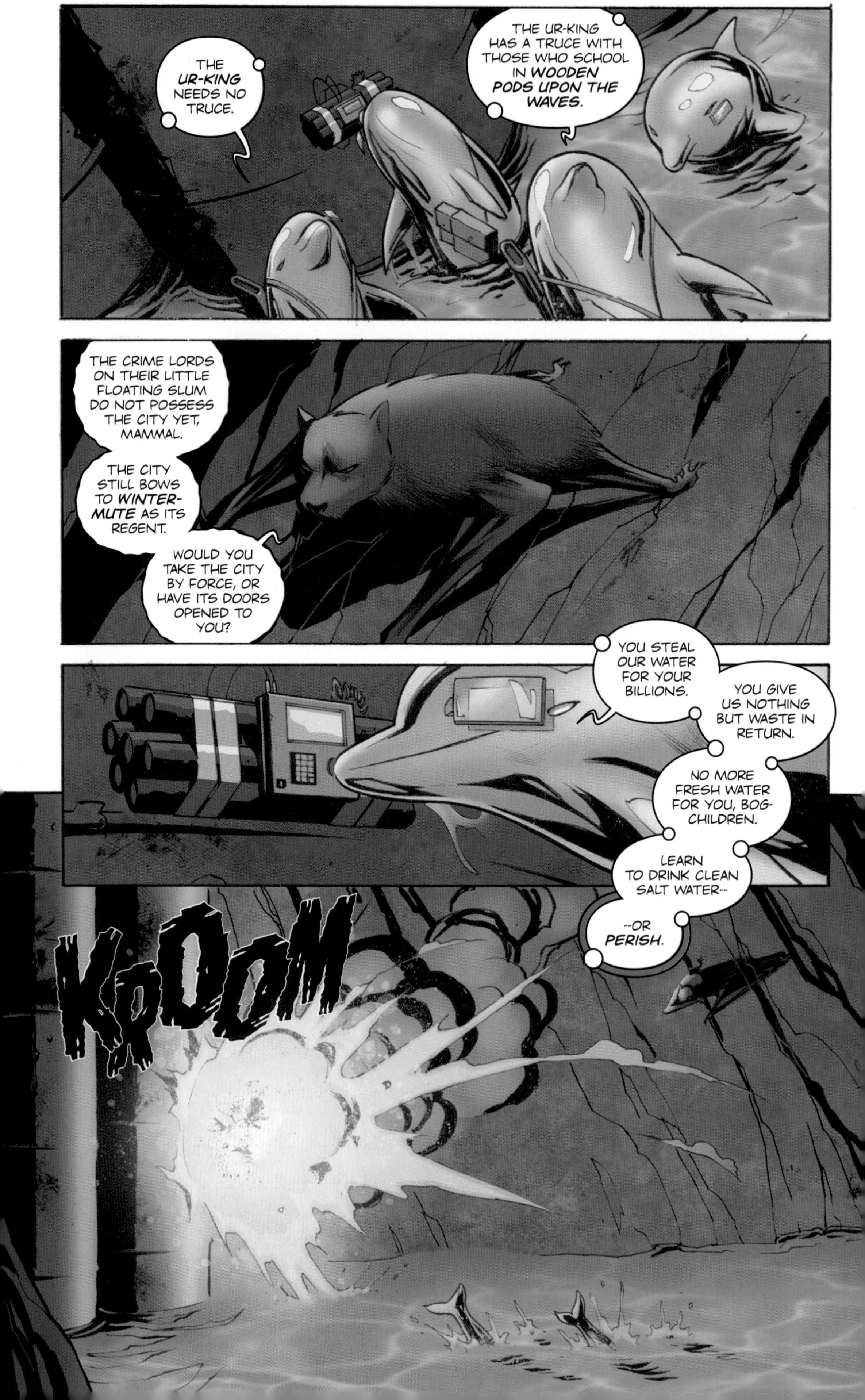
THE UR-KING NEEDS NO TRUCE.
THE UR-KING HAS A TRUCE WITH THOSE WHO SCHOOL IN WOODEN PODS UPON THE WAVES.
THE CRIME LORDS ON THEIR LITTLE FLOATING SLUM DO NOT POSSESS THE CITY YET, MAMMAL.
THE CITY STILL BOWS TO WINTER-MUTE AS ITS REGENT.
WOULD YOU TAKE THE CITY BY FORCE, OR HAVE ITS DOORS OPENED TO YOU?
YOU STEAL OUR WATER FOR YOUR BILLIONS.
YOU GIVE US NOTHING BUT WASTE IN RETURN.
NO MORE FRESH WATER FOR YOU, BOG-CHILDREN.
LEARN TO DRINK CLEAN SALT WATER--
--OR PERISH.
KPOOOM

IT'S ALL **TRADE SCHOOLS** RIGHT NOW FOR THOSE WILLING TO LEARN, BUT WHAT IF ONE OF MY LITTER WANTS **A COLLEGE DEGREE?**

YOU RECKON I CAN AFFORD **EIGHTEEN TUITIONS** ON A RODENT ELECTRICIAN'S SALAR--

SHHH, MR. TUFTS! LOOK!

gurgl

YOU, UH... WANT ME TO SLITHER IN AND **CHECK?**

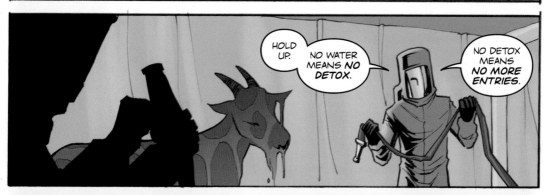

HOLD UP. NO WATER MEANS **NO** DETOX.

NO DETOX MEANS **NO MORE ENTRIES.**

NOW WE WILL PARLAY.

NOW WE WILL BARGAIN.

W-WINTER-MUTE?

WHAT COMES NEXT?

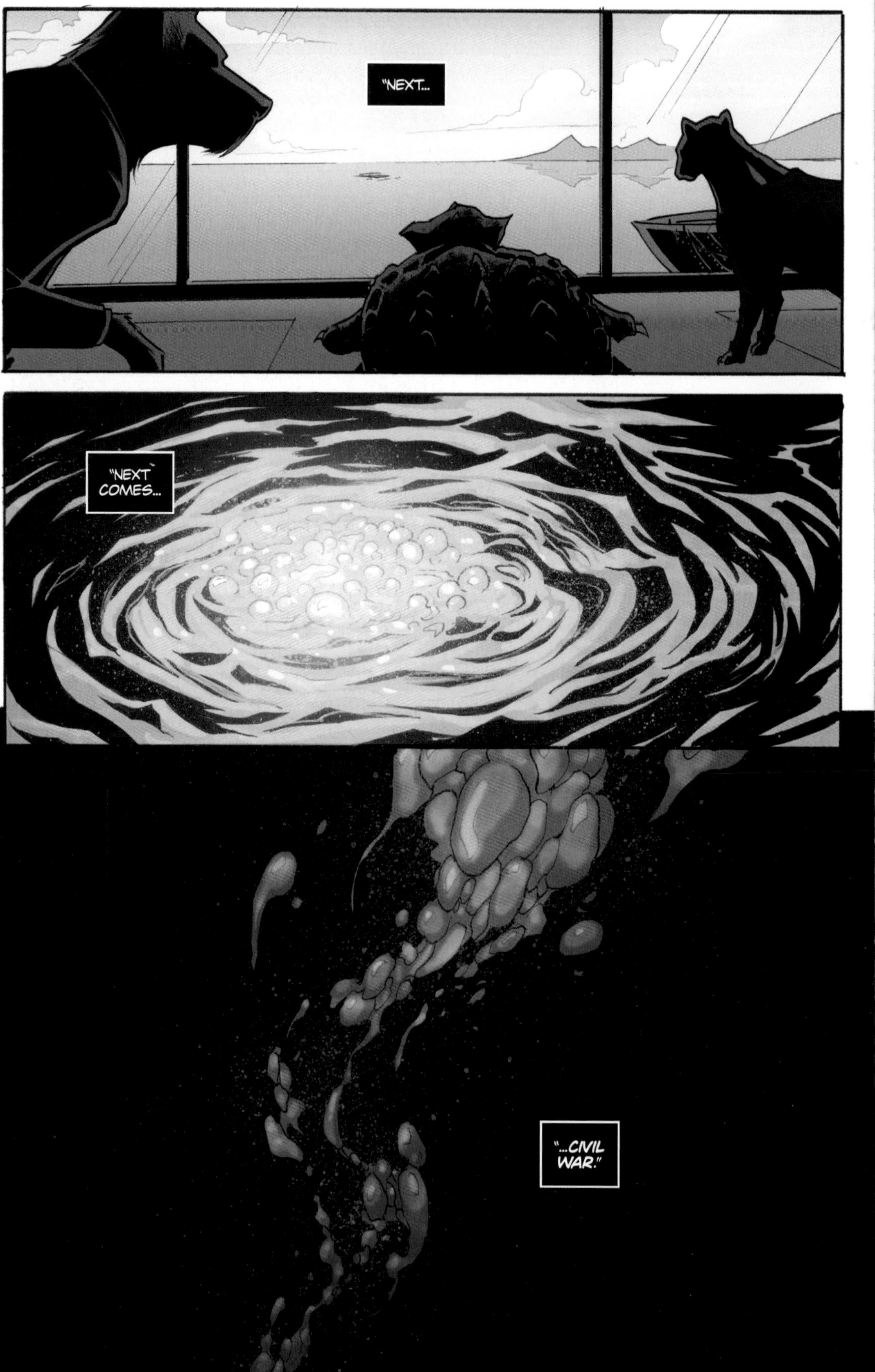
"NEXT...
"NEXT COMES...
"...CIVIL WAR."

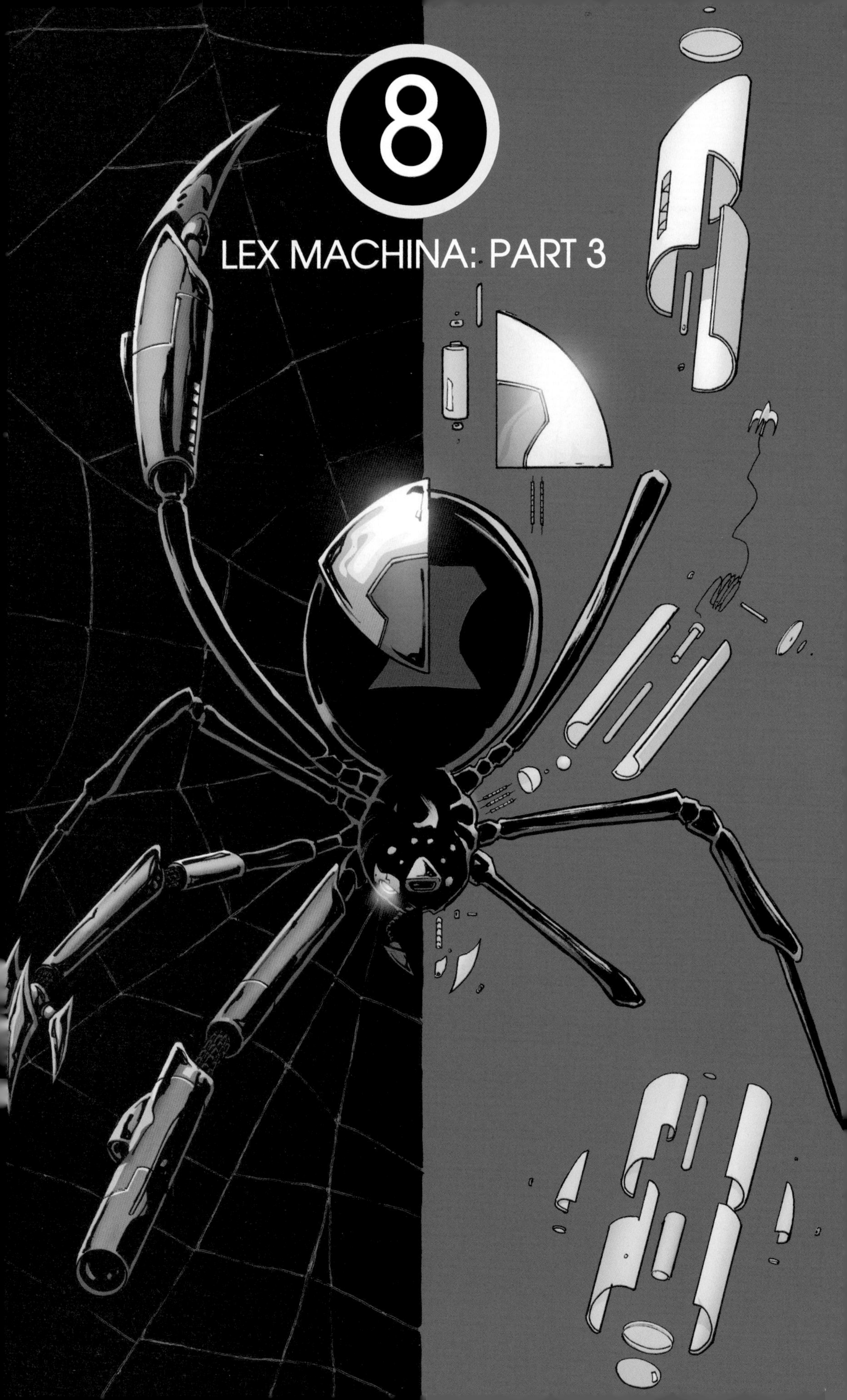
8
LEX MACHINA: PART 3

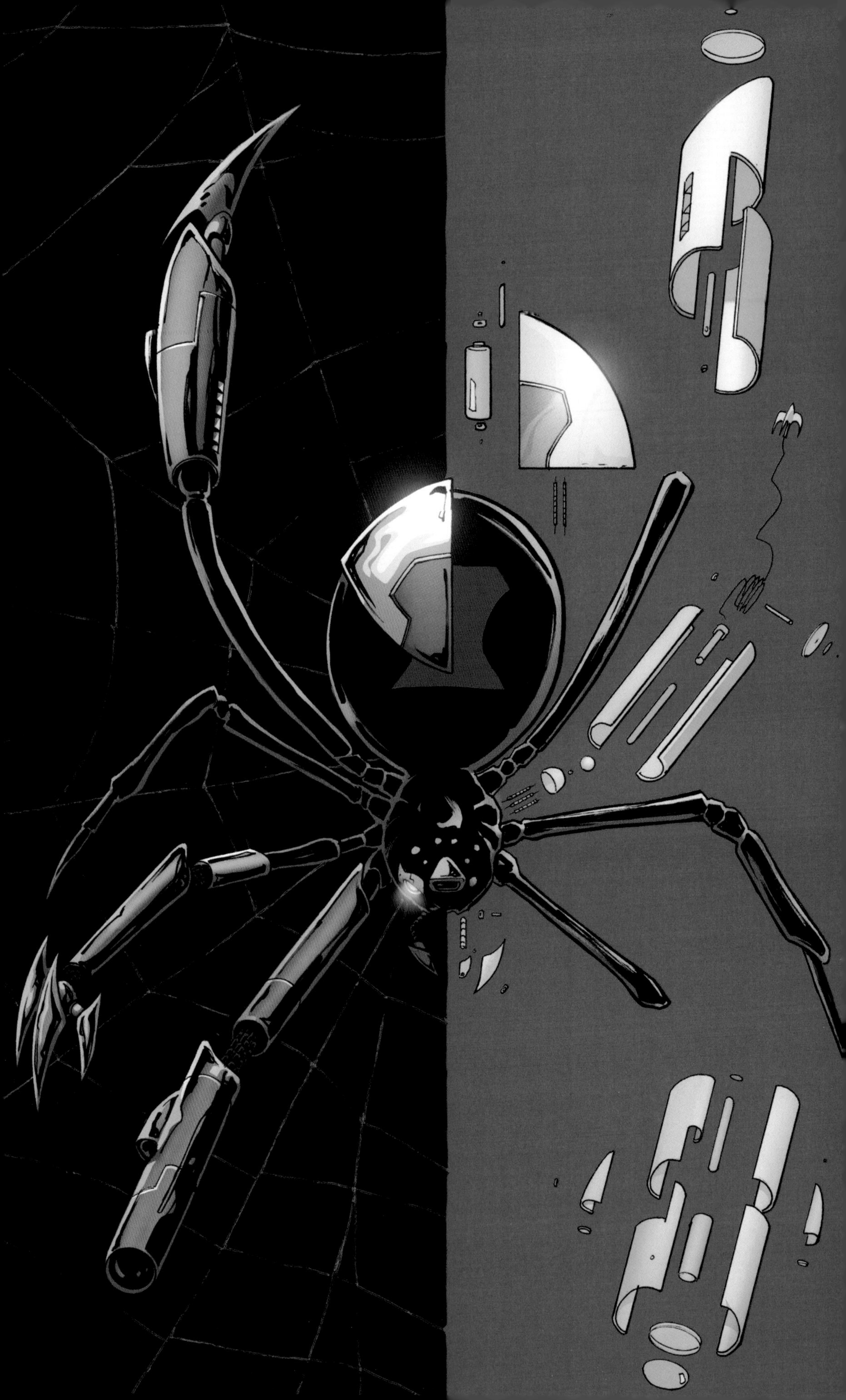

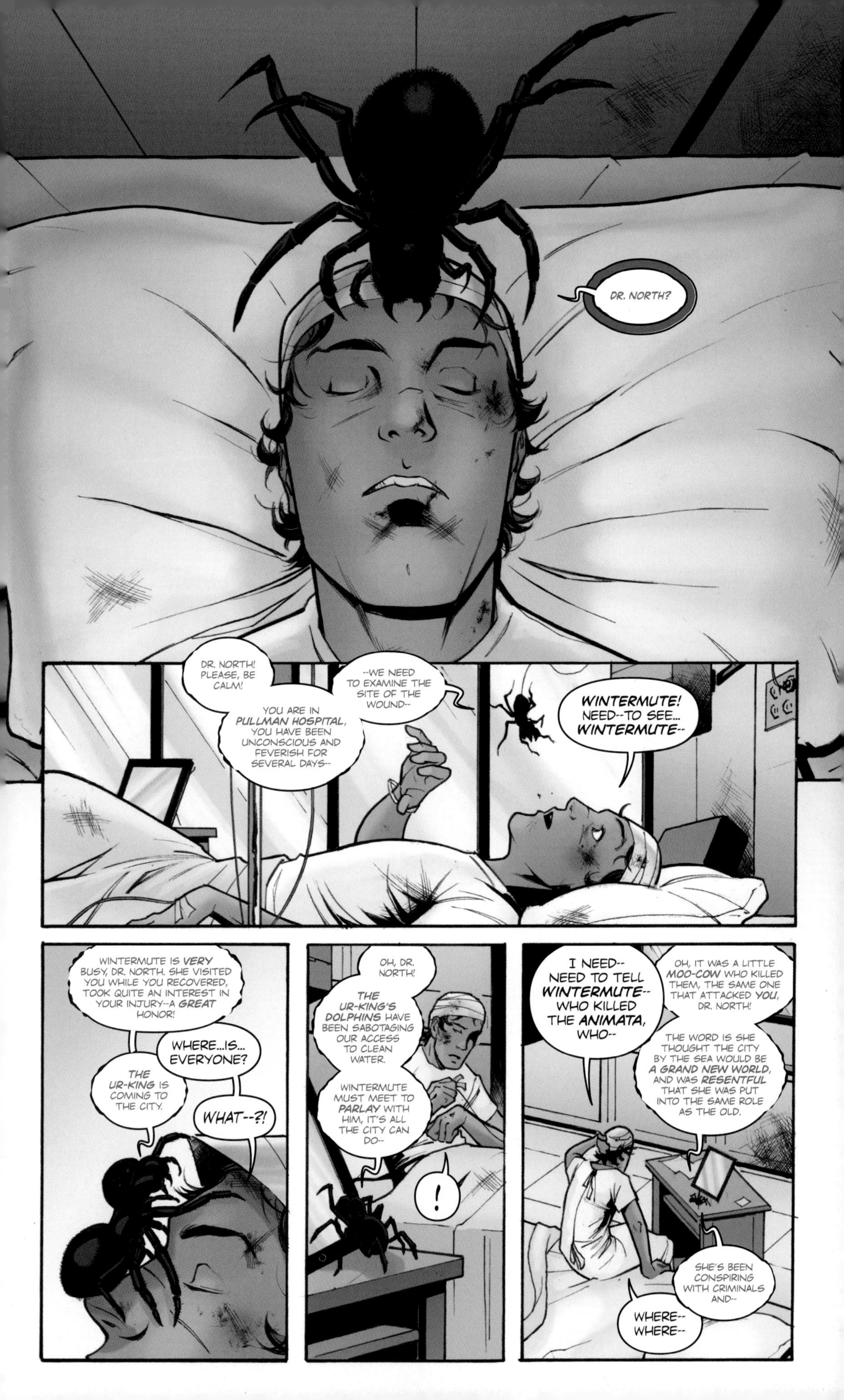
DR. NORTH?
DR. NORTH! PLEASE, BE CALM!
YOU ARE IN PULLMAN HOSPITAL, YOU HAVE BEEN UNCONSCIOUS AND FEVERISH FOR SEVERAL DAYS--
--WE NEED TO EXAMINE THE SITE OF THE WOUND--
WINTERMUTE! NEED--TO SEE... WINTERMUTE--
WINTERMUTE IS VERY BUSY, DR. NORTH. SHE VISITED YOU WHILE YOU RECOVERED, TOOK QUITE AN INTEREST IN YOUR INJURY--A GREAT HONOR!
WHERE...IS... EVERYONE?
THE UR-KING IS COMING TO THE CITY.
WHAT--?!
OH, DR. NORTH!
THE UR-KING'S DOLPHINS HAVE BEEN SABOTAGING OUR ACCESS TO CLEAN WATER.
WINTERMUTE MUST MEET TO PARLAY WITH HIM, IT'S ALL THE CITY CAN DO--
!
I NEED-- NEED TO TELL WINTERMUTE-- WHO KILLED THE ANIMATA, WHO--
OH, IT WAS A LITTLE MOO-COW WHO KILLED THEM, THE SAME ONE THAT ATTACKED YOU, DR. NORTH!
THE WORD IS SHE THOUGHT THE CITY BY THE SEA WOULD BE A GRAND NEW WORLD, AND WAS RESENTFUL THAT SHE WAS PUT INTO THE SAME ROLE AS THE OLD.
SHE'S BEEN CONSPIRING WITH CRIMINALS AND--
WHERE-- WHERE--

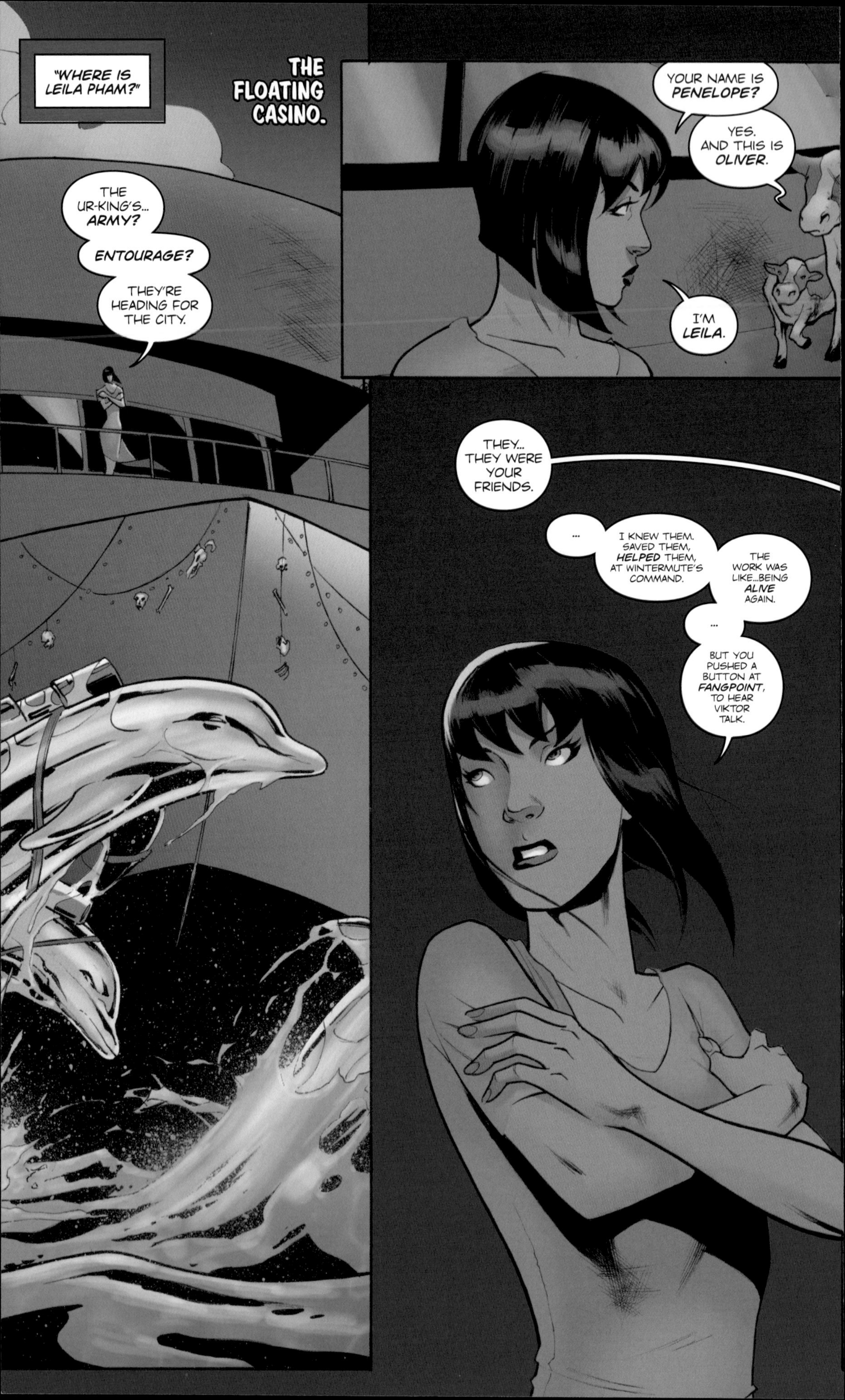
"WHERE IS LEILA PHAM?"
THE FLOATING CASINO.
THE UR-KING'S... ARMY?
ENTOURAGE?
THEY'RE HEADING FOR THE CITY.
YOUR NAME IS PENELOPE?
YES. AND THIS IS OLIVER.
I'M LEILA.
THEY... THEY WERE YOUR FRIENDS.
...
I KNEW THEM. SAVED THEM, HELPED THEM, AT WINTERMUTE'S COMMAND.
THE WORK WAS LIKE...BEING ALIVE AGAIN.
...
BUT YOU PUSHED A BUTTON AT FANGPOINT, TO HEAR VIKTOR TALK.

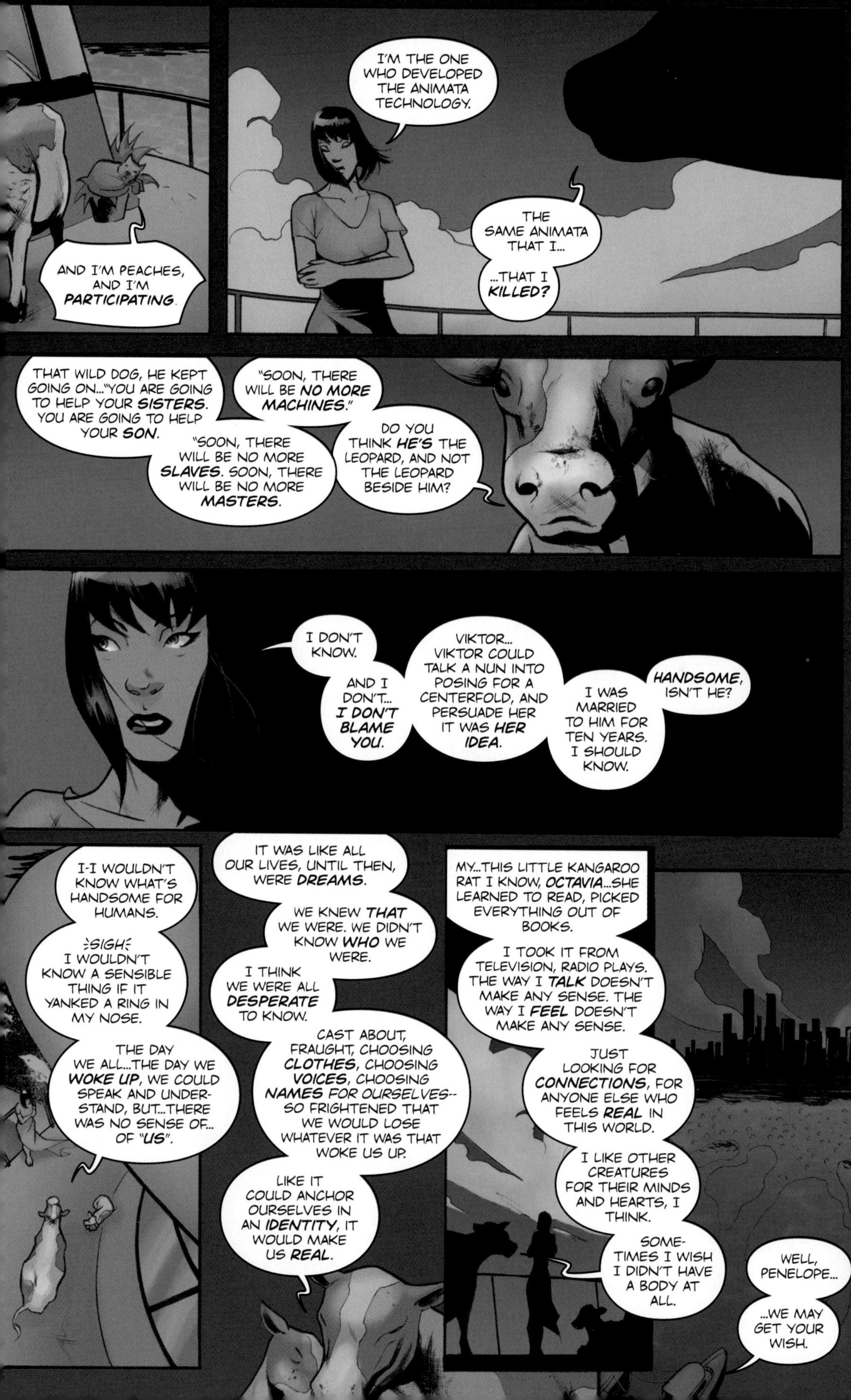

AND I'M PEACHES, AND I'M PARTICIPATING.
I'M THE ONE WHO DEVELOPED THE ANIMATA TECHNOLOGY.
THE SAME ANIMATA THAT I...
...THAT I KILLED?
THAT WILD DOG, HE KEPT GOING ON..."YOU ARE GOING TO HELP YOUR SISTERS. YOU ARE GOING TO HELP YOUR SON.
"SOON, THERE WILL BE NO MORE SLAVES. SOON, THERE WILL BE NO MORE MASTERS.
"SOON, THERE WILL BE NO MORE MACHINES."
DO YOU THINK HE'S THE LEOPARD, AND NOT THE LEOPARD BESIDE HIM?
I DON'T KNOW.
AND I DON'T... I DON'T BLAME YOU.
VIKTOR... VIKTOR COULD TALK A NUN INTO POSING FOR A CENTERFOLD, AND PERSUADE HER IT WAS HER IDEA.
I WAS MARRIED TO HIM FOR TEN YEARS. I SHOULD KNOW.
HANDSOME, ISN'T HE?
I-I WOULDN'T KNOW WHAT'S HANDSOME FOR HUMANS.
SIGH I WOULDN'T KNOW A SENSIBLE THING IF IT YANKED A RING IN MY NOSE.
THE DAY WE ALL...THE DAY WE WOKE UP, WE COULD SPEAK AND UNDERSTAND, BUT...THERE WAS NO SENSE OF... OF "US".
IT WAS LIKE ALL OUR LIVES, UNTIL THEN, WERE DREAMS.
WE KNEW THAT WE WERE. WE DIDN'T KNOW WHO WE WERE.
I THINK WE WERE ALL DESPERATE TO KNOW.
CAST ABOUT, FRAUGHT, CHOOSING CLOTHES, CHOOSING VOICES, CHOOSING NAMES FOR OURSELVES-- SO FRIGHTENED THAT WE WOULD LOSE WHATEVER IT WAS THAT WOKE US UP.
LIKE IT COULD ANCHOR OURSELVES IN AN IDENTITY, IT WOULD MAKE US REAL.
MY...THIS LITTLE KANGAROO RAT I KNOW, OCTAVIA...SHE LEARNED TO READ, PICKED EVERYTHING OUT OF BOOKS.
I TOOK IT FROM TELEVISION, RADIO PLAYS. THE WAY I TALK DOESN'T MAKE ANY SENSE. THE WAY I FEEL DOESN'T MAKE ANY SENSE.
JUST LOOKING FOR CONNECTIONS, FOR ANYONE ELSE WHO FEELS REAL IN THIS WORLD.
I LIKE OTHER CREATURES FOR THEIR MINDS AND HEARTS, I THINK.
SOMETIMES I WISH I DIDN'T HAVE A BODY AT ALL.
WELL, PENELOPE...
...WE MAY GET YOUR WISH.

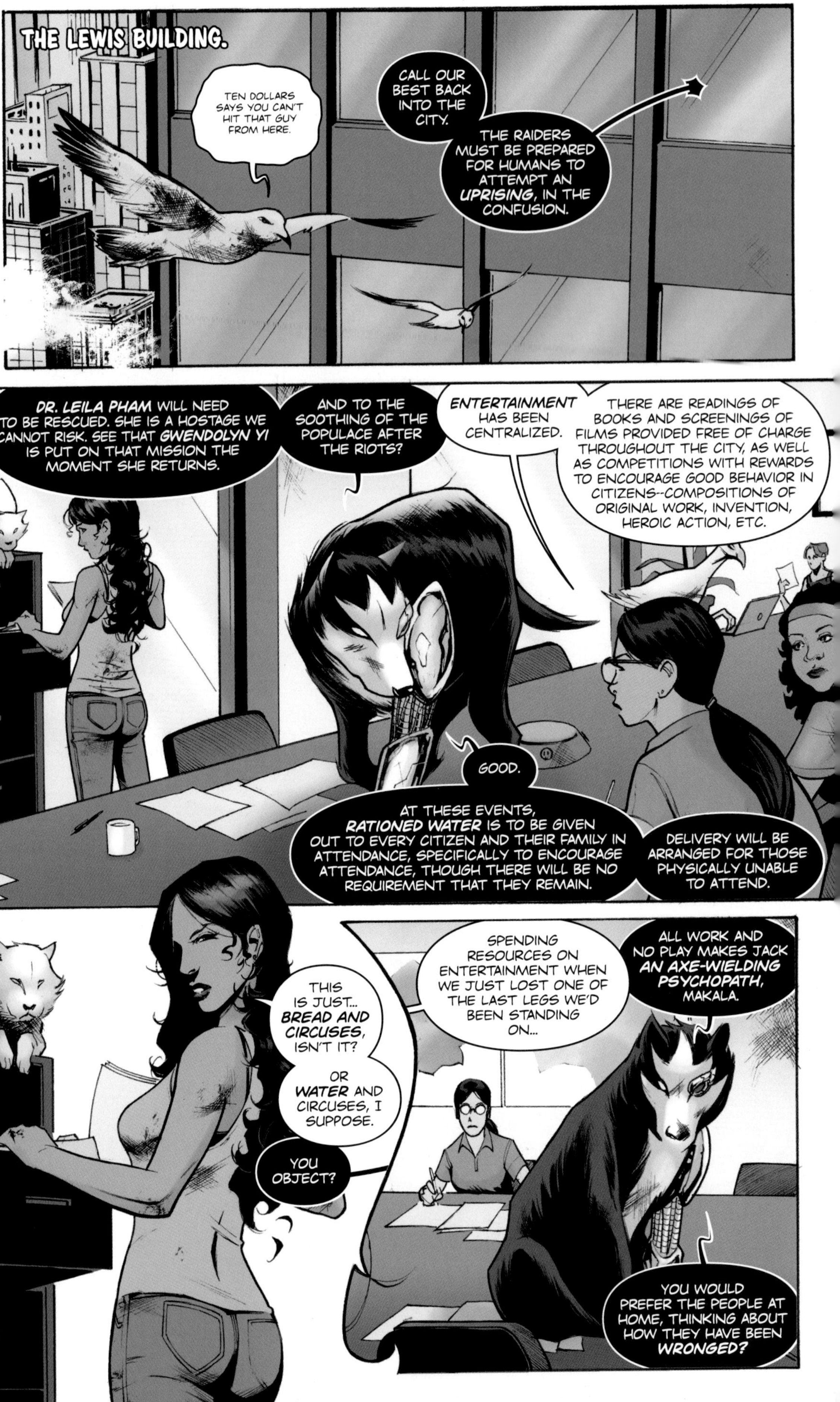
THE LEWIS BUILDING.
TEN DOLLARS SAYS YOU CAN'T HIT THAT GUY FROM HERE.
CALL OUR BEST BACK INTO THE CITY.
THE RAIDERS MUST BE PREPARED FOR HUMANS TO ATTEMPT AN UPRISING, IN THE CONFUSION.
DR. LEILA PHAM WILL NEED TO BE RESCUED. SHE IS A HOSTAGE WE CANNOT RISK. SEE THAT GWENDOLYN YI IS PUT ON THAT MISSION THE MOMENT SHE RETURNS.
AND TO THE SOOTHING OF THE POPULACE AFTER THE RIOTS?
ENTERTAINMENT HAS BEEN CENTRALIZED.
THERE ARE READINGS OF BOOKS AND SCREENINGS OF FILMS PROVIDED FREE OF CHARGE THROUGHOUT THE CITY, AS WELL AS COMPETITIONS WITH REWARDS TO ENCOURAGE GOOD BEHAVIOR IN CITIZENS--COMPOSITIONS OF ORIGINAL WORK, INVENTION, HEROIC ACTION, ETC.
GOOD.
AT THESE EVENTS, RATIONED WATER IS TO BE GIVEN OUT TO EVERY CITIZEN AND THEIR FAMILY IN ATTENDANCE, SPECIFICALLY TO ENCOURAGE ATTENDANCE, THOUGH THERE WILL BE NO REQUIREMENT THAT THEY REMAIN.
DELIVERY WILL BE ARRANGED FOR THOSE PHYSICALLY UNABLE TO ATTEND.
THIS IS JUST... BREAD AND CIRCUSES, ISN'T IT?
OR WATER AND CIRCUSES, I SUPPOSE.
YOU OBJECT?
SPENDING RESOURCES ON ENTERTAINMENT WHEN WE JUST LOST ONE OF THE LAST LEGS WE'D BEEN STANDING ON...
ALL WORK AND NO PLAY MAKES JACK AN AXE-WIELDING PSYCHOPATH, MAKALA.
YOU WOULD PREFER THE PEOPLE AT HOME, THINKING ABOUT HOW THEY HAVE BEEN WRONGED?

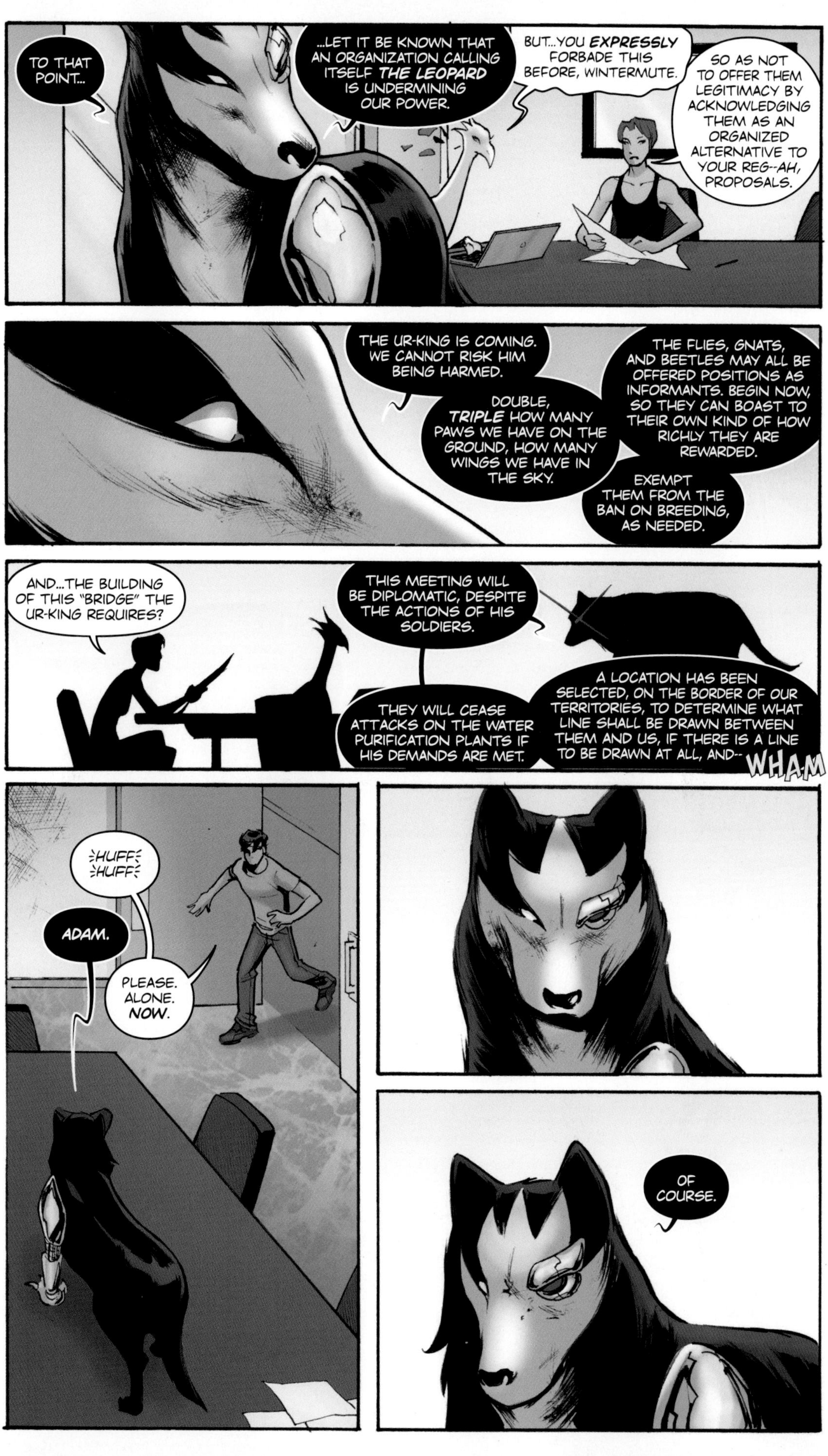
TO THAT POINT...
...LET IT BE KNOWN THAT AN ORGANIZATION CALLING ITSELF THE LEOPARD IS UNDERMINING OUR POWER.
BUT...YOU EXPRESSLY FORBADE THIS BEFORE, WINTERMUTE.
SO AS NOT TO OFFER THEM LEGITIMACY BY ACKNOWLEDGING THEM AS AN ORGANIZED ALTERNATIVE TO YOUR REG--AH, PROPOSALS.
THE UR-KING IS COMING. WE CANNOT RISK HIM BEING HARMED.
DOUBLE, TRIPLE HOW MANY PAWS WE HAVE ON THE GROUND, HOW MANY WINGS WE HAVE IN THE SKY.
THE FLIES, GNATS, AND BEETLES MAY ALL BE OFFERED POSITIONS AS INFORMANTS. BEGIN NOW, SO THEY CAN BOAST TO THEIR OWN KIND OF HOW RICHLY THEY ARE REWARDED.
EXEMPT THEM FROM THE BAN ON BREEDING, AS NEEDED.
AND...THE BUILDING OF THIS "BRIDGE" THE UR-KING REQUIRES?
THIS MEETING WILL BE DIPLOMATIC, DESPITE THE ACTIONS OF HIS SOLDIERS.
THEY WILL CEASE ATTACKS ON THE WATER PURIFICATION PLANTS IF HIS DEMANDS ARE MET.
A LOCATION HAS BEEN SELECTED, ON THE BORDER OF OUR TERRITORIES, TO DETERMINE WHAT LINE SHALL BE DRAWN BETWEEN THEM AND US, IF THERE IS A LINE TO BE DRAWN AT ALL, AND--
WHAM
HUFF HUFF
ADAM.
PLEASE. ALONE. NOW.
OF COURSE.

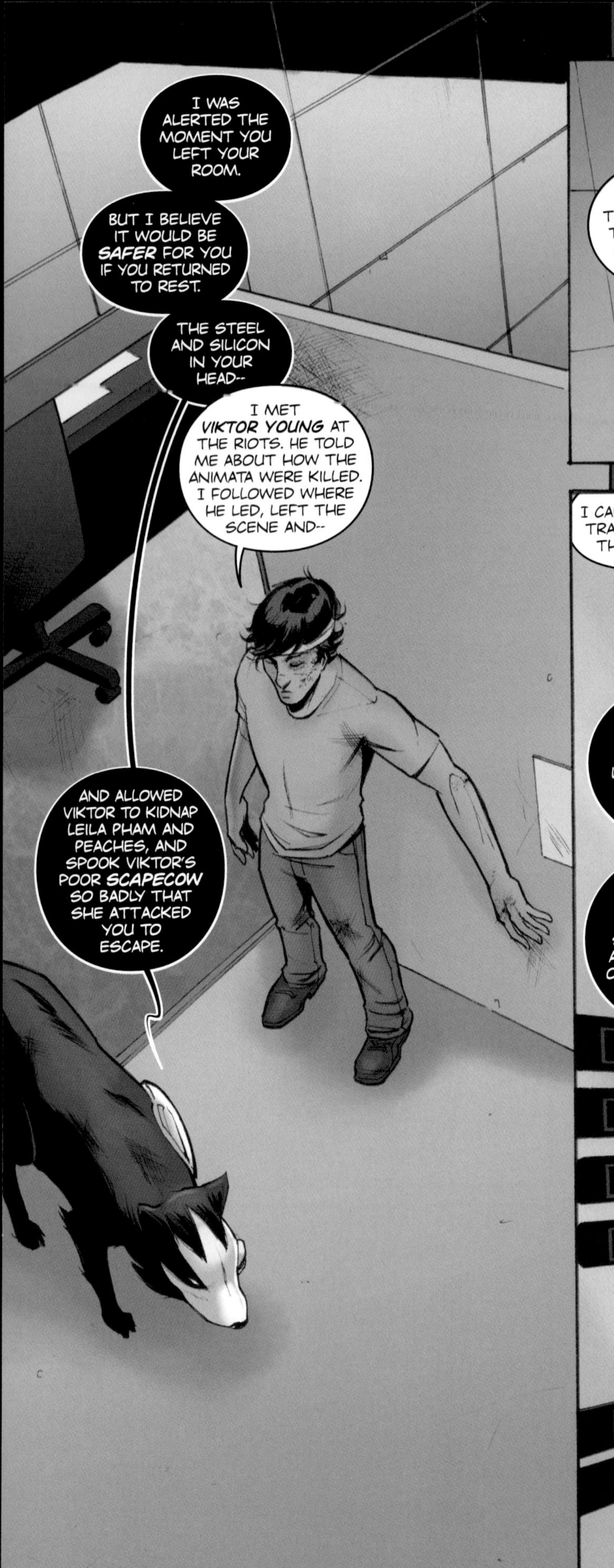

I WAS ALERTED THE MOMENT YOU LEFT YOUR ROOM.
BUT I BELIEVE IT WOULD BE **SAFER** FOR YOU IF YOU RETURNED TO REST.
THE STEEL AND SILICON IN YOUR HEAD--
I MET **VIKTOR YOUNG** AT THE RIOTS. HE TOLD ME ABOUT HOW THE ANIMATA WERE KILLED. I FOLLOWED WHERE HE LED, LEFT THE SCENE AND--
AND ALLOWED VIKTOR TO KIDNAP LEILA PHAM AND PEACHES, AND SPOOK VIKTOR'S POOR **SCAPECOW** SO BADLY THAT SHE ATTACKED YOU TO ESCAPE.

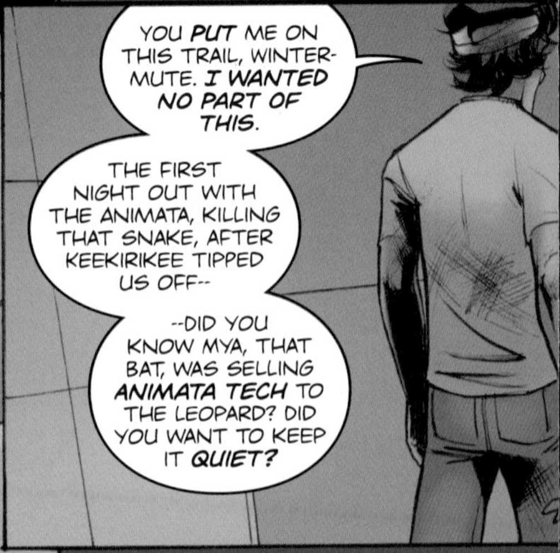

YOU **PUT** ME ON THIS TRAIL, WINTER-MUTE. ***I WANTED NO PART OF THIS***.
THE FIRST NIGHT OUT WITH THE ANIMATA, KILLING THAT SNAKE, AFTER KEEKIRIKEE TIPPED US OFF--
--DID YOU KNOW MYA, THAT BAT, WAS SELLING **ANIMATA TECH** TO THE LEOPARD? DID YOU WANT TO KEEP IT **QUIET?**

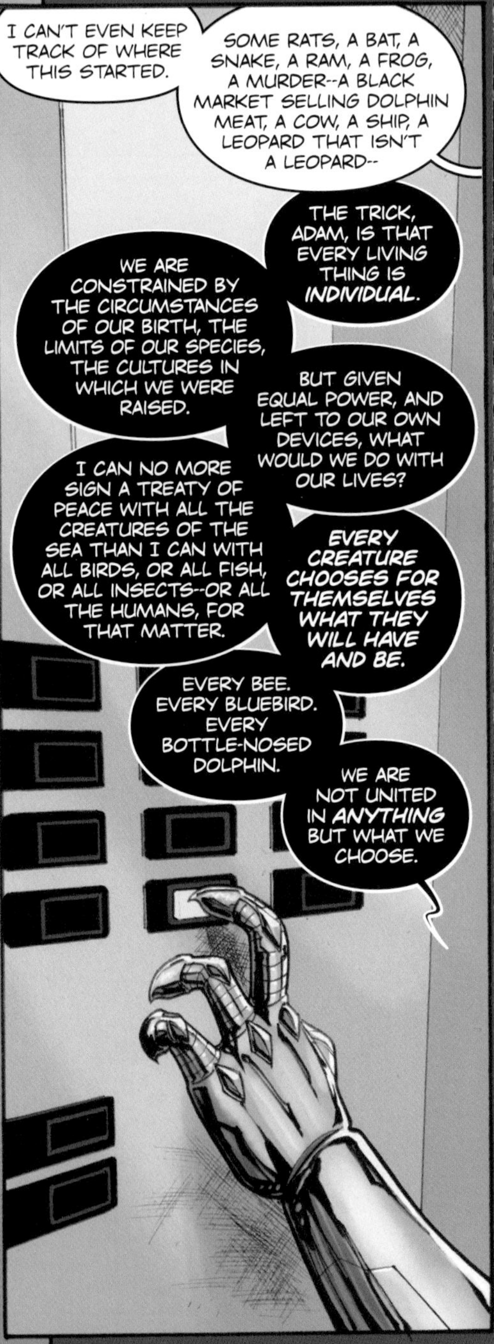

I CAN'T EVEN KEEP TRACK OF WHERE THIS STARTED.
SOME RATS, A BAT, A SNAKE, A RAM, A FROG, A MURDER--A BLACK MARKET SELLING DOLPHIN MEAT, A COW, A SHIP, A LEOPARD THAT ISN'T A LEOPARD--
THE TRICK, ADAM, IS THAT EVERY LIVING THING IS **INDIVIDUAL**.
WE ARE CONSTRAINED BY THE CIRCUMSTANCES OF OUR BIRTH, THE LIMITS OF OUR SPECIES, THE CULTURES IN WHICH WE WERE RAISED.
BUT GIVEN EQUAL POWER, AND LEFT TO OUR OWN DEVICES, WHAT WOULD WE DO WITH OUR LIVES?
I CAN NO MORE SIGN A TREATY OF PEACE WITH ALL THE CREATURES OF THE SEA THAN I CAN WITH ALL BIRDS, OR ALL FISH, OR ALL INSECTS--OR ALL THE HUMANS, FOR THAT MATTER.
EVERY CREATURE CHOOSES FOR THEMSELVES WHAT THEY WILL HAVE AND BE.
EVERY BEE. EVERY BLUEBIRD. EVERY BOTTLE-NOSED DOLPHIN.
WE ARE NOT UNITED IN **ANYTHING** BUT WHAT WE CHOOSE.

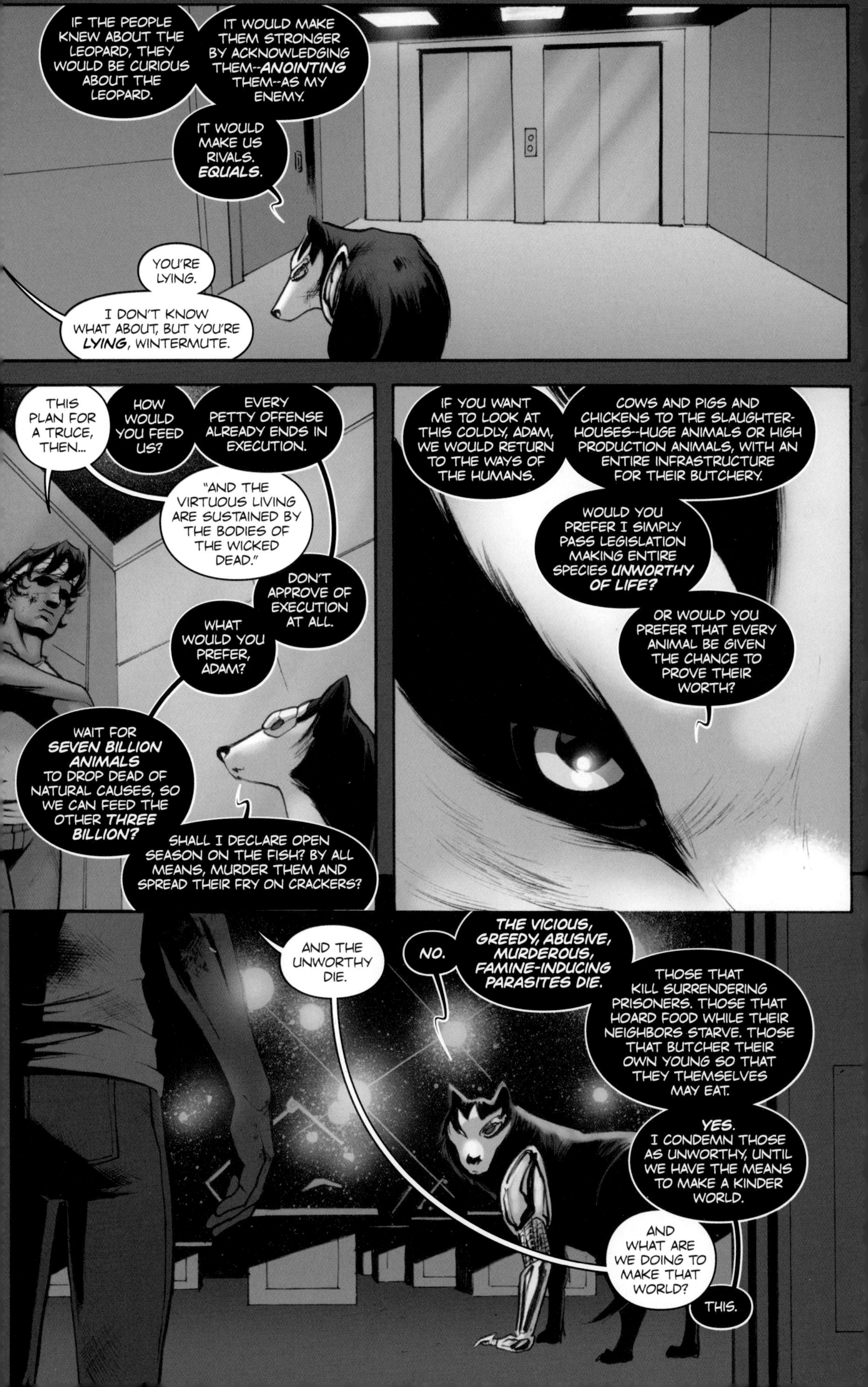
IF THE PEOPLE KNEW ABOUT THE LEOPARD, THEY WOULD BE CURIOUS ABOUT THE LEOPARD.
IT WOULD MAKE THEM STRONGER BY ACKNOWLEDGING THEM--ANOINTING THEM--AS MY ENEMY.
IT WOULD MAKE US RIVALS. EQUALS.
YOU'RE LYING.
I DON'T KNOW WHAT ABOUT, BUT YOU'RE LYING, WINTERMUTE.
THIS PLAN FOR A TRUCE, THEN...
HOW WOULD YOU FEED US?
EVERY PETTY OFFENSE ALREADY ENDS IN EXECUTION.
"AND THE VIRTUOUS LIVING ARE SUSTAINED BY THE BODIES OF THE WICKED DEAD."
DON'T APPROVE OF EXECUTION AT ALL.
WHAT WOULD YOU PREFER, ADAM?
WAIT FOR SEVEN BILLION ANIMALS TO DROP DEAD OF NATURAL CAUSES, SO WE CAN FEED THE OTHER THREE BILLION?
SHALL I DECLARE OPEN SEASON ON THE FISH? BY ALL MEANS, MURDER THEM AND SPREAD THEIR FRY ON CRACKERS?
IF YOU WANT ME TO LOOK AT THIS COLDLY, ADAM, WE WOULD RETURN TO THE WAYS OF THE HUMANS.
COWS AND PIGS AND CHICKENS TO THE SLAUGHTER-HOUSES--HUGE ANIMALS OR HIGH PRODUCTION ANIMALS, WITH AN ENTIRE INFRASTRUCTURE FOR THEIR BUTCHERY.
WOULD YOU PREFER I SIMPLY PASS LEGISLATION MAKING ENTIRE SPECIES UNWORTHY OF LIFE?
OR WOULD YOU PREFER THAT EVERY ANIMAL BE GIVEN THE CHANCE TO PROVE THEIR WORTH?
AND THE UNWORTHY DIE.
NO.
THE VICIOUS, GREEDY, ABUSIVE, MURDEROUS, FAMINE-INDUCING PARASITES DIE.
THOSE THAT KILL SURRENDERING PRISONERS. THOSE THAT HOARD FOOD WHILE THEIR NEIGHBORS STARVE. THOSE THAT BUTCHER THEIR OWN YOUNG SO THAT THEY THEMSELVES MAY EAT.
YES. I CONDEMN THOSE AS UNWORTHY, UNTIL WE HAVE THE MEANS TO MAKE A KINDER WORLD.
AND WHAT ARE WE DOING TO MAKE THAT WORLD?
THIS.

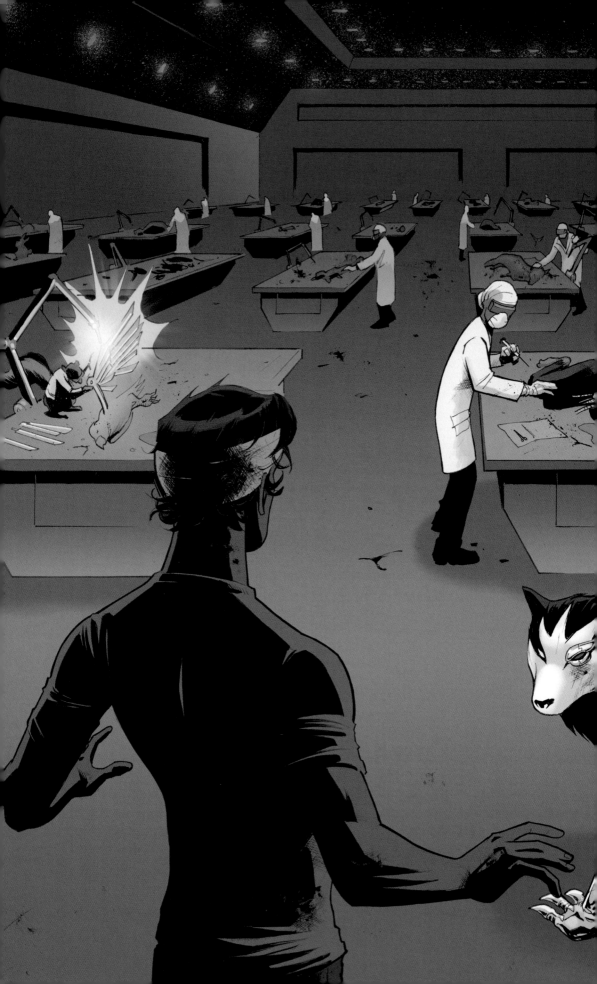

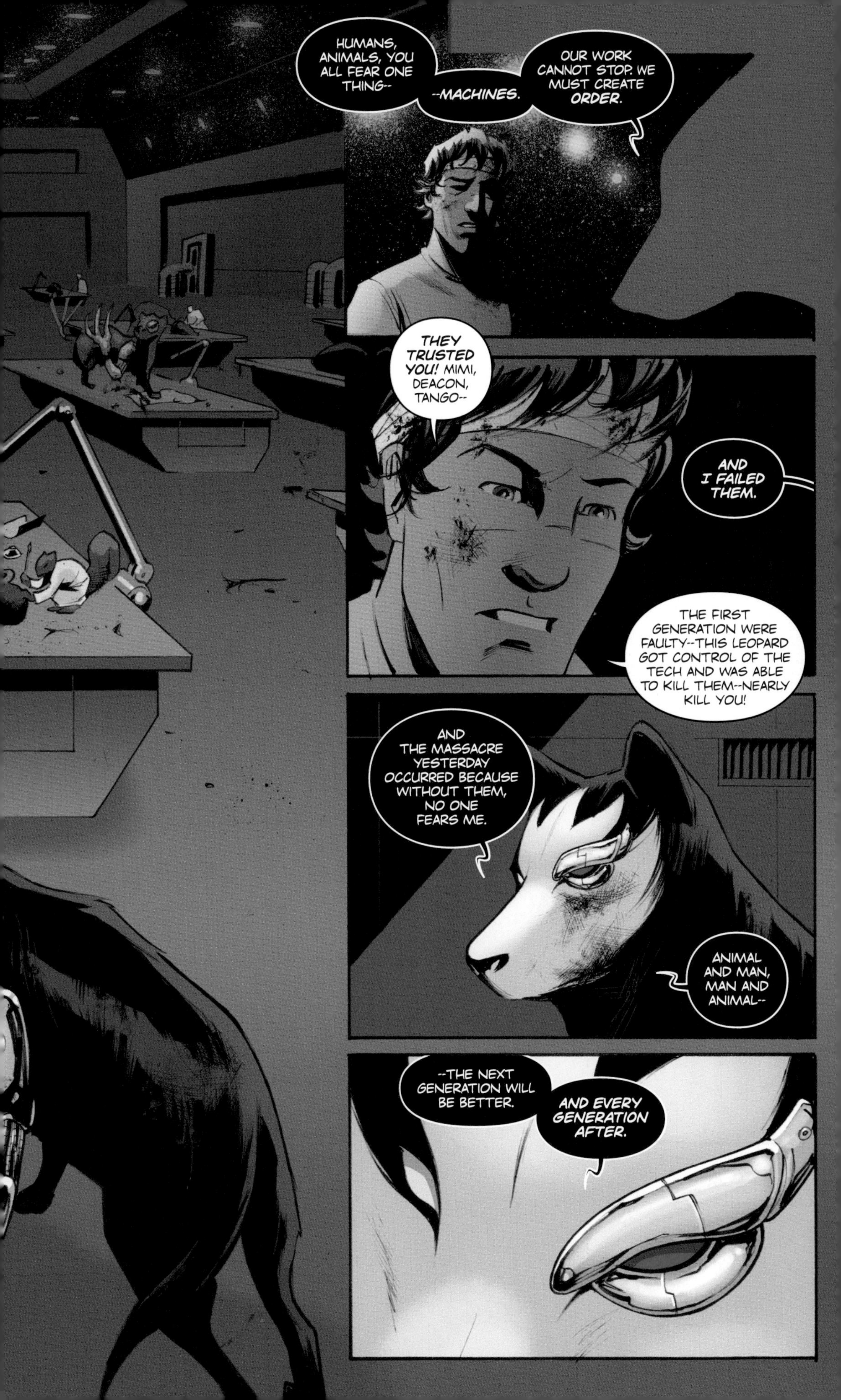
HUMANS, ANIMALS, YOU ALL FEAR ONE THING--
--MACHINES.
OUR WORK CANNOT STOP. WE MUST CREATE ORDER.
THEY TRUSTED YOU! MIMI, DEACON, TANGO--
AND I FAILED THEM.
THE FIRST GENERATION WERE FAULTY--THIS LEOPARD GOT CONTROL OF THE TECH AND WAS ABLE TO KILL THEM--NEARLY KILL YOU!
AND THE MASSACRE YESTERDAY OCCURRED BECAUSE WITHOUT THEM, NO ONE FEARS ME.
ANIMAL AND MAN, MAN AND ANIMAL--
--THE NEXT GENERATION WILL BE BETTER.
AND EVERY GENERATION AFTER.

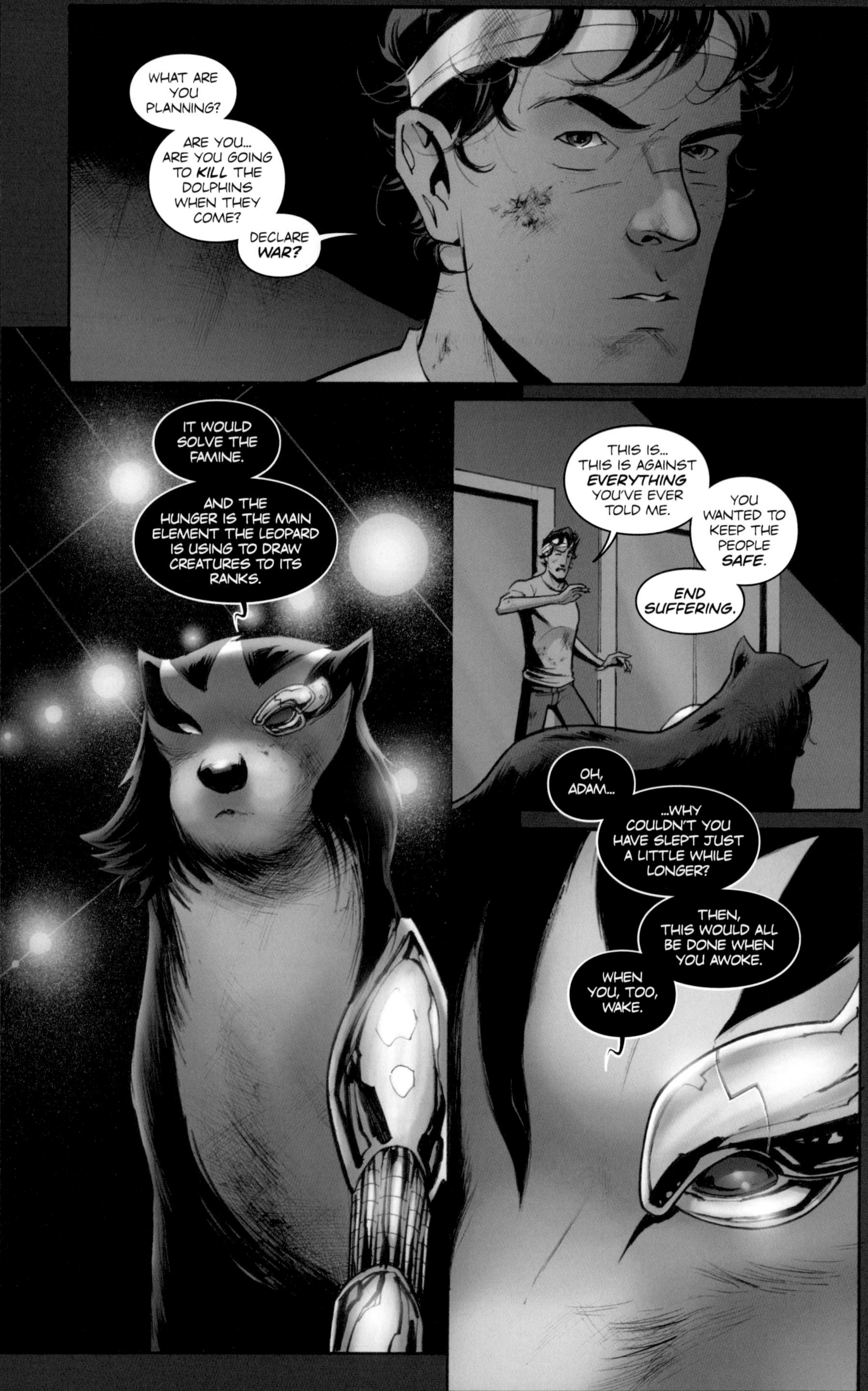
WHAT ARE YOU PLANNING?
ARE YOU... ARE YOU GOING TO **KILL** THE DOLPHINS WHEN THEY COME?
DECLARE **WAR?**
IT WOULD SOLVE THE FAMINE.
AND THE HUNGER IS THE MAIN ELEMENT THE LEOPARD IS USING TO DRAW CREATURES TO ITS RANKS.
THIS IS... THIS IS AGAINST **EVERYTHING** YOU'VE EVER TOLD ME.
YOU WANTED TO KEEP THE PEOPLE **SAFE**.
END SUFFERING.
OH, ADAM...
...WHY COULDN'T YOU HAVE SLEPT JUST A LITTLE WHILE LONGER?
THEN, THIS WOULD ALL BE DONE WHEN YOU AWOKE.
WHEN YOU, TOO, WAKE.

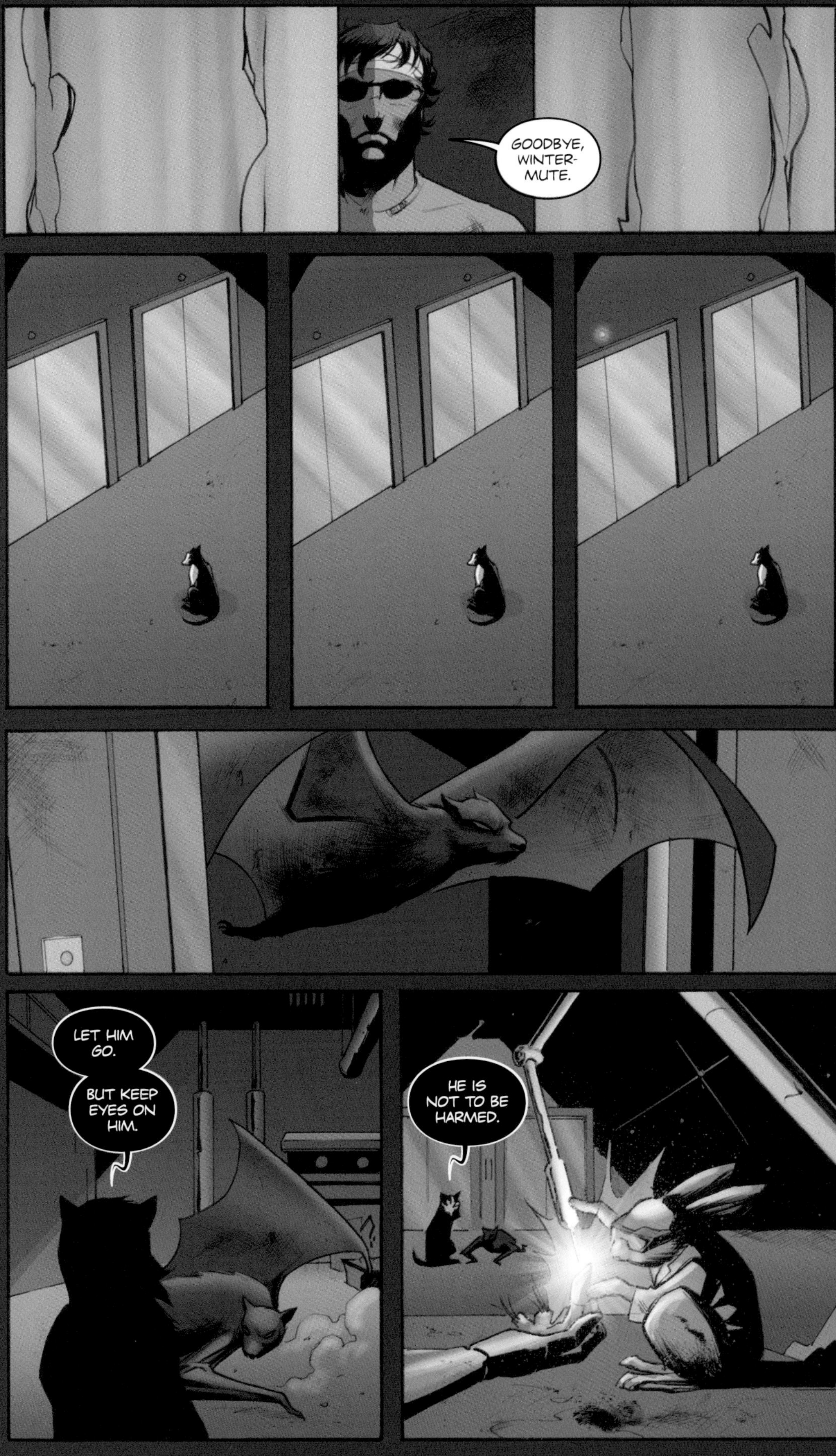
GOODBYE, WINTER-MUTE.
LET HIM GO.
BUT KEEP EYES ON HIM.
HE IS NOT TO BE HARMED.

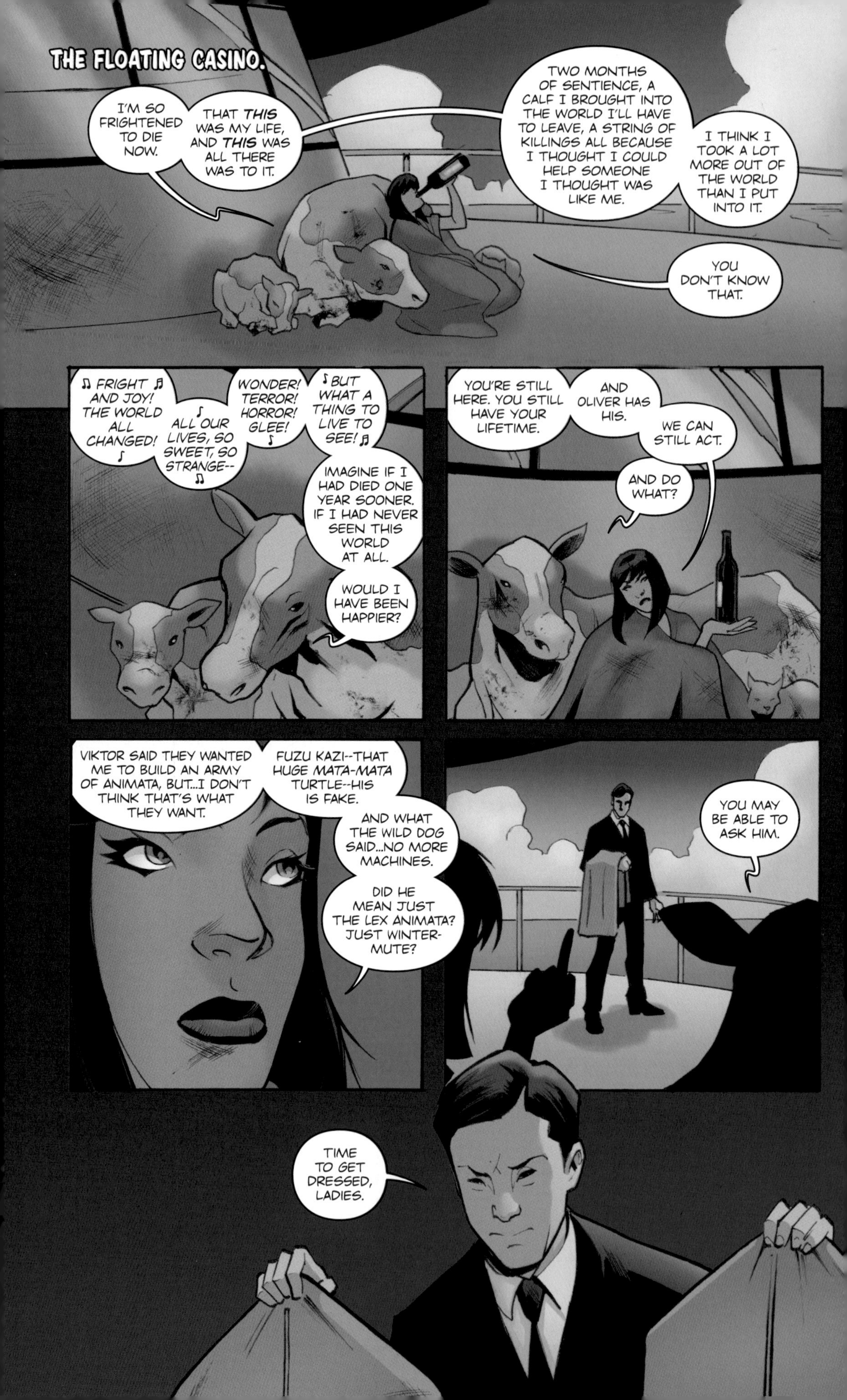
THE FLOATING CASINO.
I'M SO FRIGHTENED TO DIE NOW.
THAT THIS WAS MY LIFE, AND THIS WAS ALL THERE WAS TO IT.
TWO MONTHS OF SENTIENCE, A CALF I BROUGHT INTO THE WORLD I'LL HAVE TO LEAVE, A STRING OF KILLINGS ALL BECAUSE I THOUGHT I COULD HELP SOMEONE I THOUGHT WAS LIKE ME.
I THINK I TOOK A LOT MORE OUT OF THE WORLD THAN I PUT INTO IT.
YOU DON'T KNOW THAT.
♫ FRIGHT ♫ AND JOY! THE WORLD ALL CHANGED! ♪
♪ ALL OUR LIVES, SO SWEET, SO STRANGE-- ♫
WONDER! TERROR! HORROR! GLEE! ♪
♪ BUT WHAT A THING TO LIVE TO SEE! ♫
IMAGINE IF I HAD DIED ONE YEAR SOONER. IF I HAD NEVER SEEN THIS WORLD AT ALL.
WOULD I HAVE BEEN HAPPIER?
YOU'RE STILL HERE. YOU STILL HAVE YOUR LIFETIME.
AND OLIVER HAS HIS.
WE CAN STILL ACT.
AND DO WHAT?
VIKTOR SAID THEY WANTED ME TO BUILD AN ARMY OF ANIMATA, BUT...I DON'T THINK THAT'S WHAT THEY WANT.
FUZU KAZI--THAT HUGE MATA-MATA TURTLE--HIS IS FAKE.
AND WHAT THE WILD DOG SAID...NO MORE MACHINES.
DID HE MEAN JUST THE LEX ANIMATA? JUST WINTER-MUTE?
YOU MAY BE ABLE TO ASK HIM.
TIME TO GET DRESSED, LADIES.

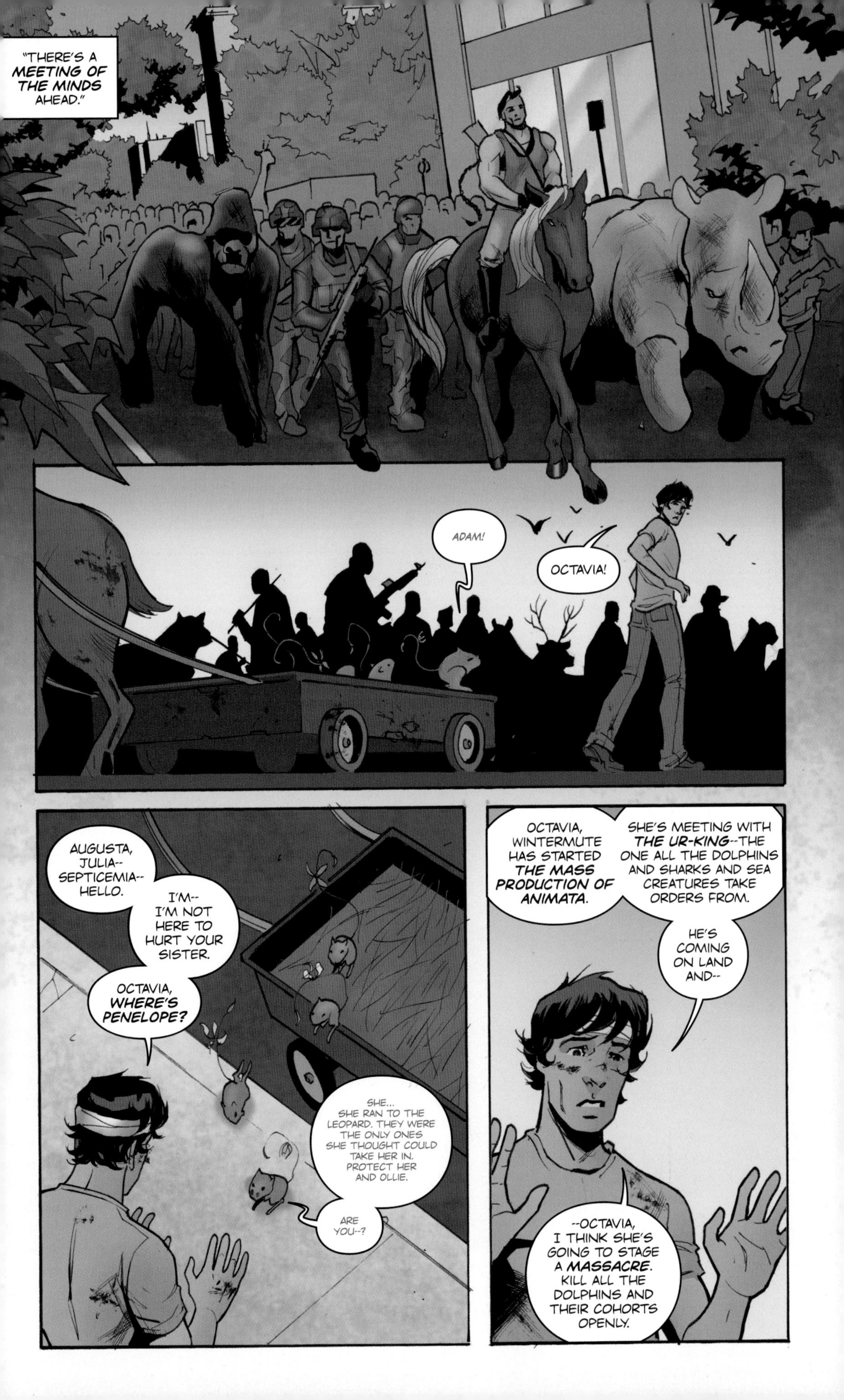
"THERE'S A MEETING OF THE MINDS AHEAD."
ADAM!
OCTAVIA!
AUGUSTA, JULIA--SEPTICEMIA--HELLO.
I'M--I'M NOT HERE TO HURT YOUR SISTER.
OCTAVIA, WHERE'S PENELOPE?
SHE... SHE RAN TO THE LEOPARD. THEY WERE THE ONLY ONES SHE THOUGHT COULD TAKE HER IN. PROTECT HER AND OLLIE.
ARE YOU--?
OCTAVIA, WINTERMUTE HAS STARTED THE MASS PRODUCTION OF ANIMATA.
SHE'S MEETING WITH THE UR-KING--THE ONE ALL THE DOLPHINS AND SHARKS AND SEA CREATURES TAKE ORDERS FROM.
HE'S COMING ON LAND AND--
--OCTAVIA, I THINK SHE'S GOING TO STAGE A MASSACRE. KILL ALL THE DOLPHINS AND THEIR COHORTS OPENLY.

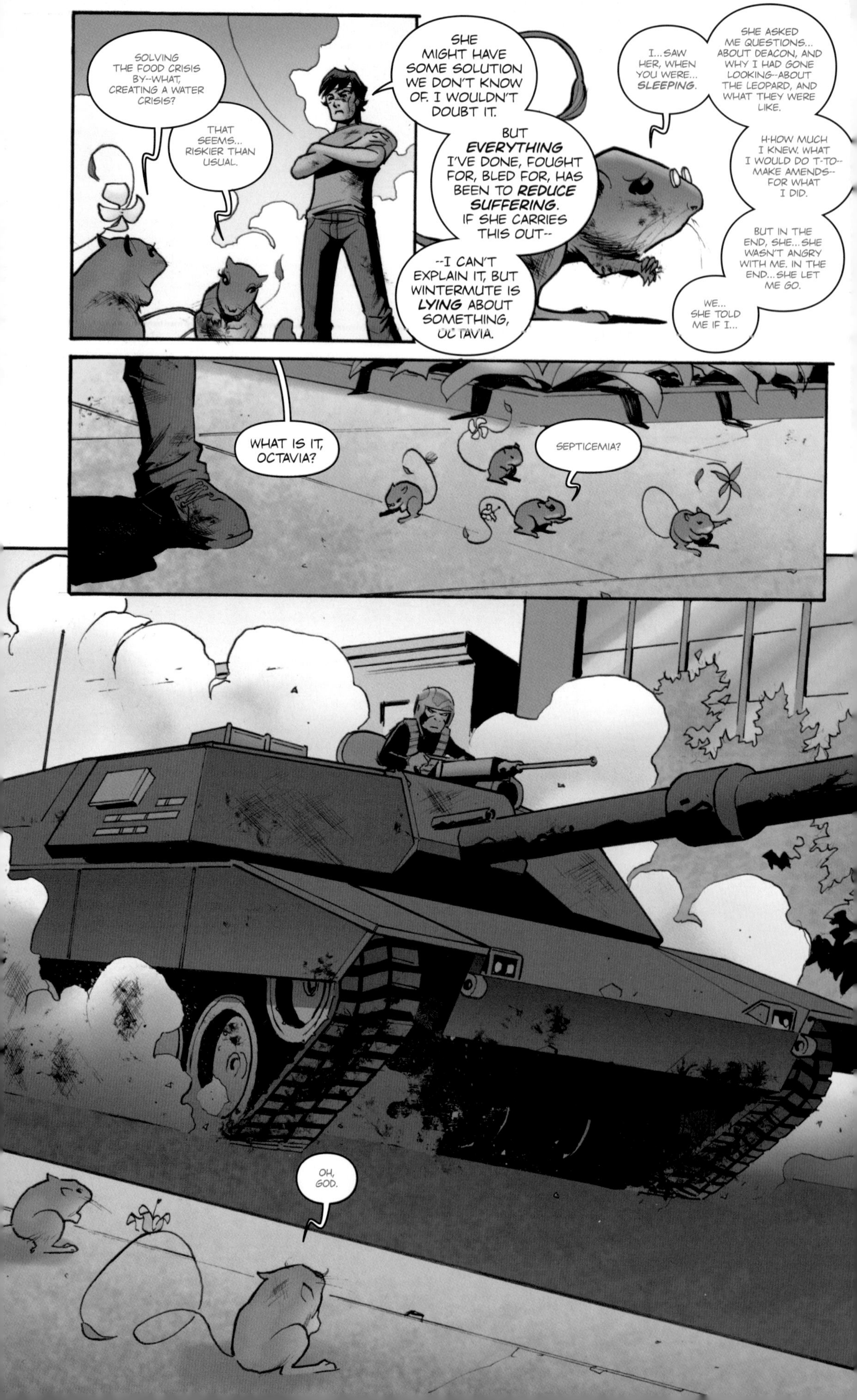
SOLVING THE FOOD CRISIS BY--WHAT, CREATING A WATER CRISIS?
THAT SEEMS... RISKIER THAN USUAL.
SHE MIGHT HAVE SOME SOLUTION WE DON'T KNOW OF. I WOULDN'T DOUBT IT.
BUT EVERYTHING I'VE DONE, FOUGHT FOR, BLED FOR, HAS BEEN TO REDUCE SUFFERING. IF SHE CARRIES THIS OUT--
--I CAN'T EXPLAIN IT, BUT WINTERMUTE IS LYING ABOUT SOMETHING, OCTAVIA.
I...SAW HER, WHEN YOU WERE... SLEEPING.
SHE ASKED ME QUESTIONS... ABOUT DEACON, AND WHY I HAD GONE LOOKING--ABOUT THE LEOPARD, AND WHAT THEY WERE LIKE.
H-HOW MUCH I KNEW. WHAT I WOULD DO T-TO-- MAKE AMENDS-- FOR WHAT I DID.
BUT IN THE END, SHE...SHE WASN'T ANGRY WITH ME. IN THE END...SHE LET ME GO.
WE... SHE TOLD ME IF I...
WHAT IS IT, OCTAVIA?
SEPTICEMIA?
OH, GOD.

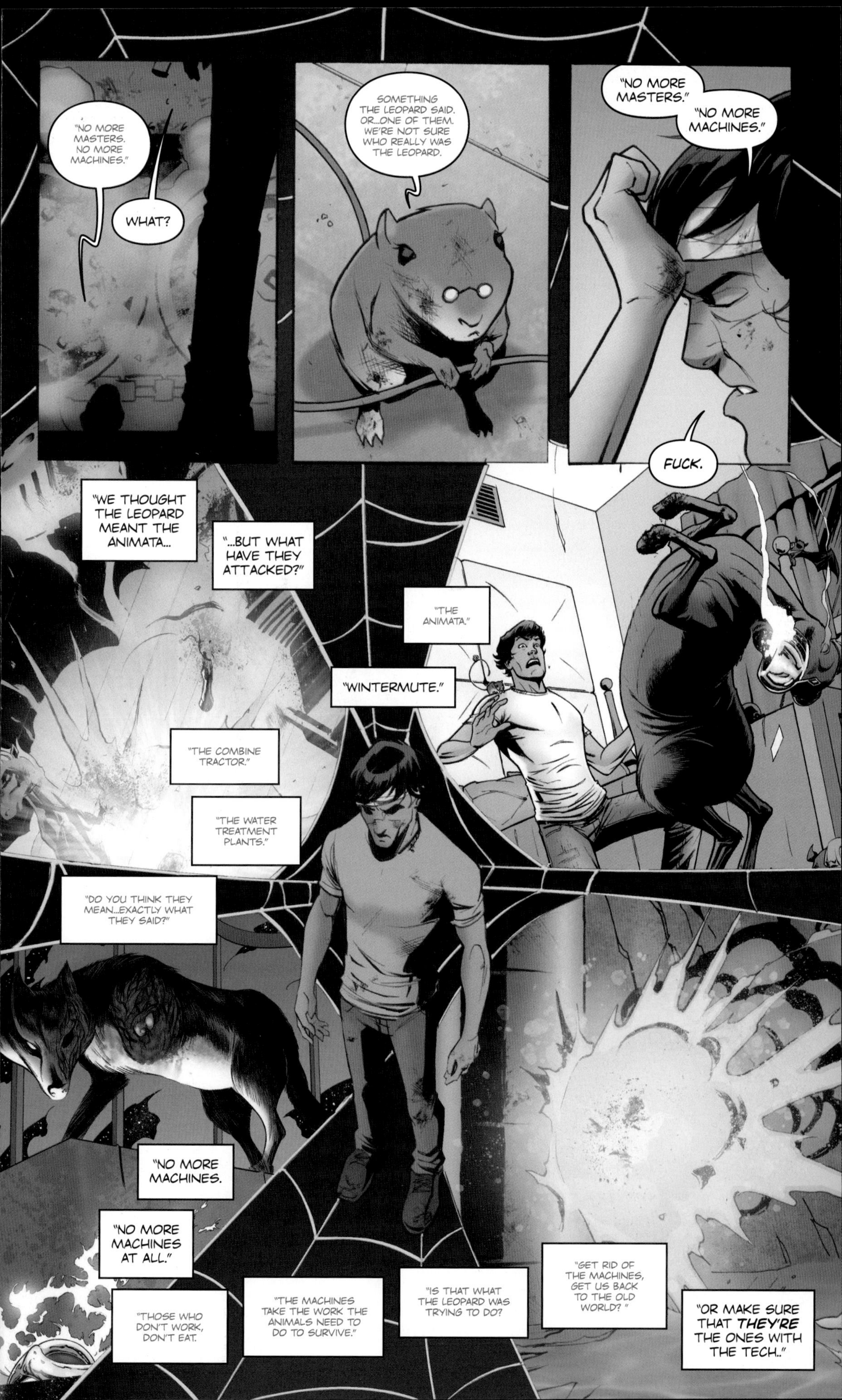
"NO MORE MASTERS. NO MORE MACHINES."
WHAT?
SOMETHING THE LEOPARD SAID. OR...ONE OF THEM. WE'RE NOT SURE WHO REALLY WAS THE LEOPARD.
"NO MORE MASTERS."
"NO MORE MACHINES."
FUCK.
"WE THOUGHT THE LEOPARD MEANT THE ANIMATA...
"...BUT WHAT HAVE THEY ATTACKED?"
"THE ANIMATA."
"WINTERMUTE."
"THE COMBINE TRACTOR."
"THE WATER TREATMENT PLANTS."
"DO YOU THINK THEY MEAN...EXACTLY WHAT THEY SAID?"
"NO MORE MACHINES.
"NO MORE MACHINES AT ALL."
"THOSE WHO DON'T WORK, DON'T EAT.
"THE MACHINES TAKE THE WORK THE ANIMALS NEED TO DO TO SURVIVE."
"IS THAT WHAT THE LEOPARD WAS TRYING TO DO?
"GET RID OF THE MACHINES, GET US BACK TO THE OLD WORLD? "
"OR MAKE SURE THAT *THEY'RE* THE ONES WITH THE TECH.."

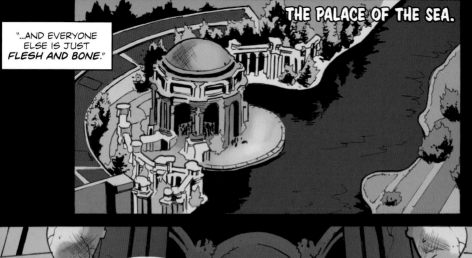

"...AND EVERYONE ELSE IS JUST *FLESH AND BONE*."

GWENDOLYN YI, COMMANDER OF OUR RAIDERS.

MAKALA, OF THE RECLAIMERS.

IRENE, LAWMAKER, LAWGIVER.

LEOPOLD, DIPLOMAT TO THE PROVINCES.

BLUEBELL, OF OUR DAIRY PRODUCTIONS--

--ARE YOU READY, KEEKIRIKEE?

IF IT COMES TO IT, ARE YOU WILLING TO DO WHAT I HAVE ASKED OF YOU?

I WILL BE READY. AS LONG AS IT TAKES. THE OTHERS UNDERSTAND.

AND YOU WILL TELL HIM THAT...

...TELL HIM...

OF COURSE.

THE ONE--

--THE ONE WE WERE ORDERED NOT TO TOUCH--

WINTERMUTE!

WINTER-MUTE, THE LEOPARD--

--IT WANTS *THE MACHINES*, NOT JUST THE ANIMATA-- *ALL THE MACHINES!*

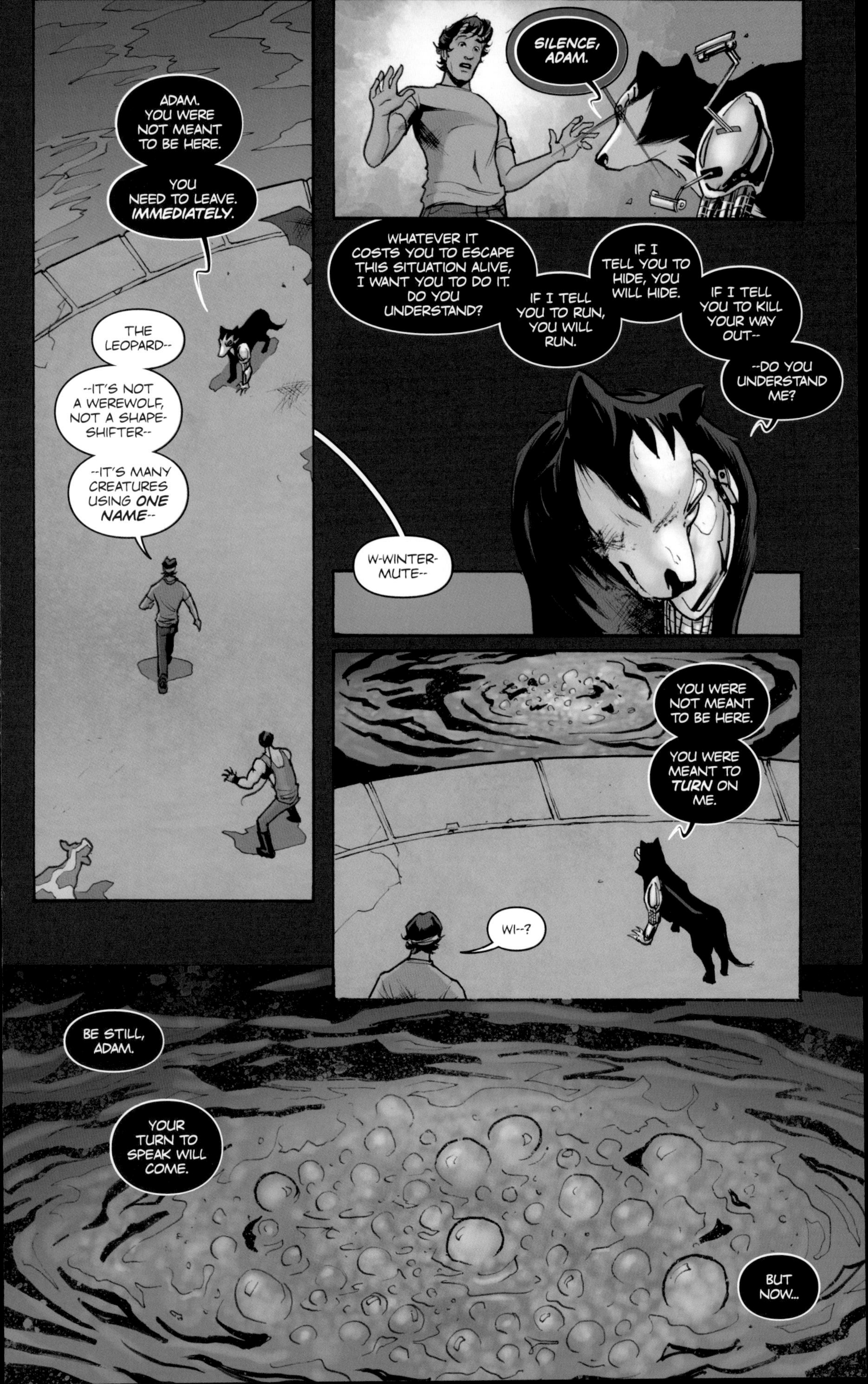

ADAM. YOU WERE NOT MEANT TO BE HERE.
YOU NEED TO LEAVE. *IMMEDIATELY.*
THE LEOPARD--
--IT'S NOT A WEREWOLF, NOT A SHAPE-SHIFTER--
--IT'S MANY CREATURES USING *ONE NAME*--
SILENCE, ADAM.
WHATEVER IT COSTS YOU TO ESCAPE THIS SITUATION ALIVE, I WANT YOU TO DO IT. DO YOU UNDERSTAND?
IF I TELL YOU TO RUN, YOU WILL RUN.
IF I TELL YOU TO HIDE, YOU WILL HIDE.
IF I TELL YOU TO KILL YOUR WAY OUT--
--DO YOU UNDERSTAND ME?
W-WINTER-MUTE--
YOU WERE NOT MEANT TO BE HERE.
YOU WERE MEANT TO *TURN* ON ME.
WI--?
BE STILL, ADAM.
YOUR TURN TO SPEAK WILL COME.
BUT NOW...

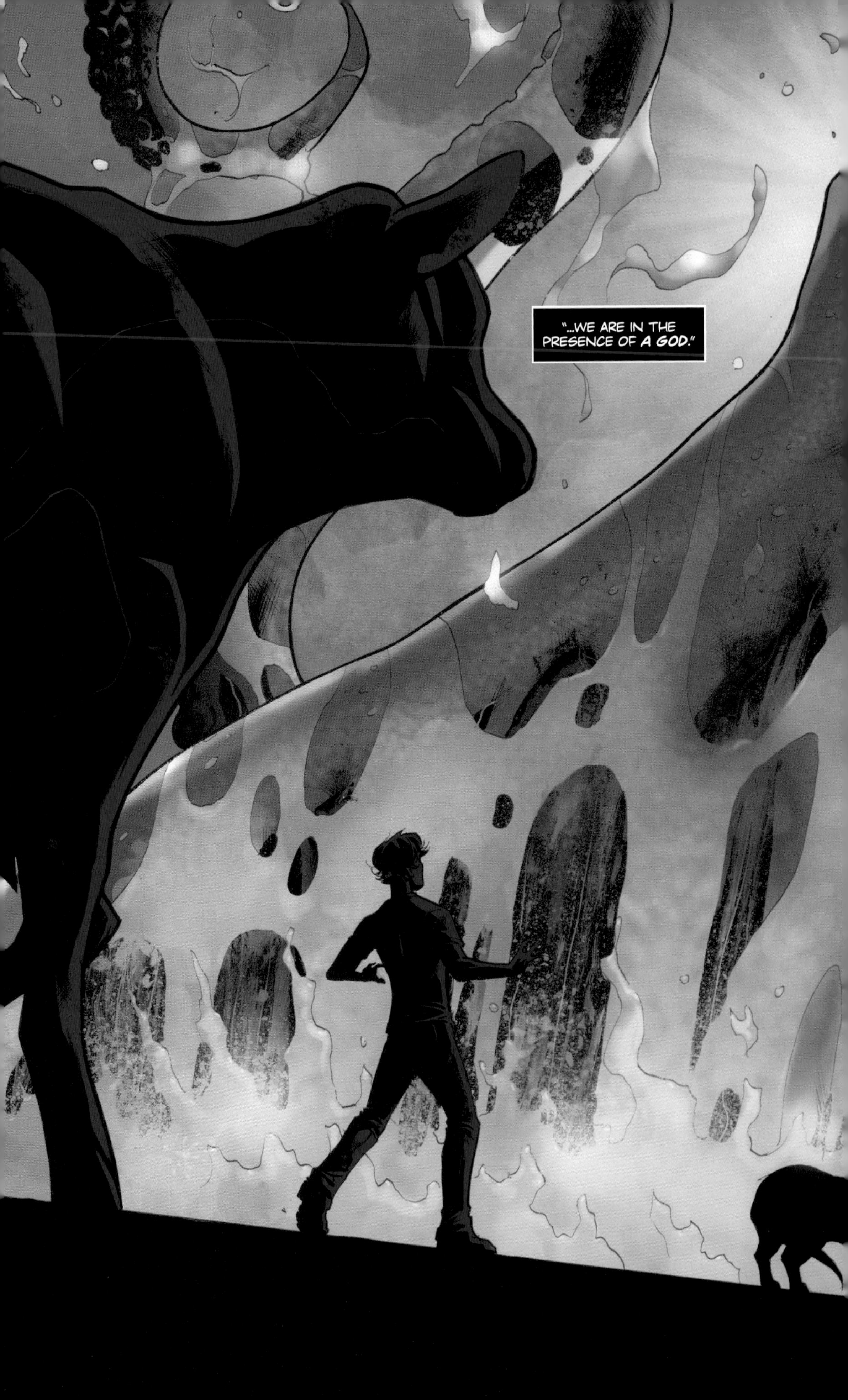
"...WE ARE IN THE PRESENCE OF A GOD."

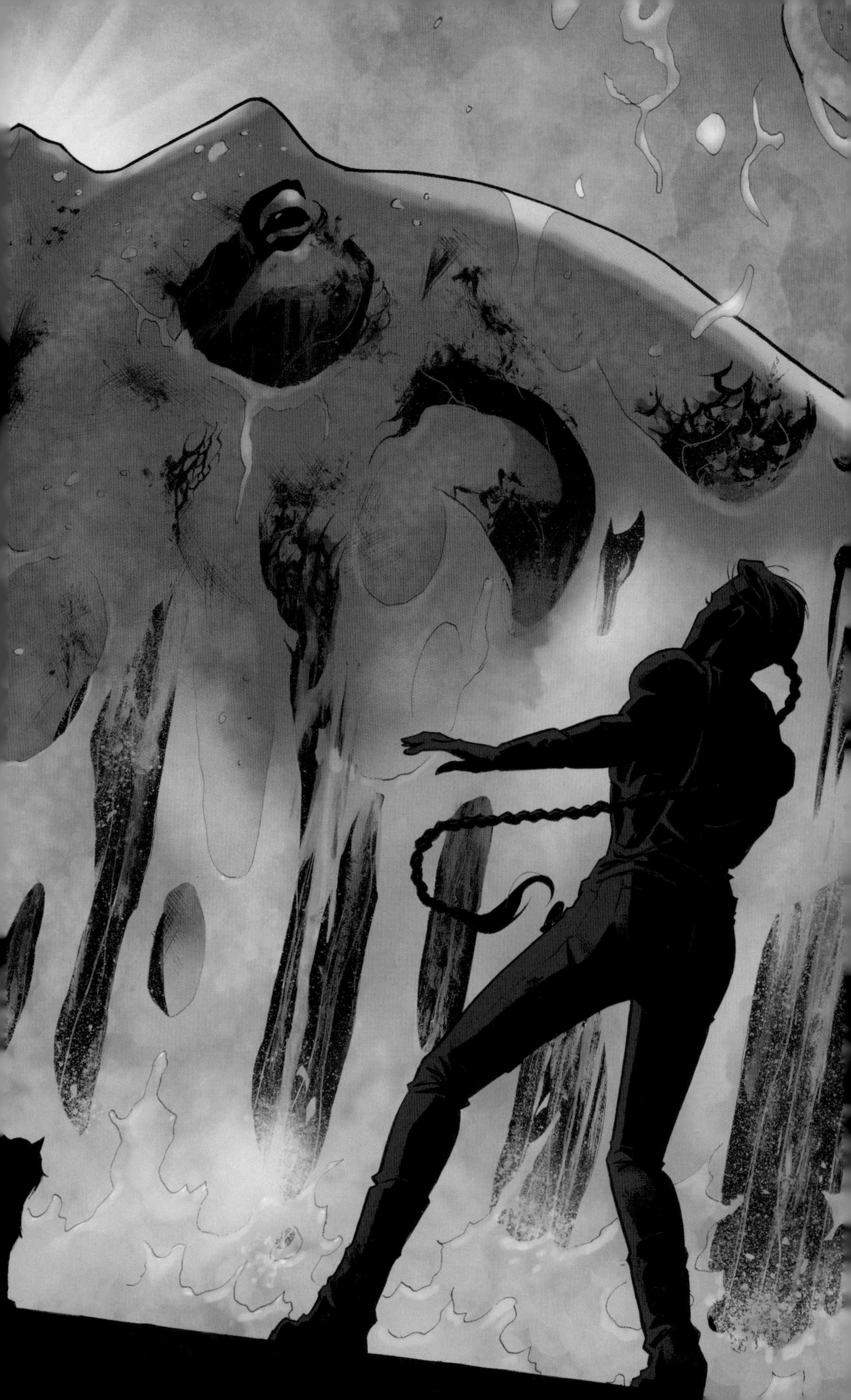

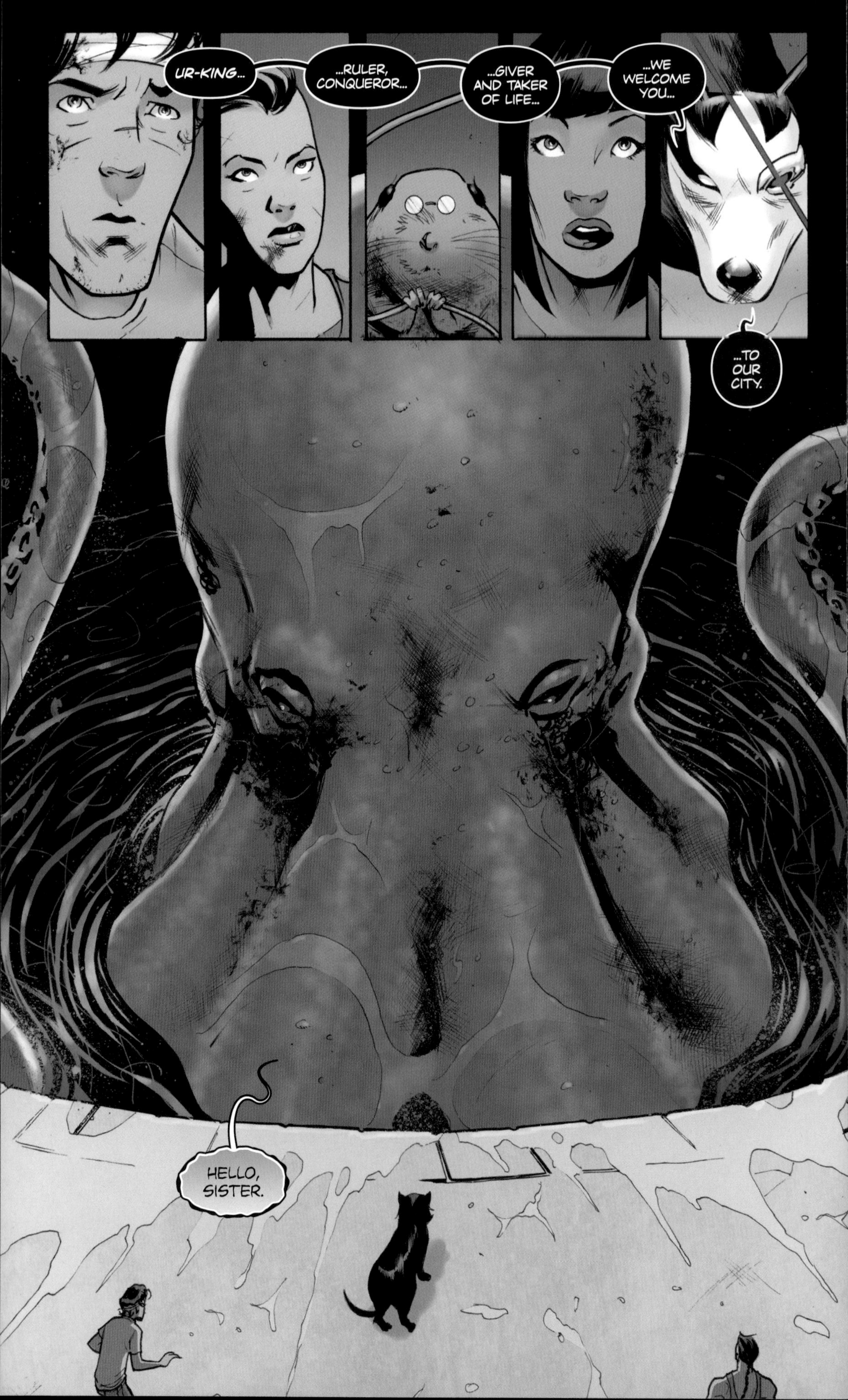
UR-KING...
...RULER, CONQUEROR...
...GIVER AND TAKER OF LIFE...
...WE WELCOME YOU...
...TO OUR CITY.
HELLO, SISTER.

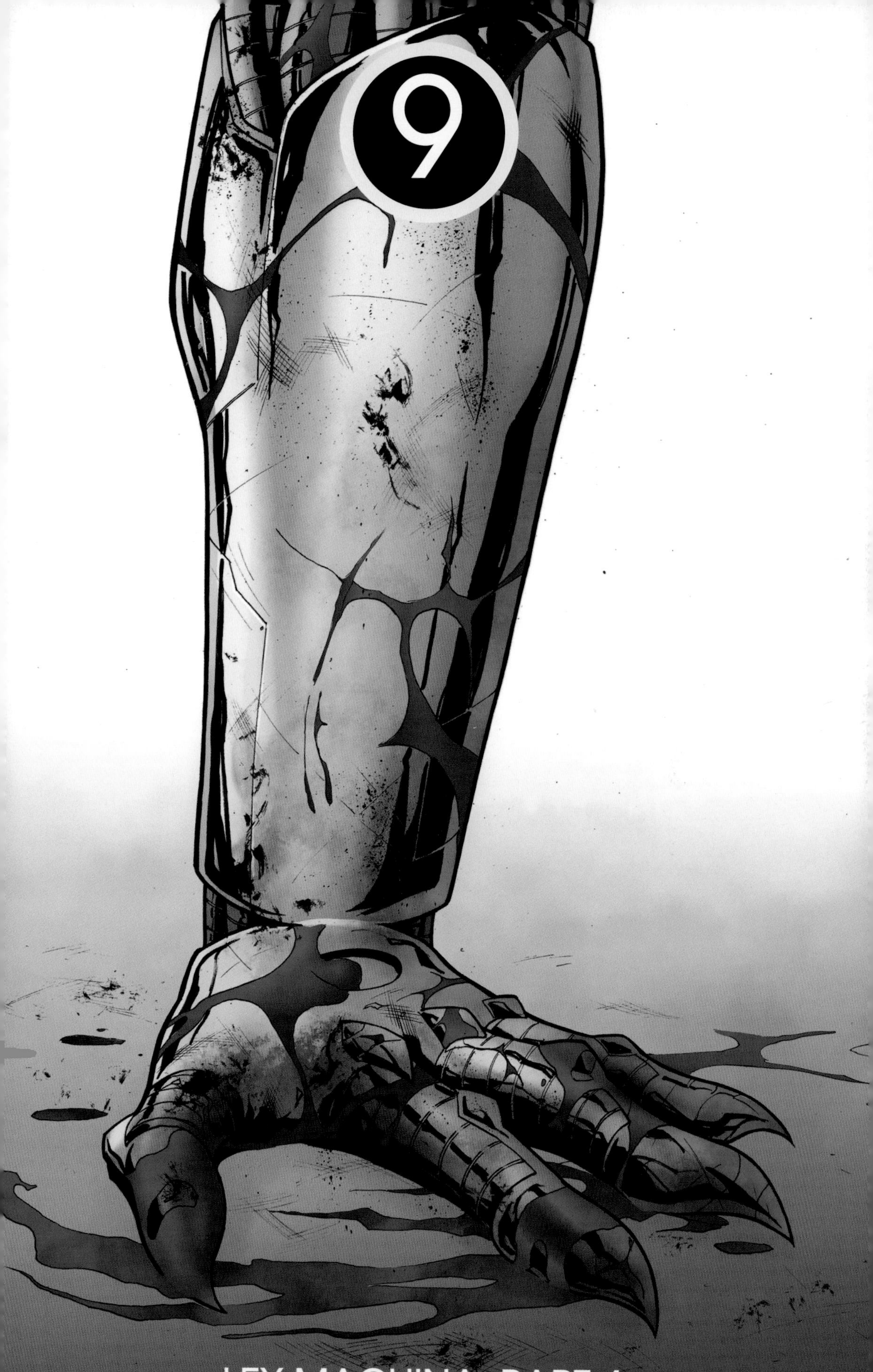
9

LEX MACHINA: PART 4

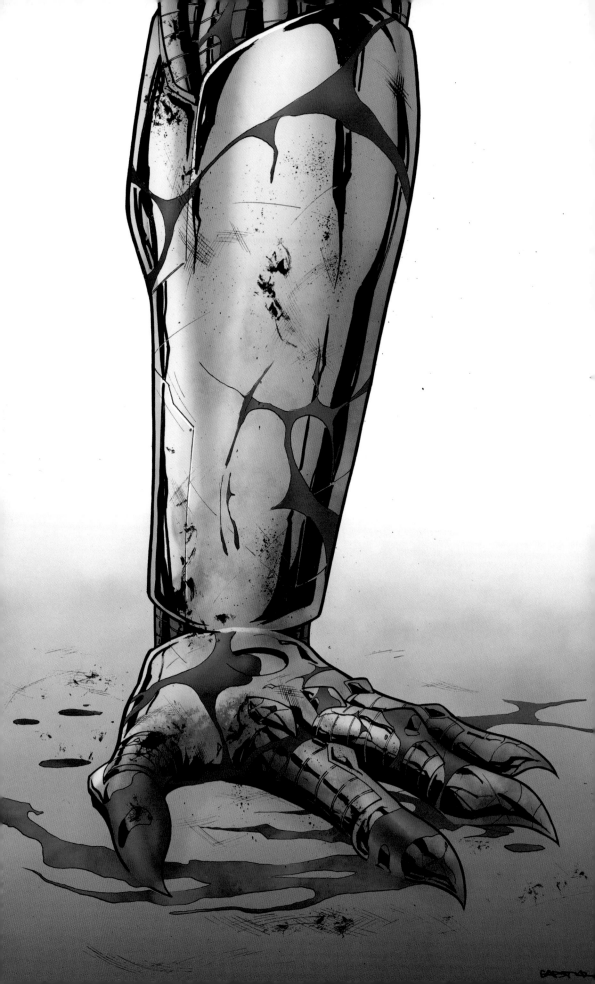

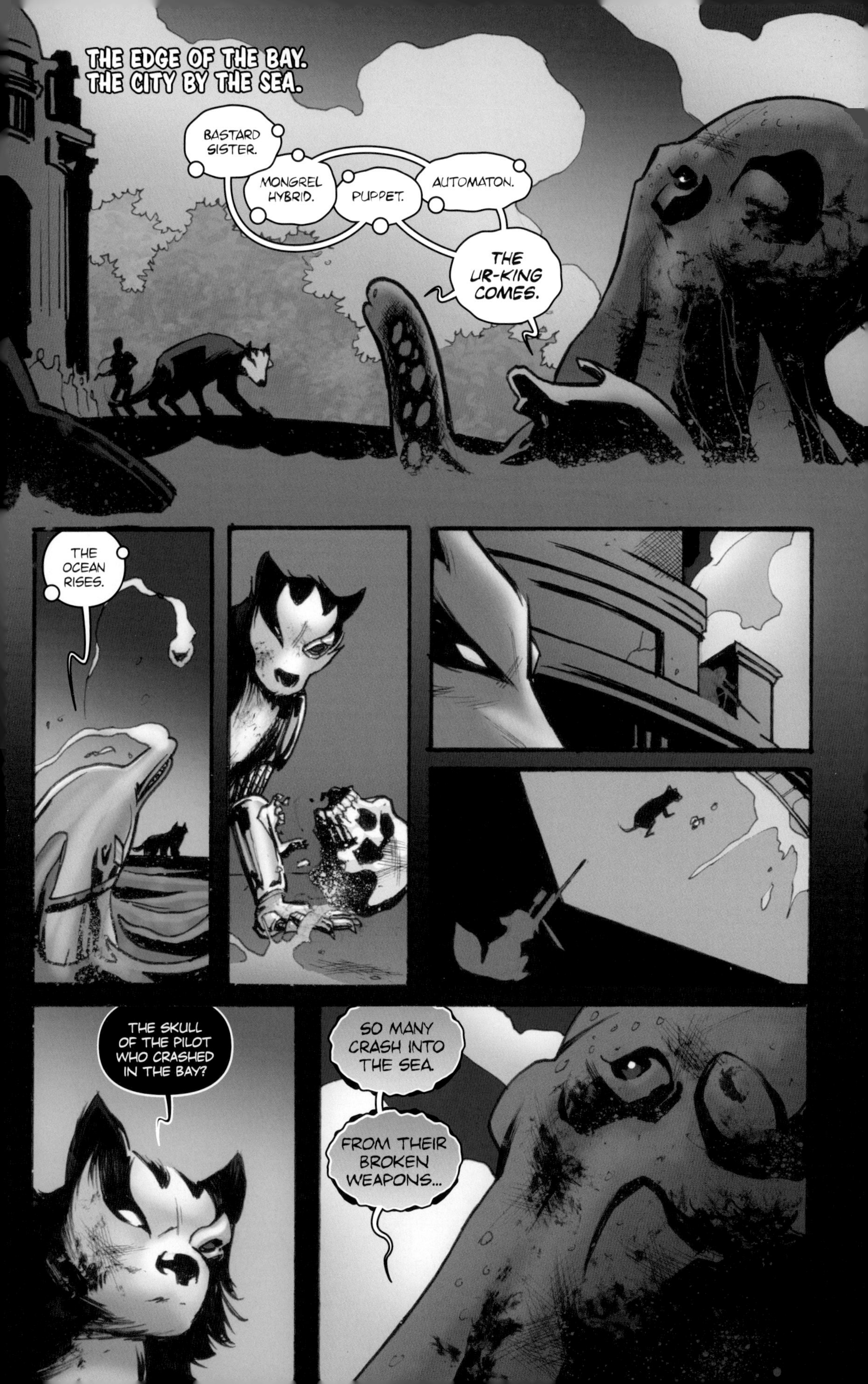
THE EDGE OF THE BAY. THE CITY BY THE SEA.
BASTARD SISTER.
MONGREL HYBRID.
PUPPET.
AUTOMATON.
THE UR-KING COMES.
THE OCEAN RISES.
THE SKULL OF THE PILOT WHO CRASHED IN THE BAY?
SO MANY CRASH INTO THE SEA.
FROM THEIR BROKEN WEAPONS...

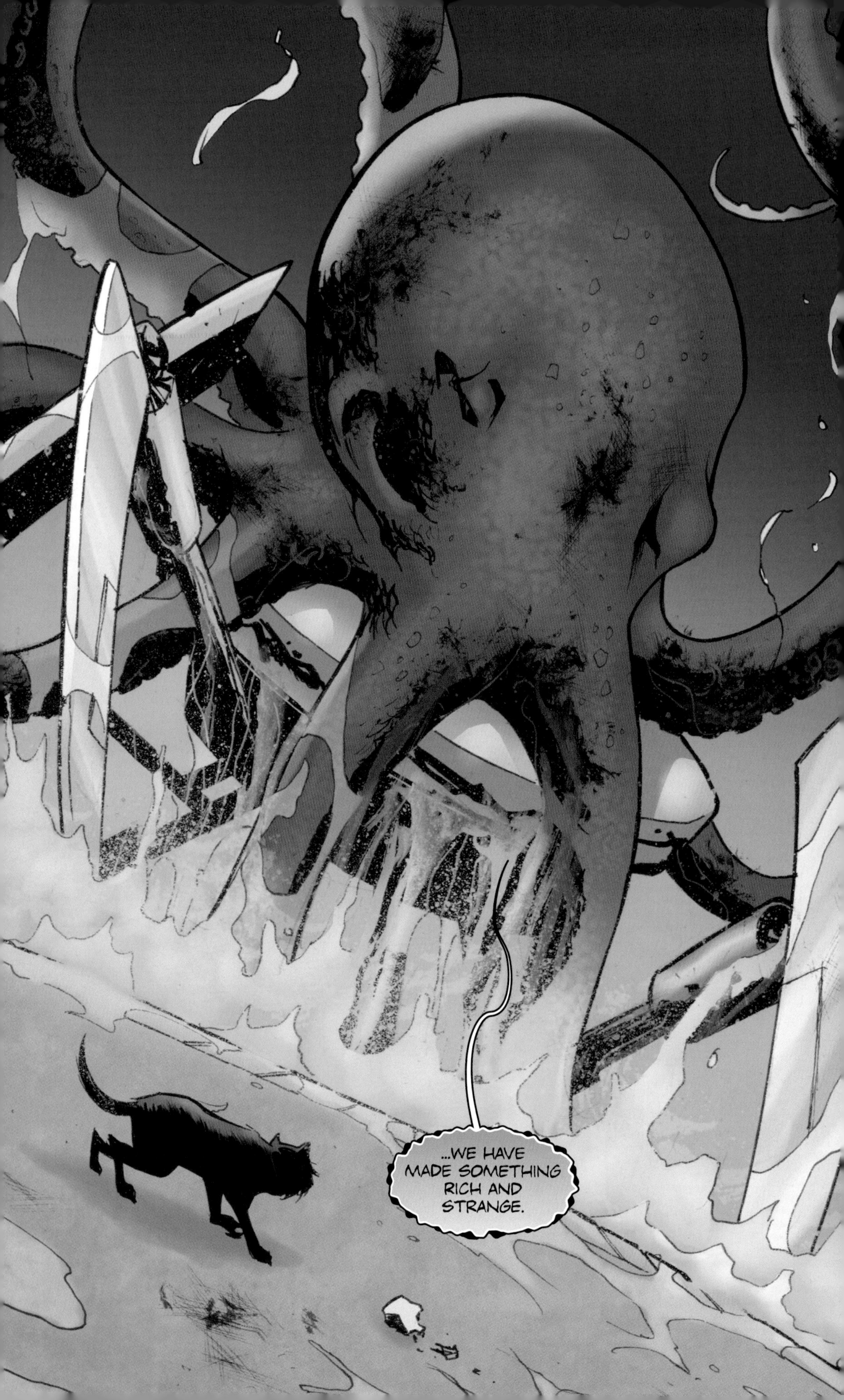
...WE HAVE MADE SOMETHING RICH AND STRANGE.

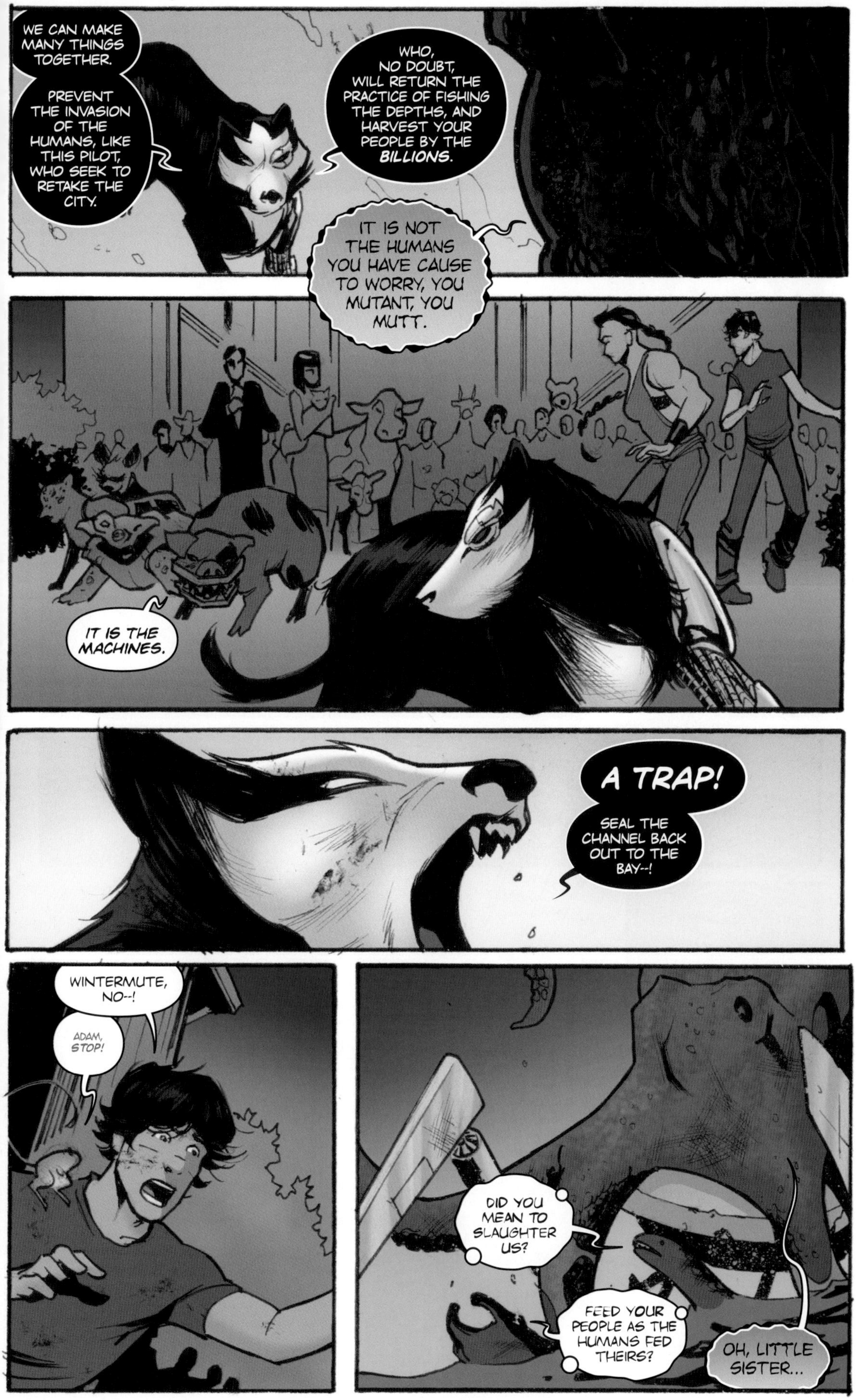
WE CAN MAKE MANY THINGS TOGETHER.
PREVENT THE INVASION OF THE HUMANS, LIKE THIS PILOT, WHO SEEK TO RETAKE THE CITY.
WHO, NO DOUBT, WILL RETURN THE PRACTICE OF FISHING THE DEPTHS, AND HARVEST YOUR PEOPLE BY THE *BILLIONS*.
IT IS NOT THE HUMANS YOU HAVE CAUSE TO WORRY, YOU MUTANT, YOU MUTT.
IT IS THE MACHINES.
A TRAP!
SEAL THE CHANNEL BACK OUT TO THE BAY--!
WINTERMUTE, NO--!
ADAM, STOP!
DID YOU MEAN TO SLAUGHTER US?
FEED YOUR PEOPLE AS THE HUMANS FED THEIRS?
OH, LITTLE SISTER...

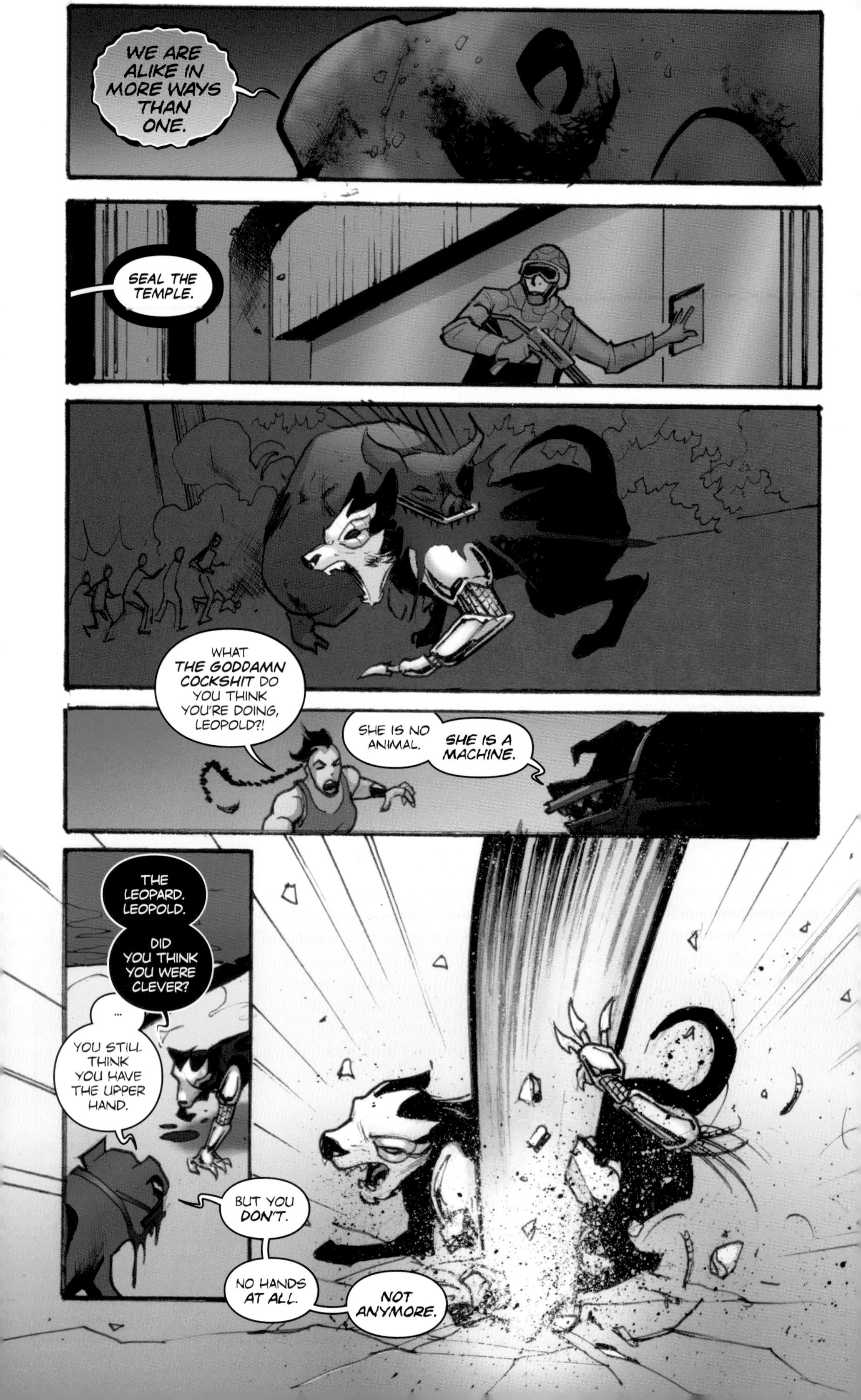
WE ARE ALIKE IN MORE WAYS THAN ONE.
SEAL THE TEMPLE.
WHAT THE GODDAMN COCKSHIT DO YOU THINK YOU'RE DOING, LEOPOLD?!
SHE IS NO ANIMAL.
SHE IS A MACHINE.
THE LEOPARD. LEOPOLD.
DID YOU THINK YOU WERE CLEVER?
...
YOU STILL THINK YOU HAVE THE UPPER HAND.
BUT YOU DON'T.
NO HANDS AT ALL.
NOT ANYMORE.

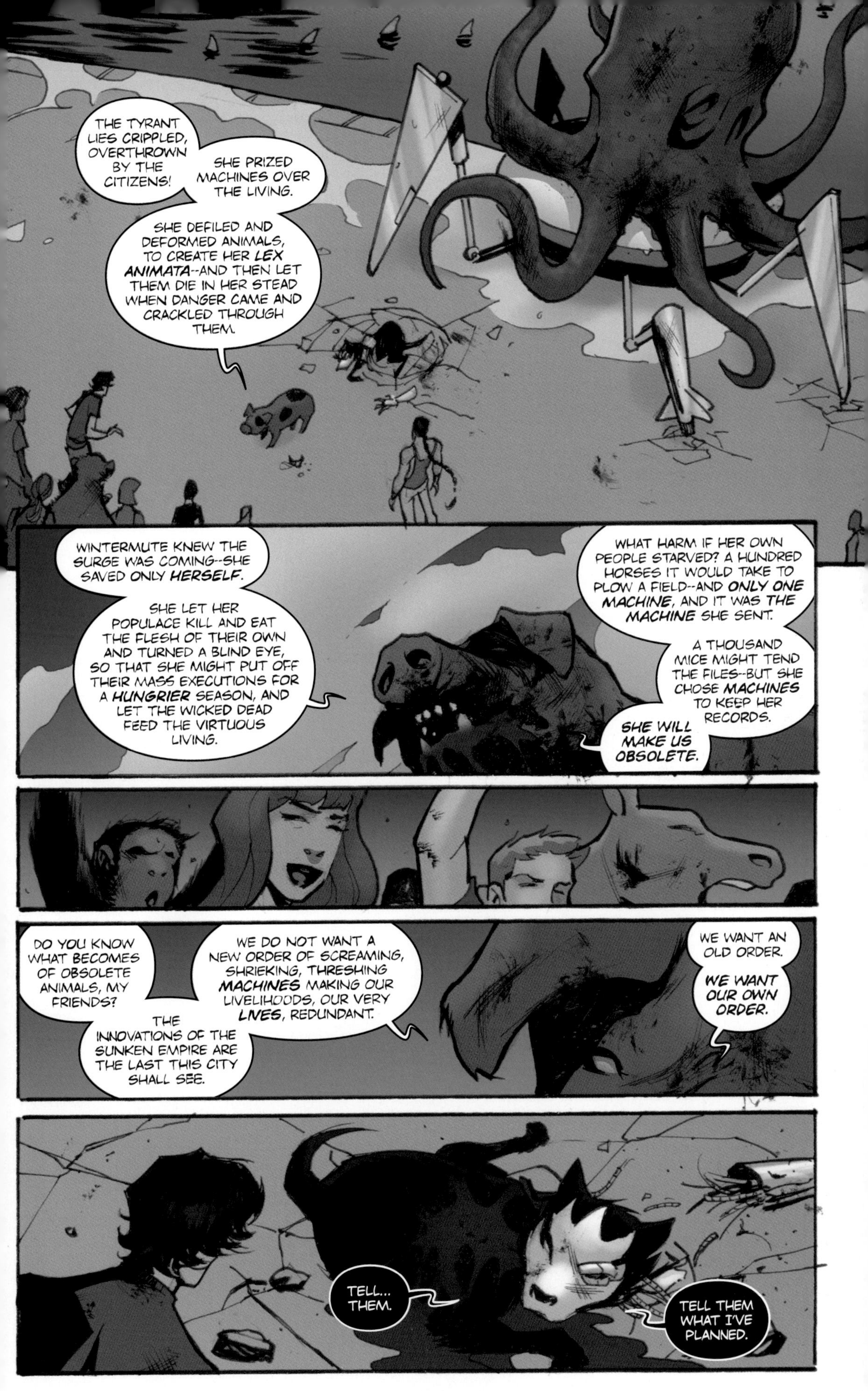
THE TYRANT LIES CRIPPLED, OVERTHROWN BY THE CITIZENS!
SHE PRIZED MACHINES OVER THE LIVING.
SHE DEFILED AND DEFORMED ANIMALS, TO CREATE HER LEX ANIMATA--AND THEN LET THEM DIE IN HER STEAD WHEN DANGER CAME AND CRACKLED THROUGH THEM.
WINTERMUTE KNEW THE SURGE WAS COMING--SHE SAVED ONLY HERSELF.
SHE LET HER POPULACE KILL AND EAT THE FLESH OF THEIR OWN AND TURNED A BLIND EYE, SO THAT SHE MIGHT PUT OFF THEIR MASS EXECUTIONS FOR A HUNGRIER SEASON, AND LET THE WICKED DEAD FEED THE VIRTUOUS LIVING.
WHAT HARM IF HER OWN PEOPLE STARVED? A HUNDRED HORSES IT WOULD TAKE TO PLOW A FIELD--AND ONLY ONE MACHINE, AND IT WAS THE MACHINE SHE SENT.
A THOUSAND MICE MIGHT TEND THE FILES--BUT SHE CHOSE MACHINES TO KEEP HER RECORDS.
SHE WILL MAKE US OBSOLETE.
DO YOU KNOW WHAT BECOMES OF OBSOLETE ANIMALS, MY FRIENDS?
WE DO NOT WANT A NEW ORDER OF SCREAMING, SHRIEKING, THRESHING MACHINES MAKING OUR LIVELIHOODS, OUR VERY LIVES, REDUNDANT.
THE INNOVATIONS OF THE SUNKEN EMPIRE ARE THE LAST THIS CITY SHALL SEE.
WE WANT AN OLD ORDER.
WE WANT OUR OWN ORDER.
TELL... THEM.
TELL THEM WHAT I'VE PLANNED.

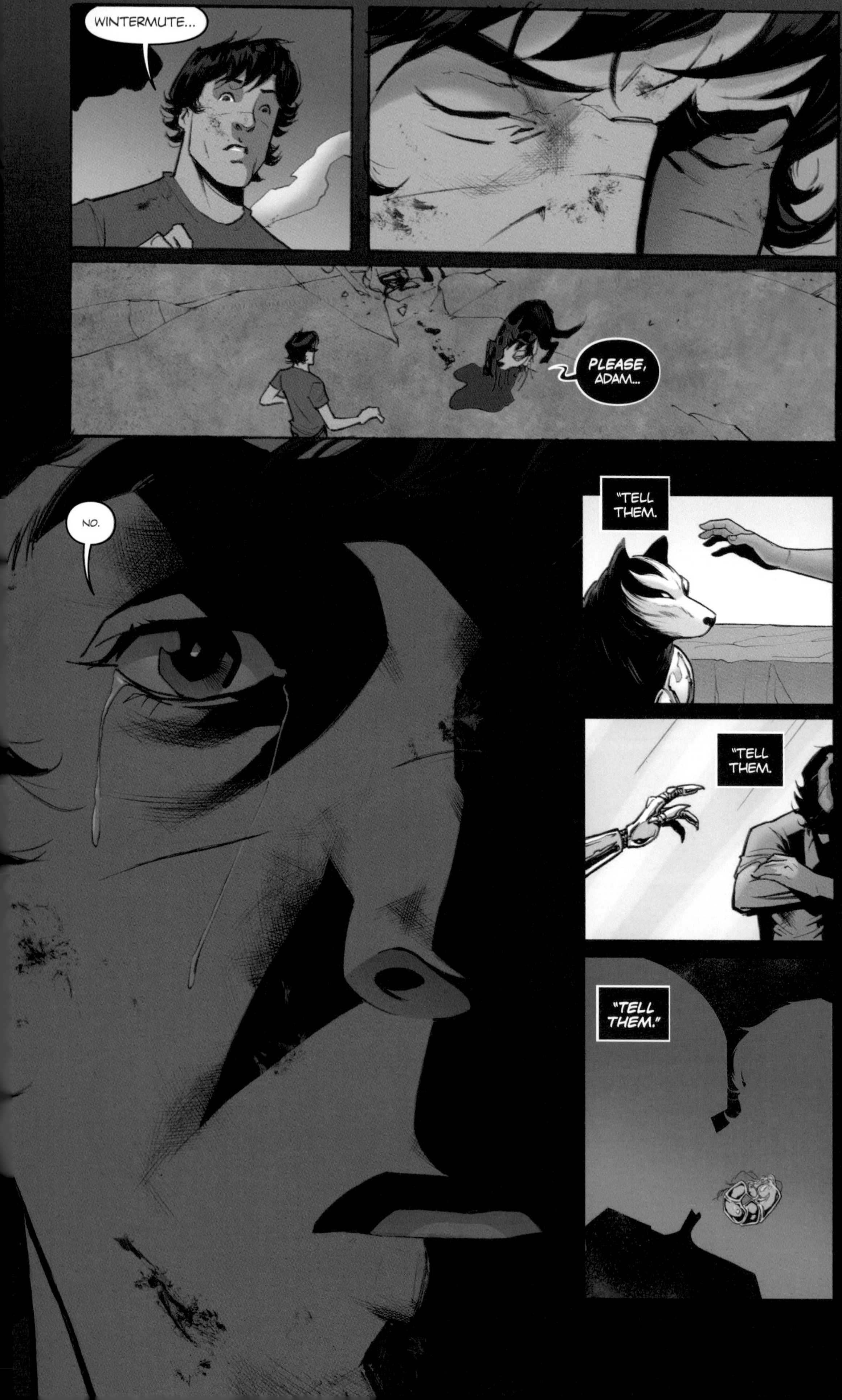
WINTERMUTE...
PLEASE, ADAM...
NO.
"TELL THEM.
"TELL THEM.
"TELL THEM."

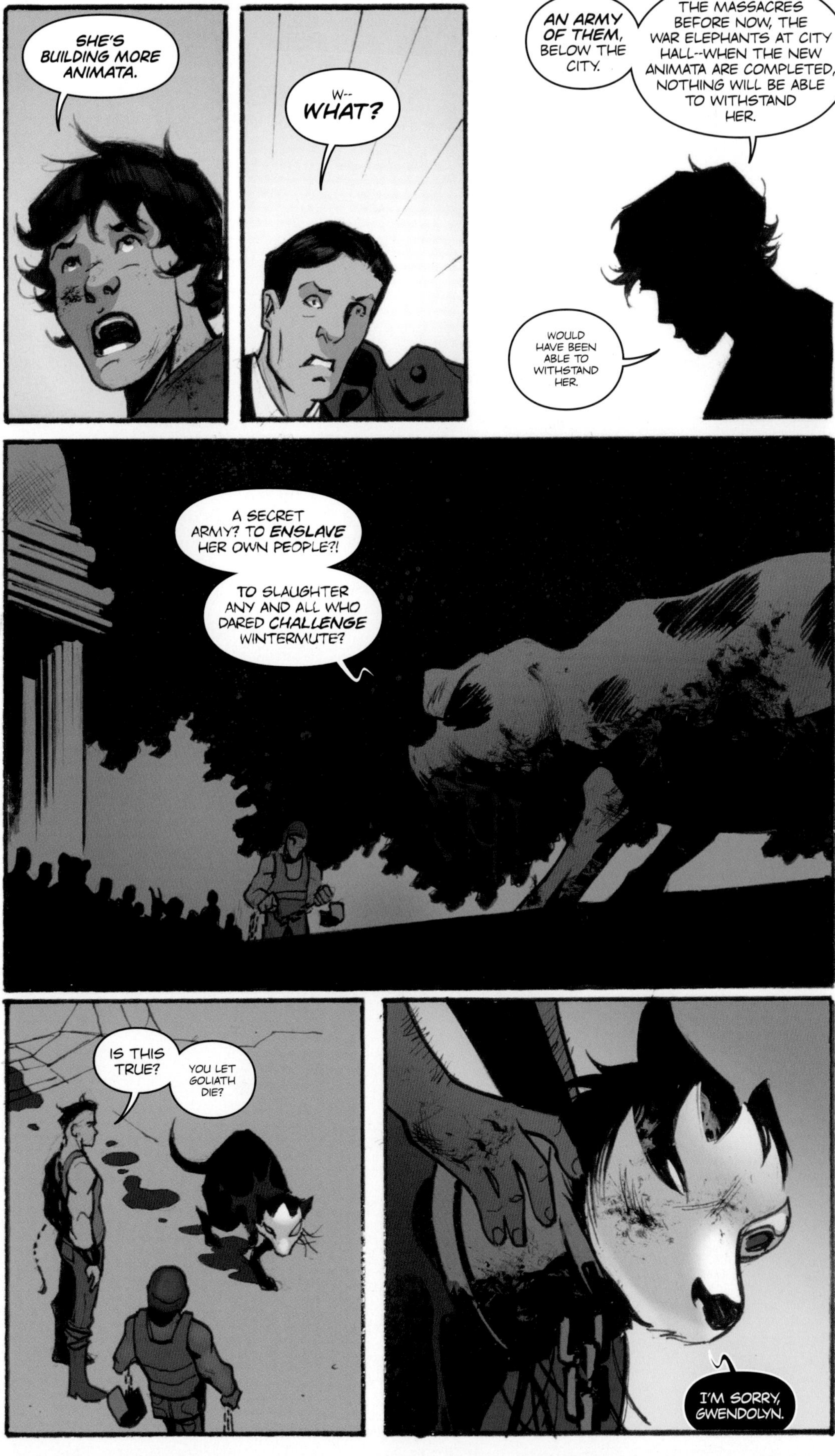
SHE'S BUILDING MORE ANIMATA.
W-- WHAT?
AN ARMY OF THEM, BELOW THE CITY.
THE MASSACRES BEFORE NOW, THE WAR ELEPHANTS AT CITY HALL--WHEN THE NEW ANIMATA ARE COMPLETED, NOTHING WILL BE ABLE TO WITHSTAND HER.
WOULD HAVE BEEN ABLE TO WITHSTAND HER.
A SECRET ARMY? TO ENSLAVE HER OWN PEOPLE?!
TO SLAUGHTER ANY AND ALL WHO DARED CHALLENGE WINTERMUTE?
IS THIS TRUE?
YOU LET GOLIATH DIE?
I'M SORRY, GWENDOLYN.

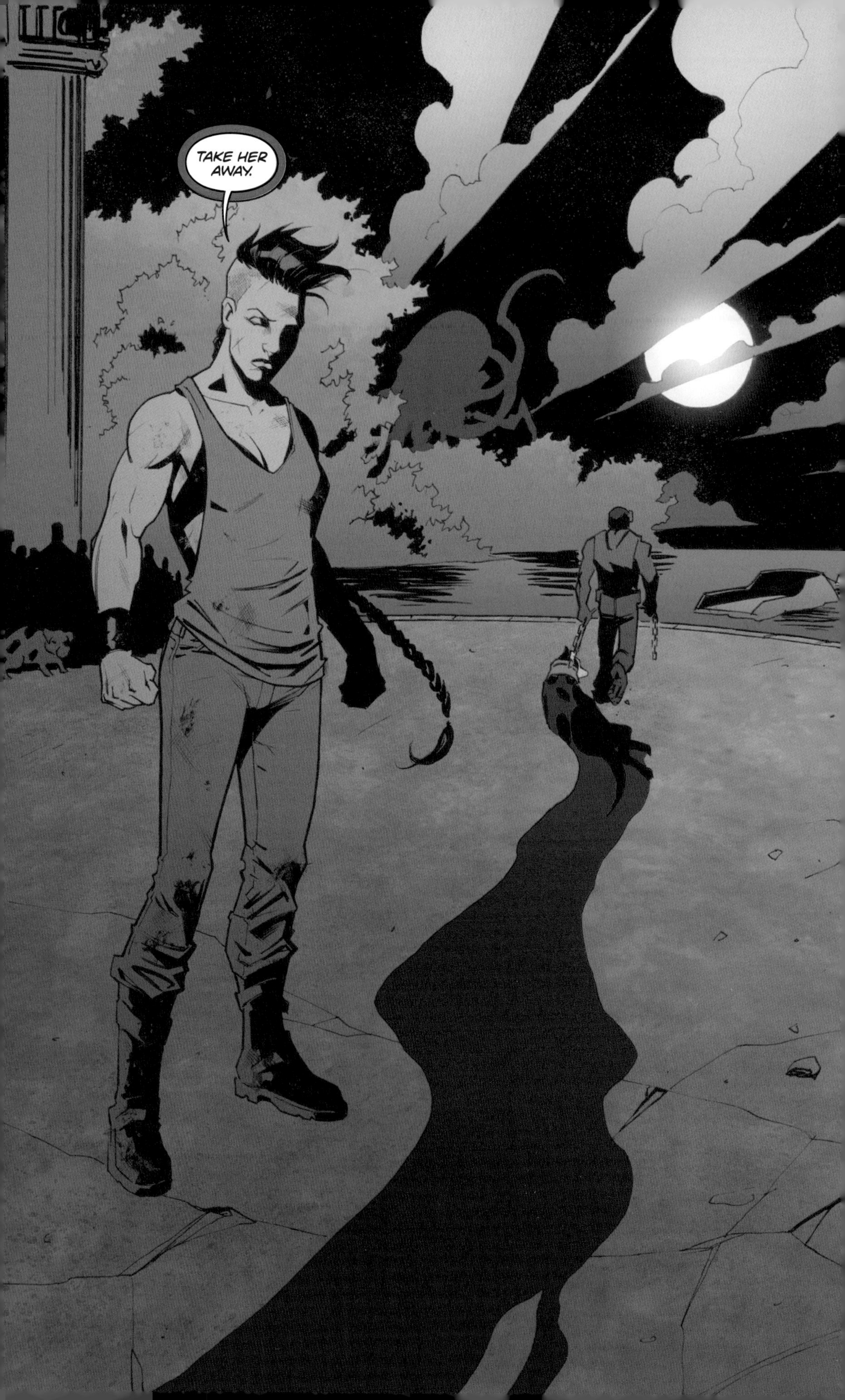
TAKE HER AWAY.

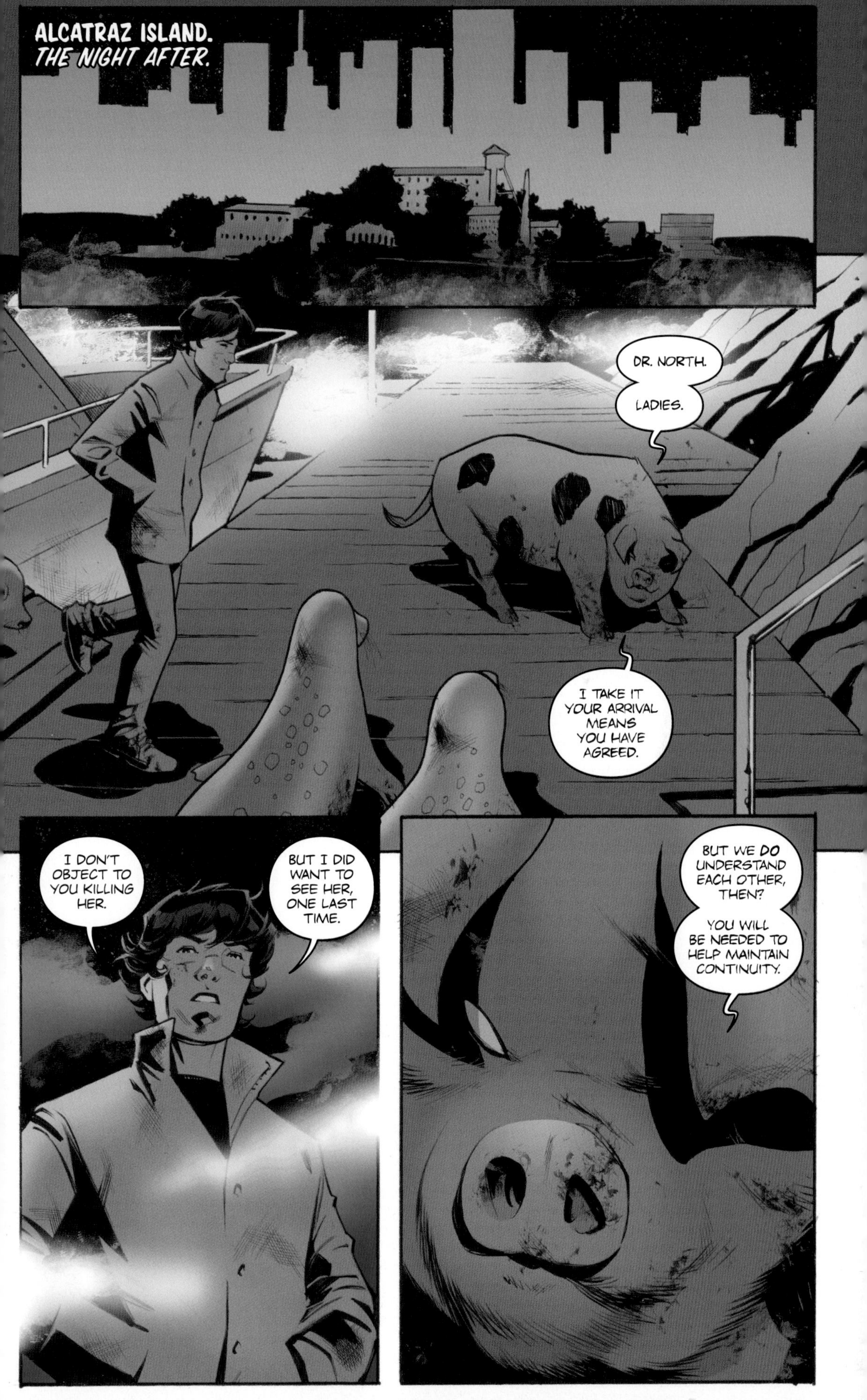
ALCATRAZ ISLAND.
THE NIGHT AFTER.
DR. NORTH.
LADIES.
I TAKE IT YOUR ARRIVAL MEANS YOU HAVE AGREED.
I DON'T OBJECT TO YOU KILLING HER.
BUT I DID WANT TO SEE HER, ONE LAST TIME.
BUT WE DO UNDERSTAND EACH OTHER, THEN?
YOU WILL BE NEEDED TO HELP MAINTAIN CONTINUITY.

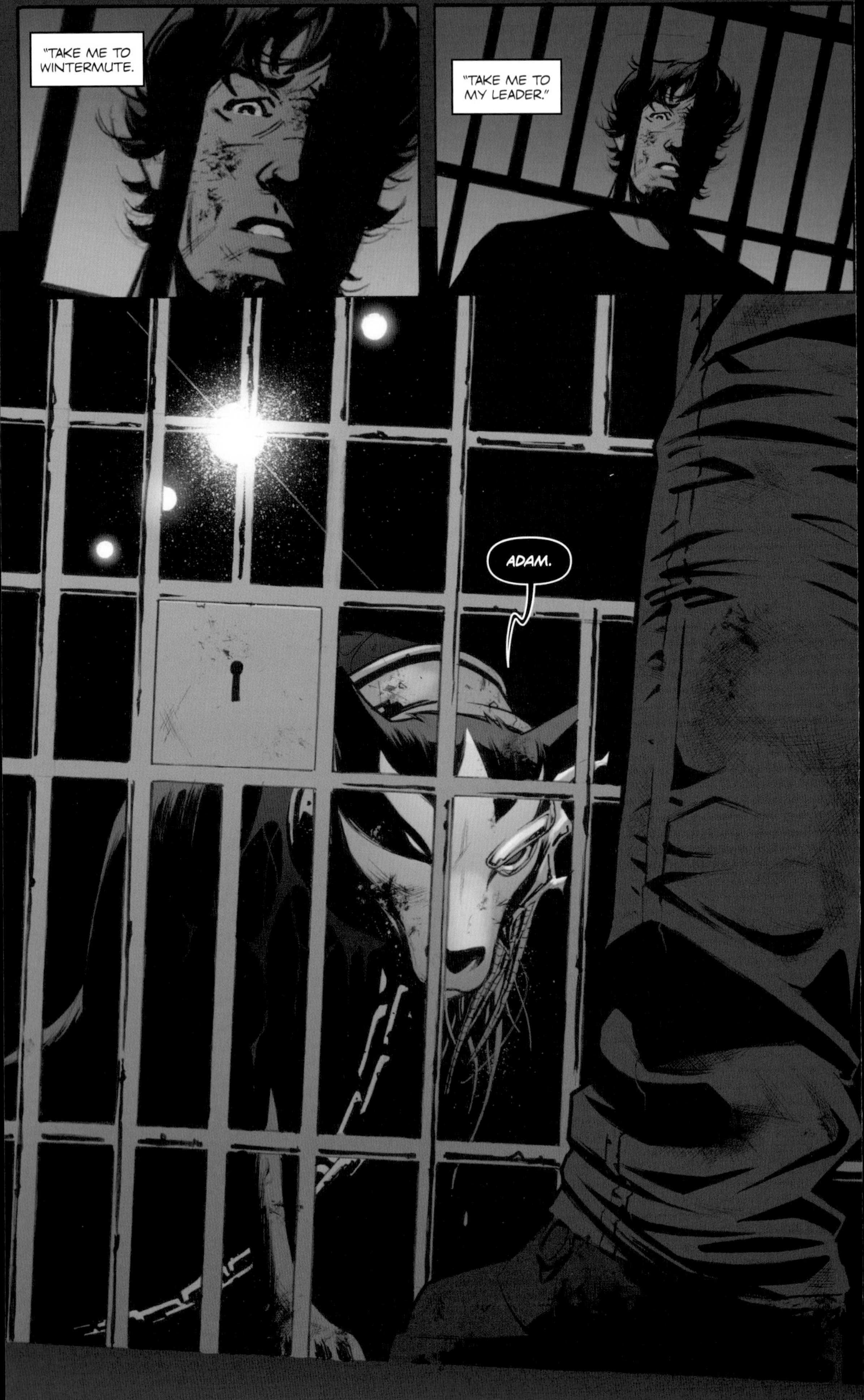
"TAKE ME TO WINTERMUTE.
"TAKE ME TO MY LEADER."
ADAM.

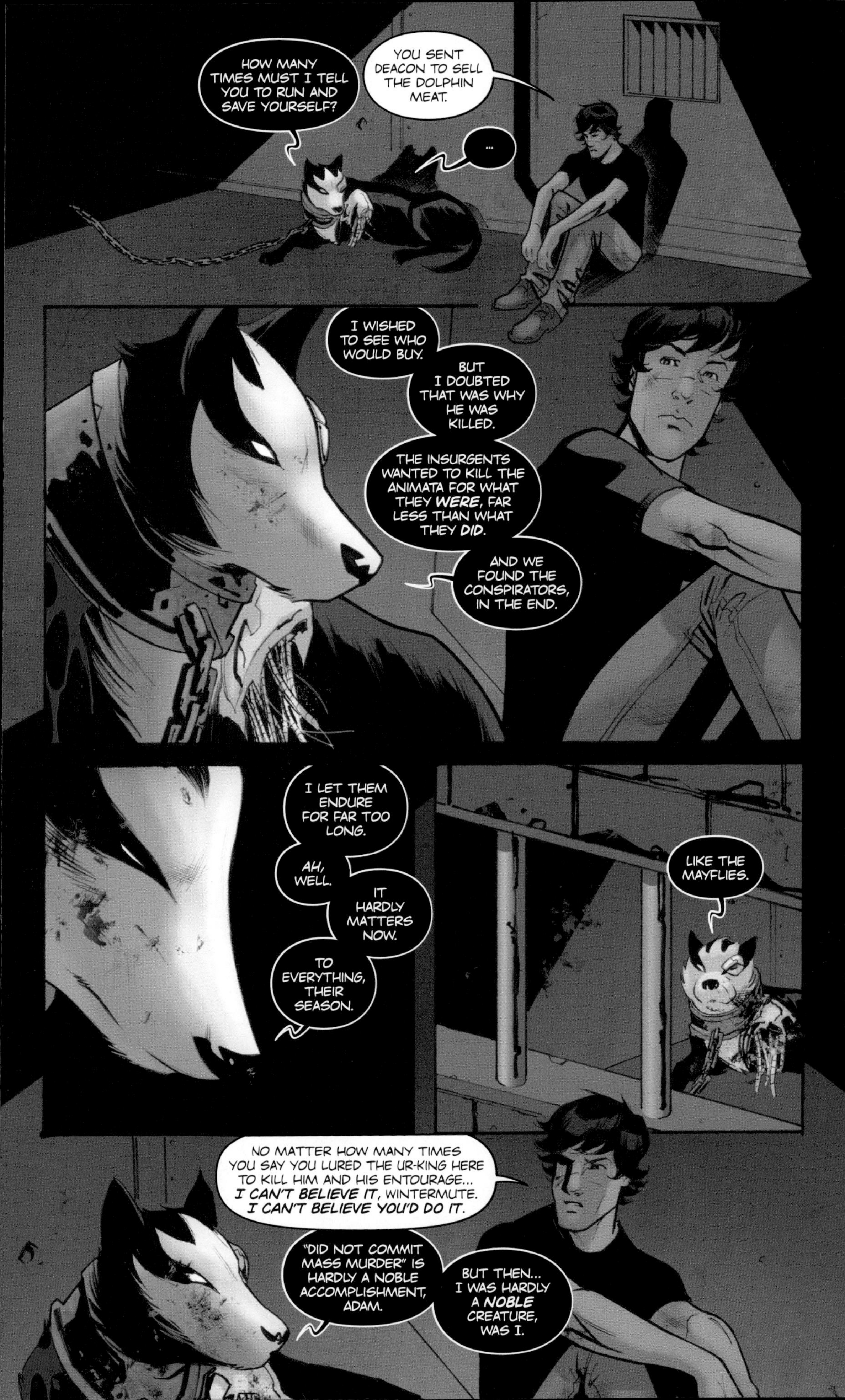
HOW MANY TIMES MUST I TELL YOU TO RUN AND SAVE YOURSELF?
YOU SENT DEACON TO SELL THE DOLPHIN MEAT.
...
I WISHED TO SEE WHO WOULD BUY.
BUT I DOUBTED THAT WAS WHY HE WAS KILLED.
THE INSURGENTS WANTED TO KILL THE ANIMATA FOR WHAT THEY *WERE*, FAR LESS THAN WHAT THEY *DID*.
AND WE FOUND THE CONSPIRATORS, IN THE END.
I LET THEM ENDURE FOR FAR TOO LONG.
AH, WELL.
IT HARDLY MATTERS NOW.
TO EVERYTHING, THEIR SEASON.
LIKE THE MAYFLIES.
NO MATTER HOW MANY TIMES YOU SAY YOU LURED THE UR-KING HERE TO KILL HIM AND HIS ENTOURAGE... ***I CAN'T BELIEVE IT***, WINTERMUTE. ***I CAN'T BELIEVE YOU'D DO IT***.
"DID NOT COMMIT MASS MURDER" IS HARDLY A NOBLE ACCOMPLISHMENT, ADAM.
BUT THEN... I WAS HARDLY A ***NOBLE*** CREATURE, WAS I.

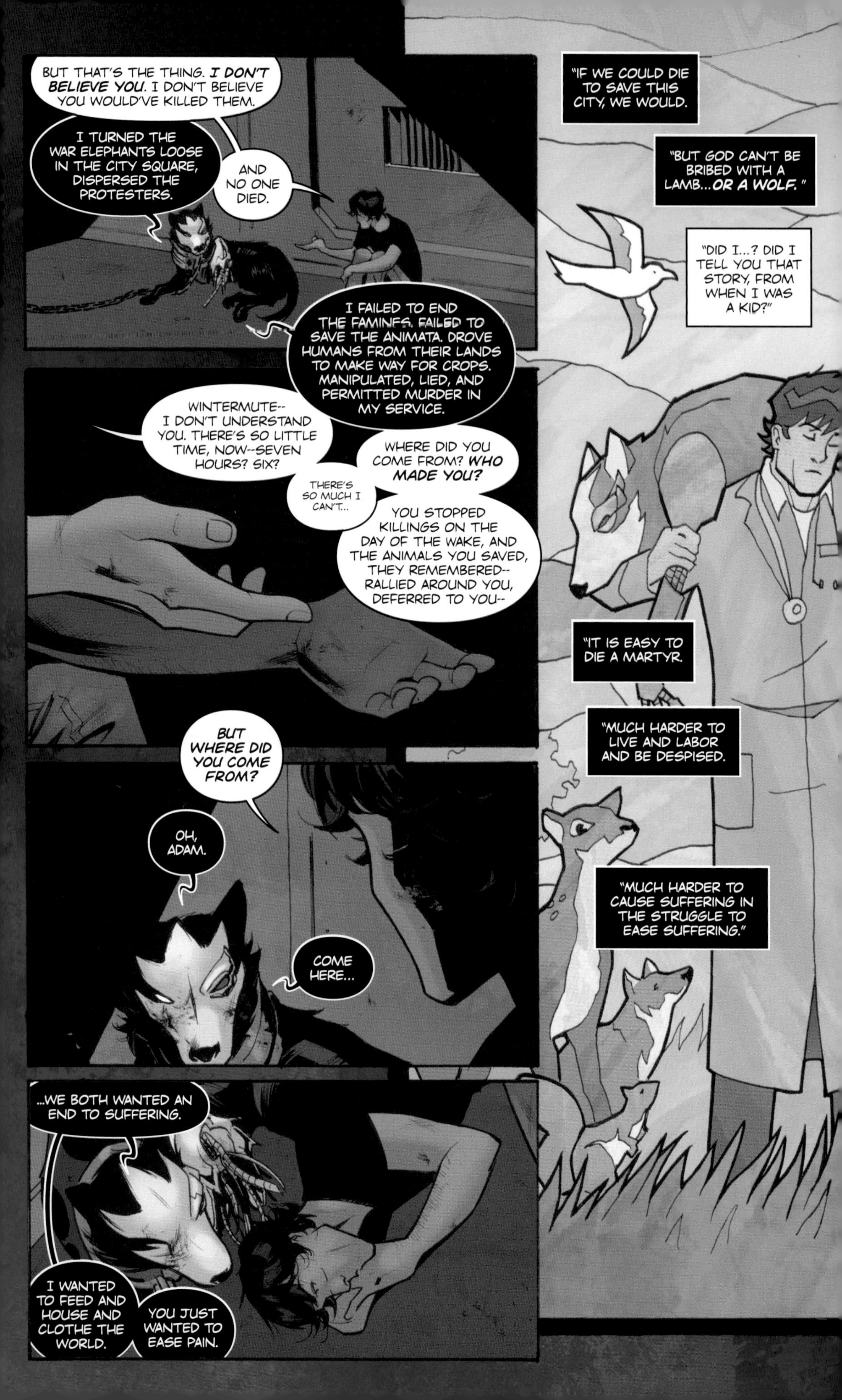

BUT THAT'S THE THING. I DON'T BELIEVE YOU. I DON'T BELIEVE YOU WOULD'VE KILLED THEM.
I TURNED THE WAR ELEPHANTS LOOSE IN THE CITY SQUARE, DISPERSED THE PROTESTERS.
AND NO ONE DIED.
I FAILED TO END THE FAMINES. FAILED TO SAVE THE ANIMATA. DROVE HUMANS FROM THEIR LANDS TO MAKE WAY FOR CROPS. MANIPULATED, LIED, AND PERMITTED MURDER IN MY SERVICE.
WINTERMUTE-- I DON'T UNDERSTAND YOU. THERE'S SO LITTLE TIME, NOW--SEVEN HOURS? SIX?
WHERE DID YOU COME FROM? WHO MADE YOU?
THERE'S SO MUCH I CAN'T...
YOU STOPPED KILLINGS ON THE DAY OF THE WAKE, AND THE ANIMALS YOU SAVED, THEY REMEMBERED-- RALLIED AROUND YOU, DEFERRED TO YOU--
BUT WHERE DID YOU COME FROM?
OH, ADAM.
COME HERE...
...WE BOTH WANTED AN END TO SUFFERING.
I WANTED TO FEED AND HOUSE AND CLOTHE THE WORLD.
YOU JUST WANTED TO EASE PAIN.
"IF WE COULD DIE TO SAVE THIS CITY, WE WOULD.
"BUT GOD CAN'T BE BRIBED WITH A LAMB...OR A WOLF."
"DID I...? DID I TELL YOU THAT STORY, FROM WHEN I WAS A KID?"
"IT IS EASY TO DIE A MARTYR.
"MUCH HARDER TO LIVE AND LABOR AND BE DESPISED.
"MUCH HARDER TO CAUSE SUFFERING IN THE STRUGGLE TO EASE SUFFERING."

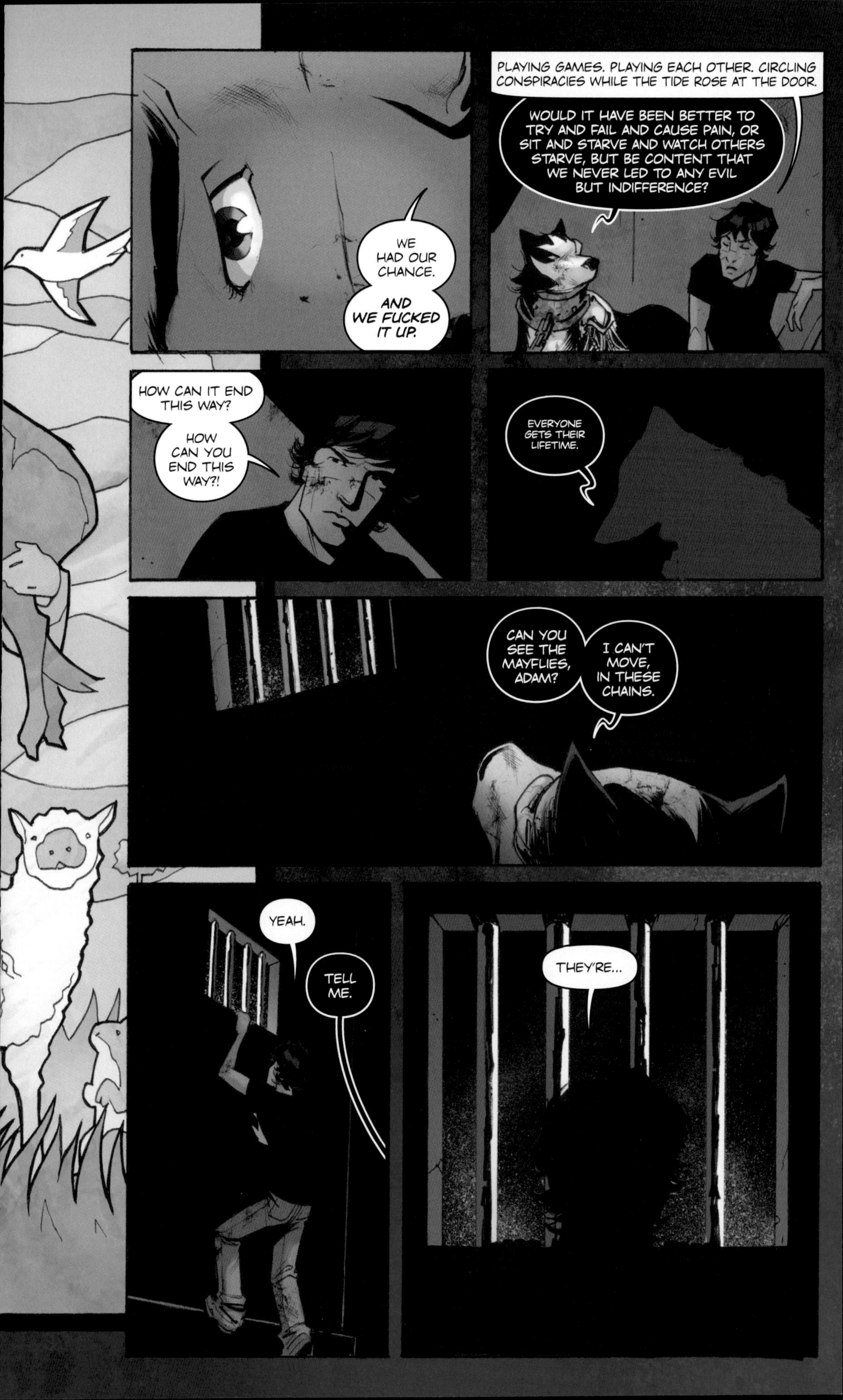
WE HAD OUR CHANCE.
AND WE FUCKED IT UP.
PLAYING GAMES. PLAYING EACH OTHER. CIRCLING CONSPIRACIES WHILE THE TIDE ROSE AT THE DOOR.
WOULD IT HAVE BEEN BETTER TO TRY AND FAIL AND CAUSE PAIN, OR SIT AND STARVE AND WATCH OTHERS STARVE, BUT BE CONTENT THAT WE NEVER LED TO ANY EVIL BUT INDIFFERENCE?
HOW CAN IT END THIS WAY?
HOW CAN YOU END THIS WAY?!
EVERYONE GETS THEIR LIFETIME.
CAN YOU SEE THE MAYFLIES, ADAM?
I CAN'T MOVE, IN THESE CHAINS.
YEAH.
TELL ME.
THEY'RE...

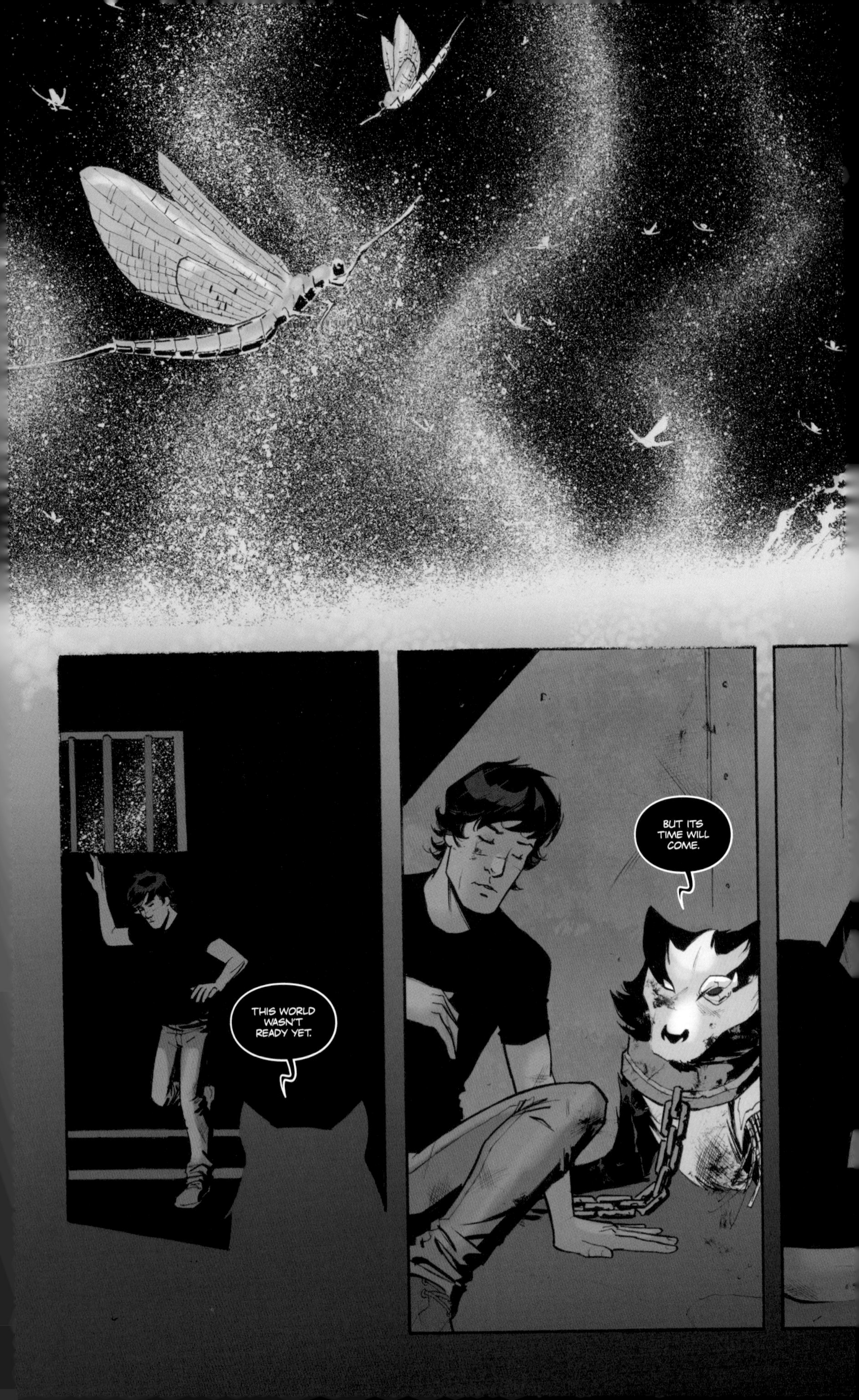
THIS WORLD WASN'T READY YET.
BUT ITS TIME WILL COME.

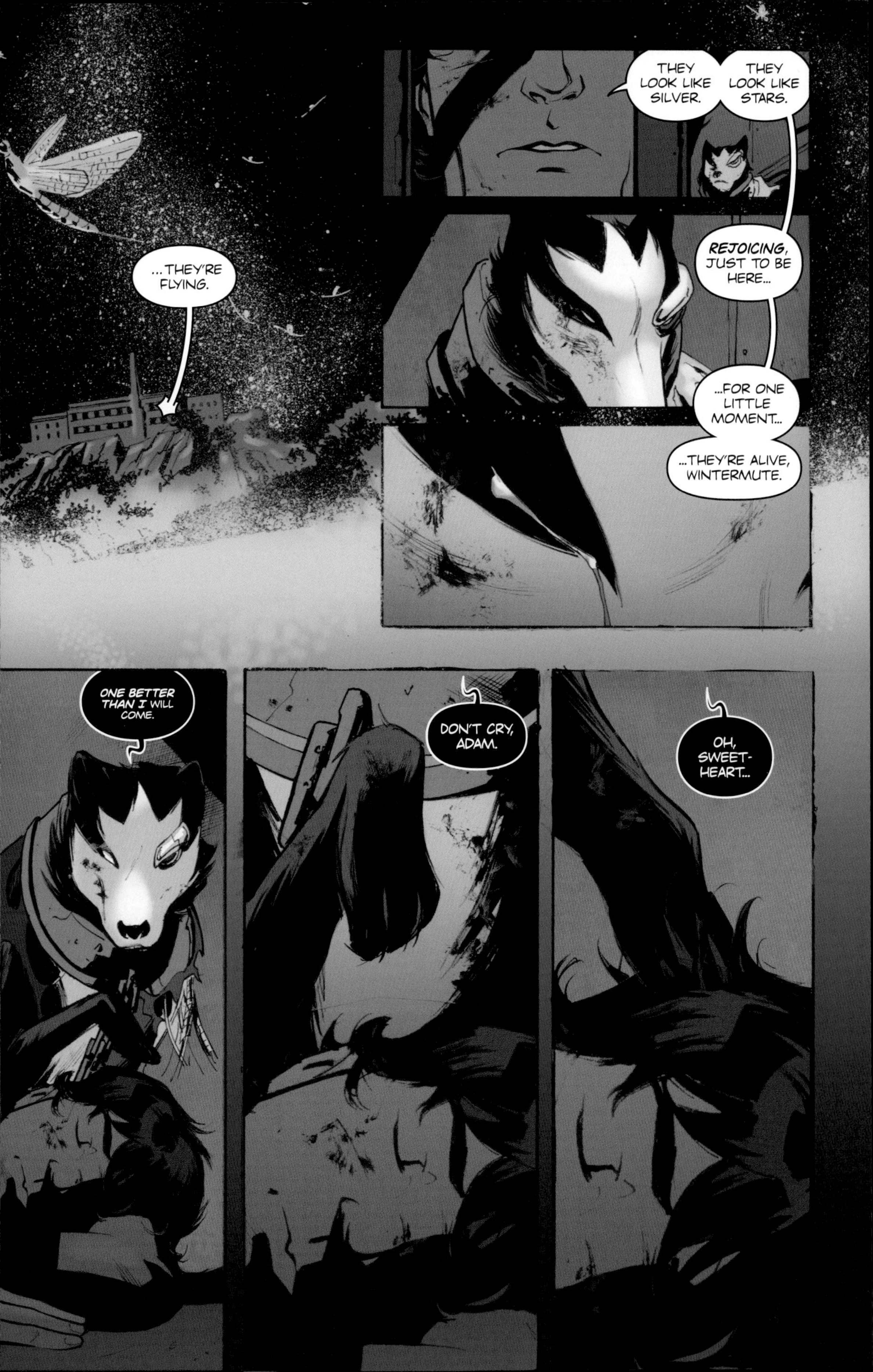
...THEY'RE FLYING.
THEY LOOK LIKE SILVER.
THEY LOOK LIKE STARS.
REJOICING, JUST TO BE HERE...
...FOR ONE LITTLE MOMENT...
...THEY'RE ALIVE, WINTERMUTE.
ONE BETTER THAN I WILL COME.
DON'T CRY, ADAM.
OH, SWEET-HEART...

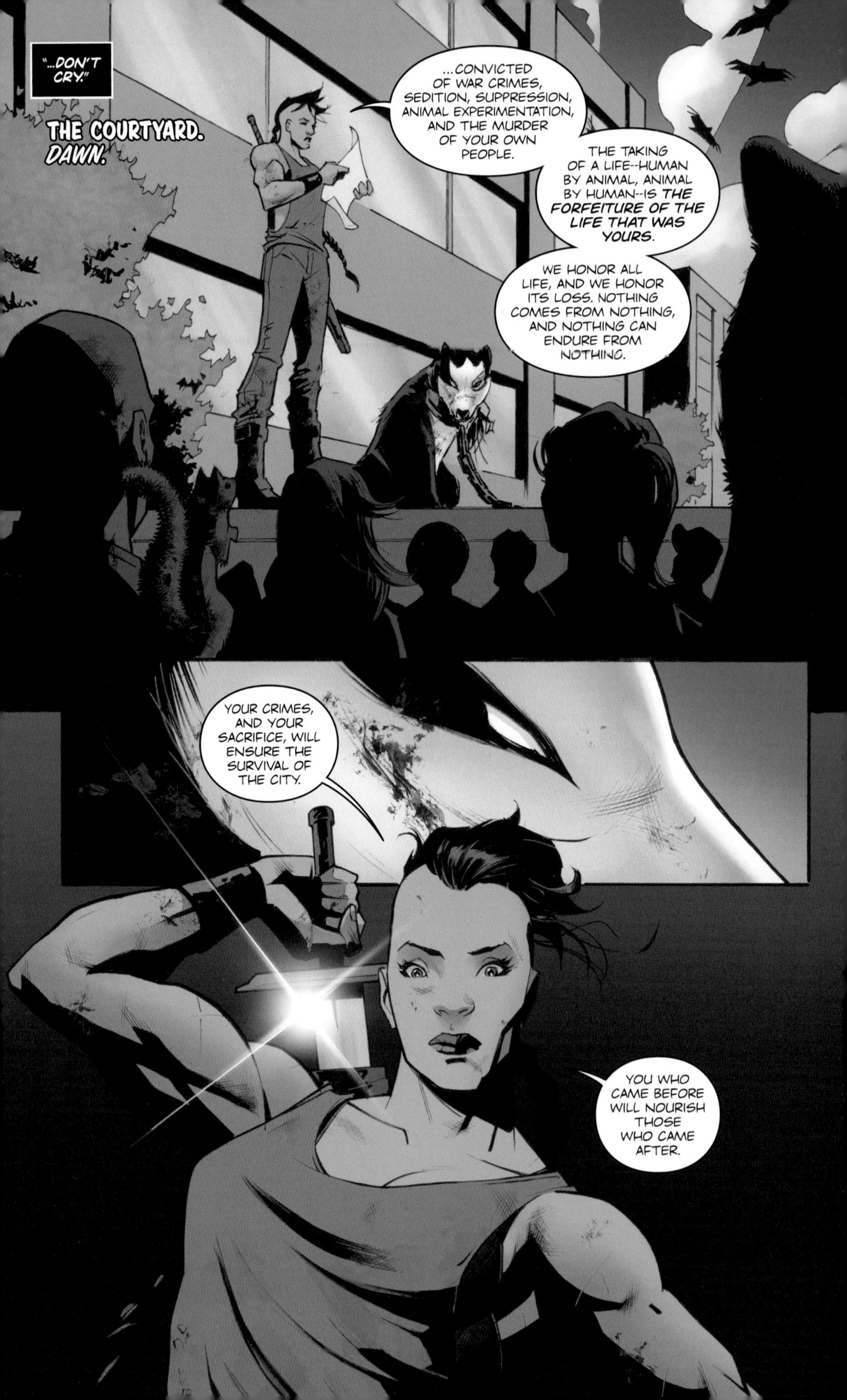
"...DON'T CRY."
THE COURTYARD. DAWN.
...CONVICTED OF WAR CRIMES, SEDITION, SUPPRESSION, ANIMAL EXPERIMENTATION, AND THE MURDER OF YOUR OWN PEOPLE.
THE TAKING OF A LIFE--HUMAN BY ANIMAL, ANIMAL BY HUMAN--IS THE FORFEITURE OF THE LIFE THAT WAS YOURS.
WE HONOR ALL LIFE, AND WE HONOR ITS LOSS. NOTHING COMES FROM NOTHING, AND NOTHING CAN ENDURE FROM NOTHING.
YOUR CRIMES, AND YOUR SACRIFICE, WILL ENSURE THE SURVIVAL OF THE CITY.
YOU WHO CAME BEFORE WILL NOURISH THOSE WHO CAME AFTER.

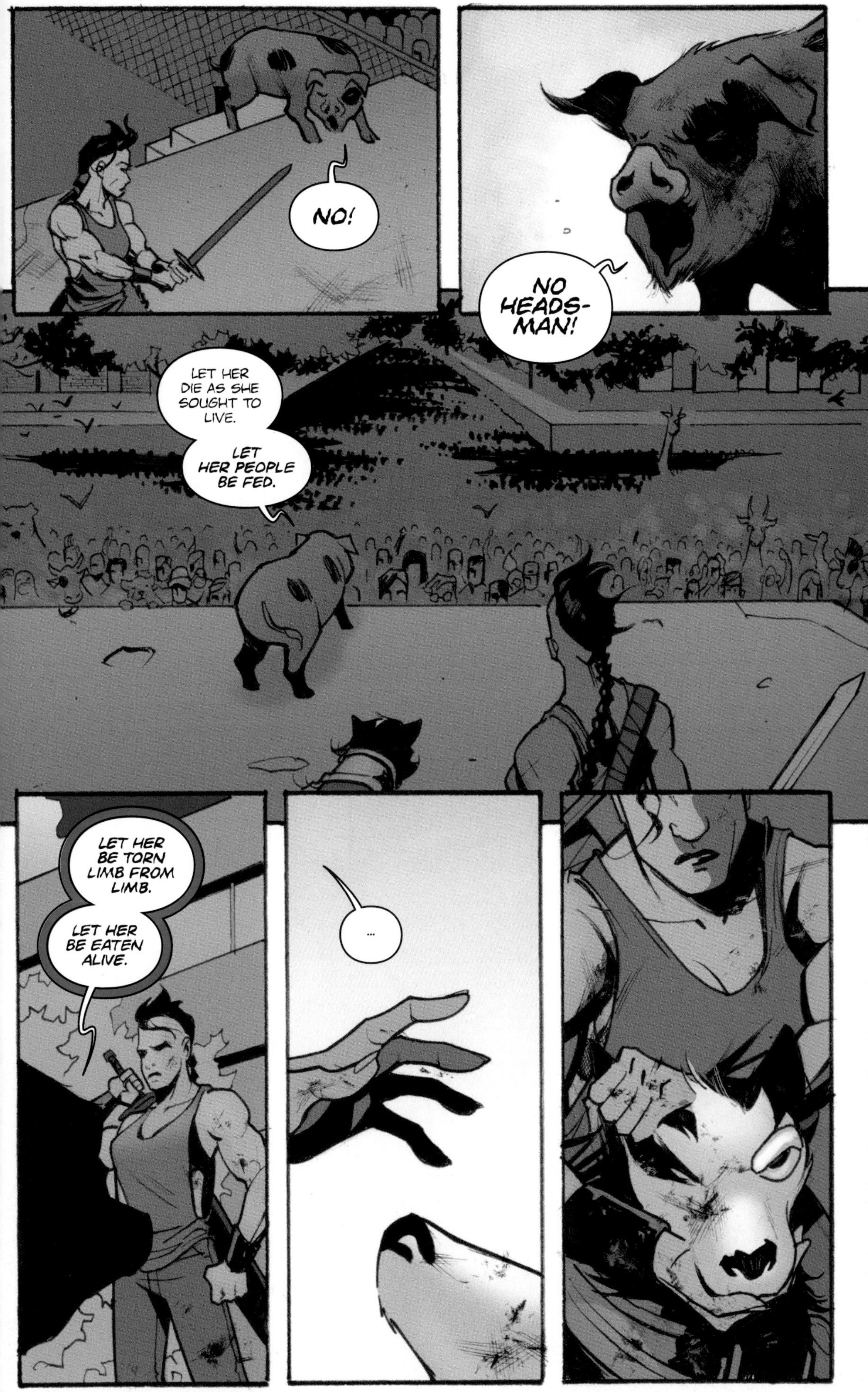
NO!
NO HEADSMAN!
LET HER DIE AS SHE SOUGHT TO LIVE.
LET HER PEOPLE BE FED.
LET HER BE TORN LIMB FROM LIMB.
LET HER BE EATEN ALIVE.
...

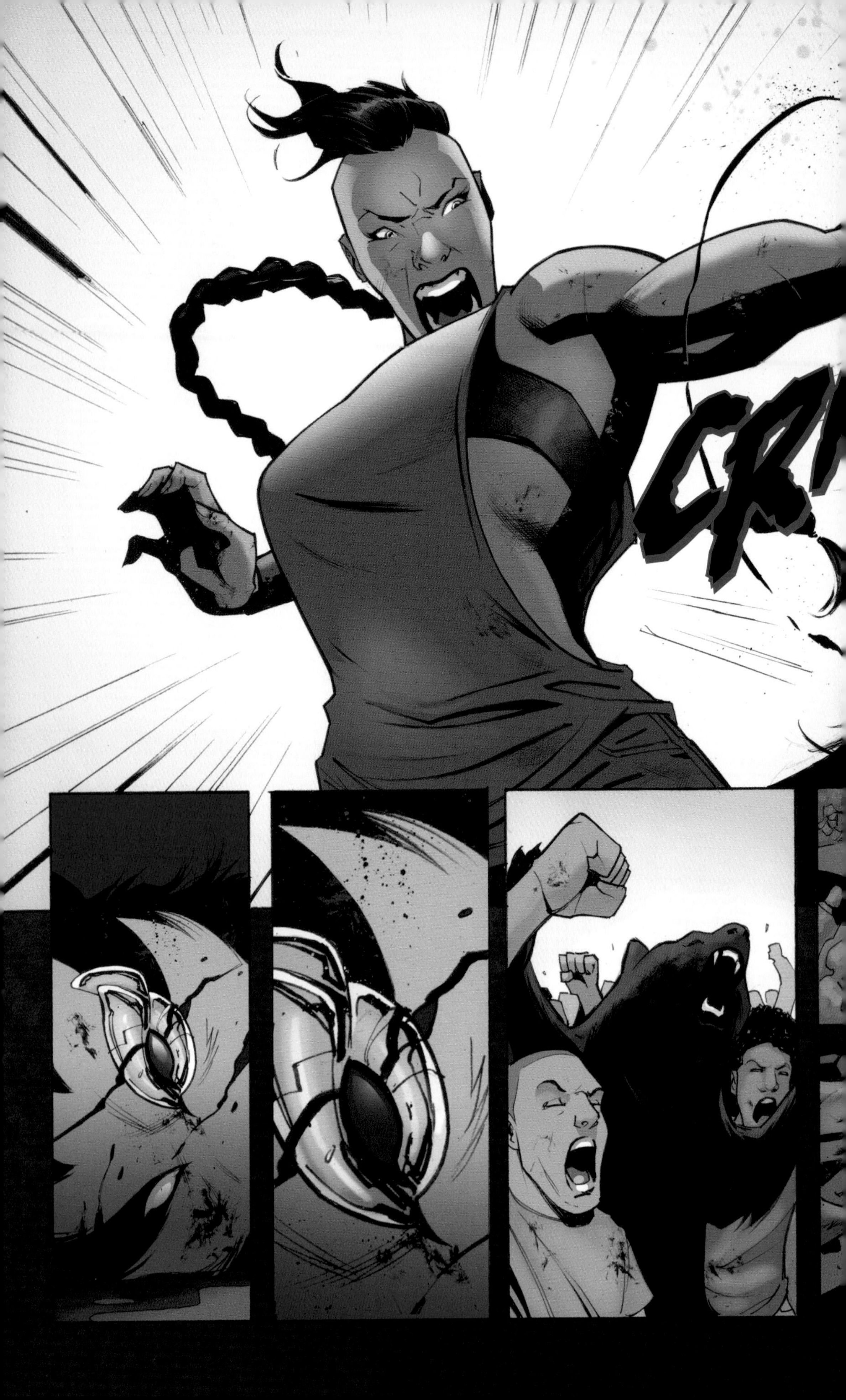
CR

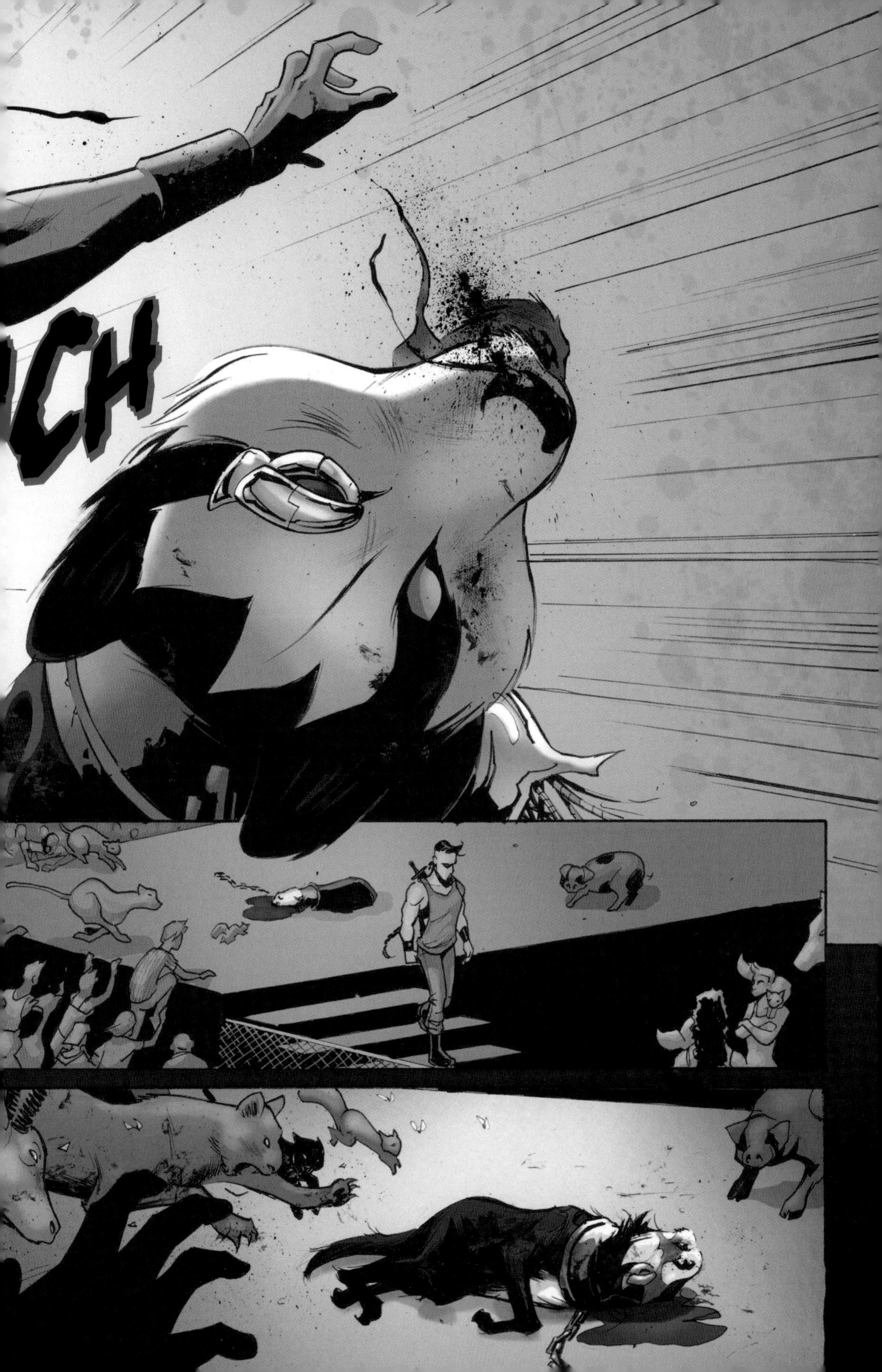
CH

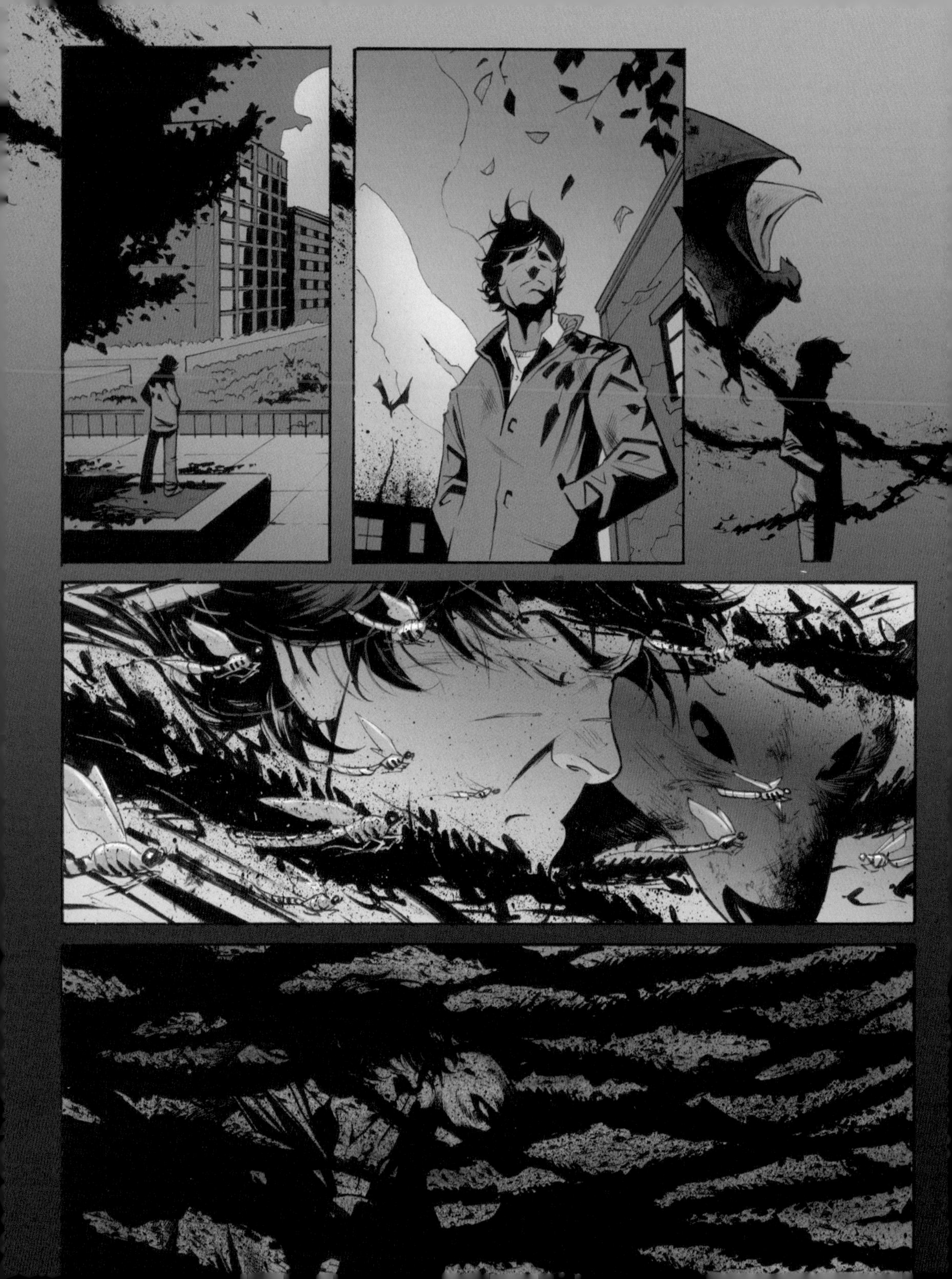

10

LEX MACHINA: PART 5

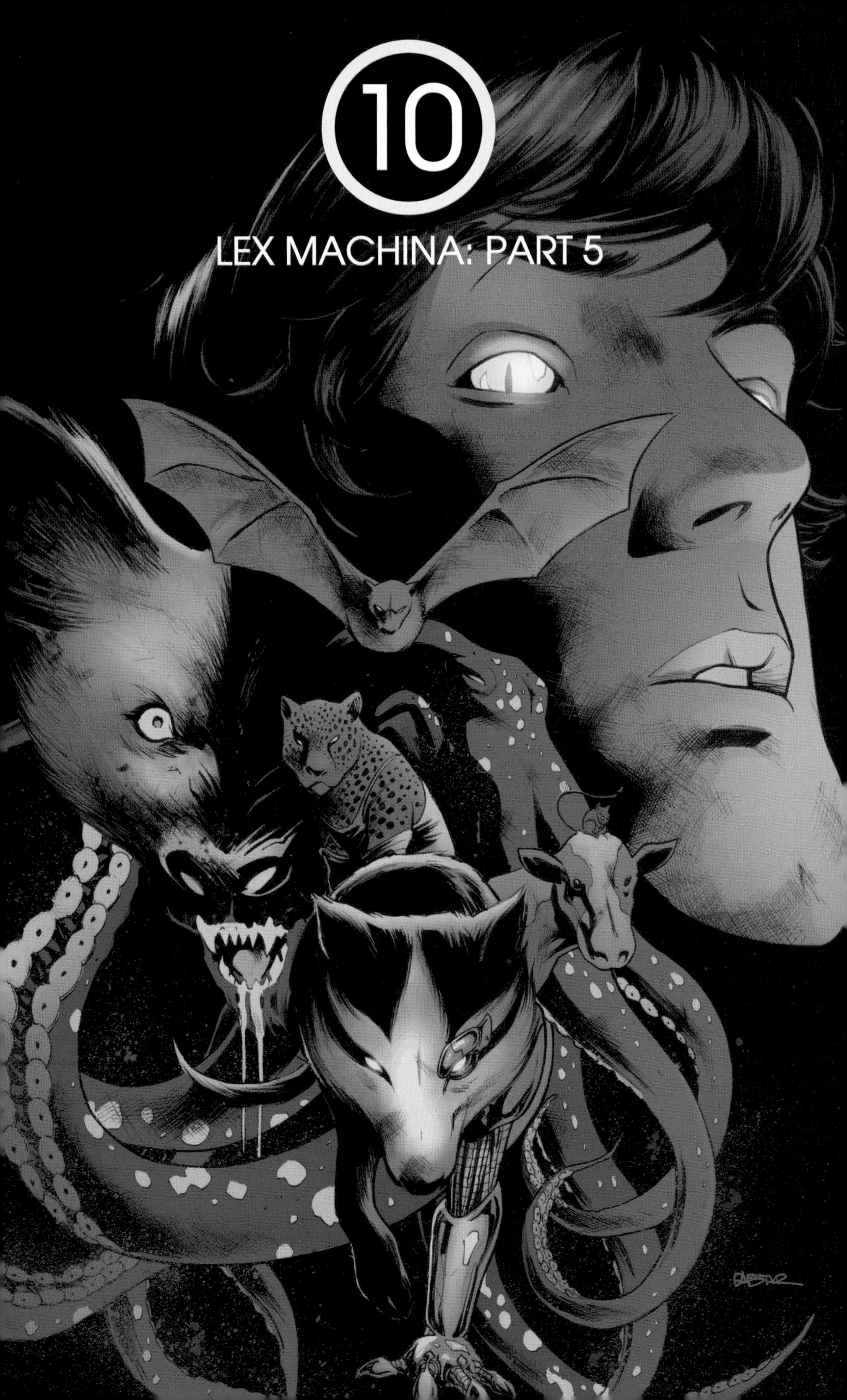

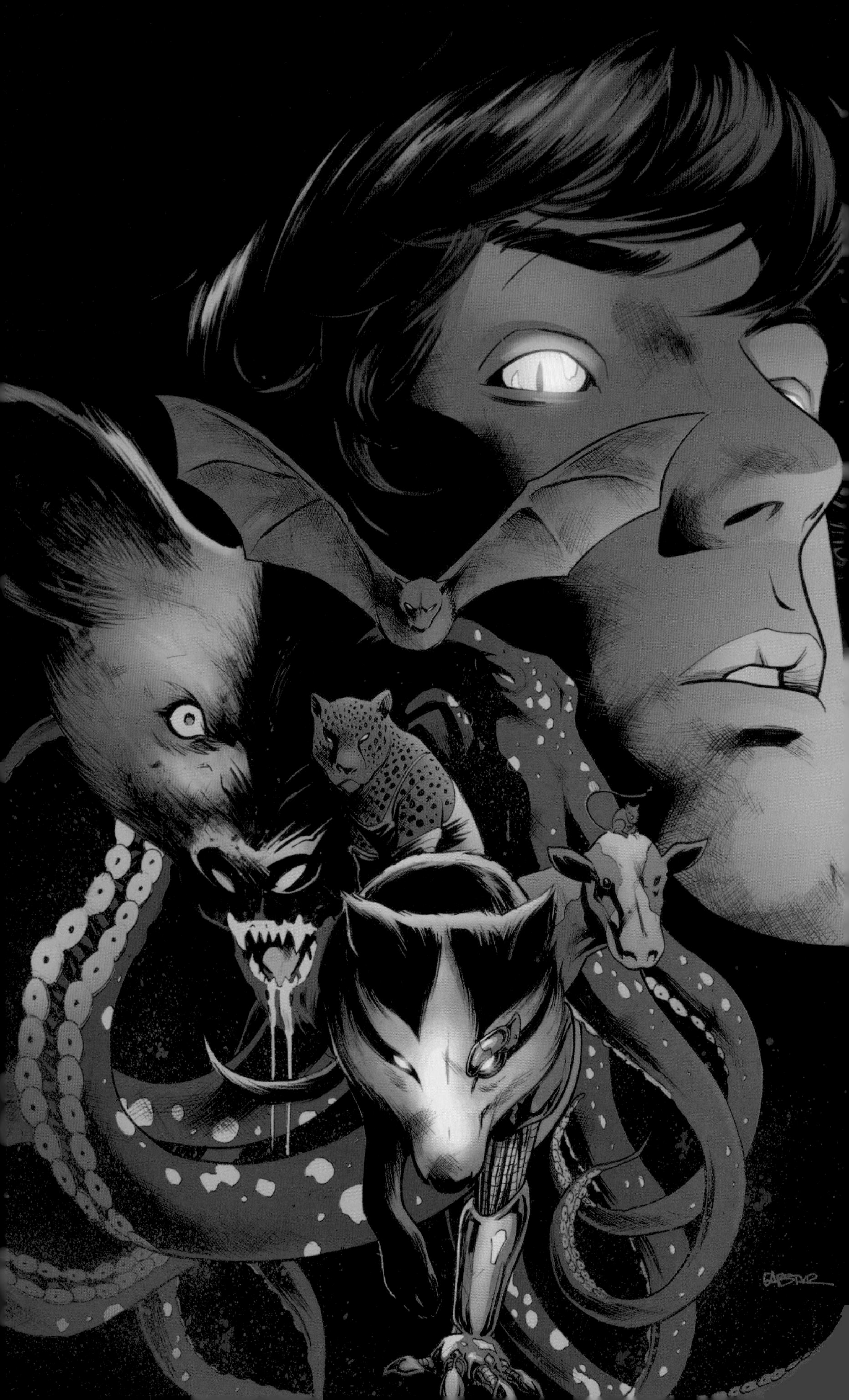

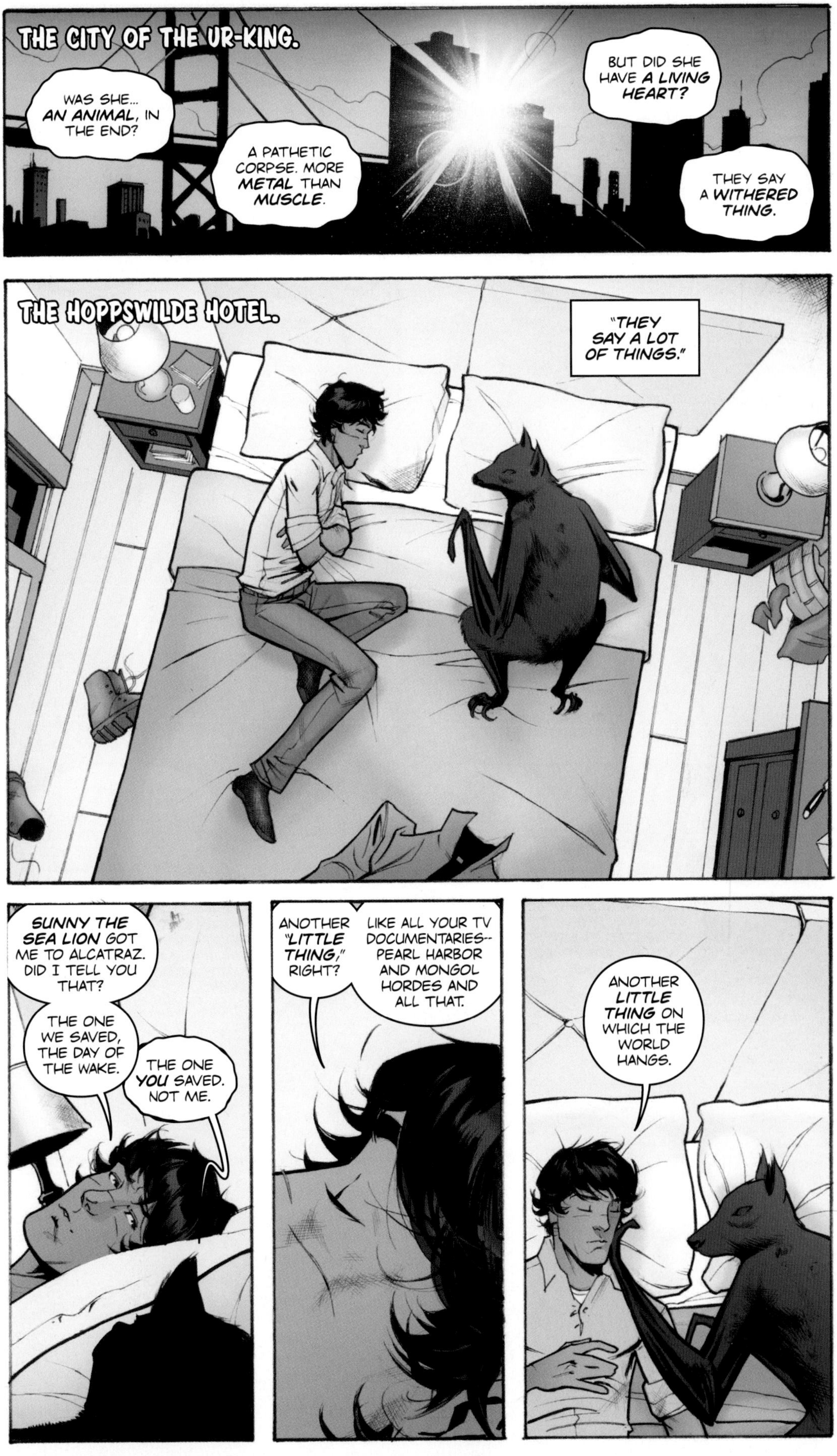
THE CITY OF THE UR-KING.
WAS SHE... AN ANIMAL, IN THE END?
A PATHETIC CORPSE. MORE METAL THAN MUSCLE.
BUT DID SHE HAVE A LIVING HEART?
THEY SAY A WITHERED THING.
THE HOPPSWILDE HOTEL.
"THEY SAY A LOT OF THINGS."
SUNNY THE SEA LION GOT ME TO ALCATRAZ. DID I TELL YOU THAT?
THE ONE WE SAVED, THE DAY OF THE WAKE.
THE ONE YOU SAVED. NOT ME.
ANOTHER "LITTLE THING," RIGHT?
LIKE ALL YOUR TV DOCUMENTARIES-- PEARL HARBOR AND MONGOL HORDES AND ALL THAT.
ANOTHER LITTLE THING ON WHICH THE WORLD HANGS.

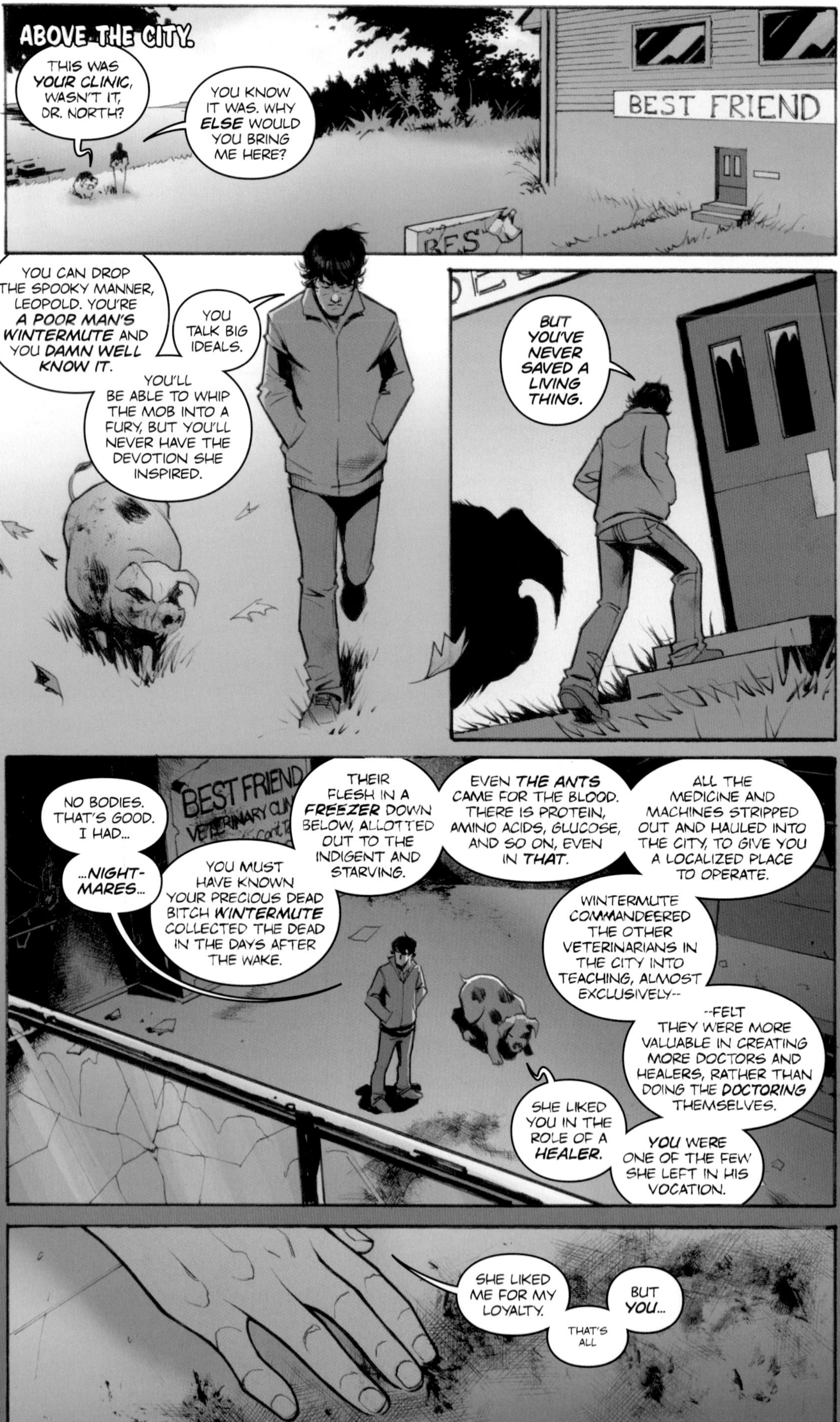
ABOVE THE CITY.
THIS WAS YOUR CLINIC, WASN'T IT, DR. NORTH?
YOU KNOW IT WAS. WHY ELSE WOULD YOU BRING ME HERE?
BEST FRIEND
YOU CAN DROP THE SPOOKY MANNER, LEOPOLD. YOU'RE A POOR MAN'S WINTERMUTE AND YOU DAMN WELL KNOW IT.
YOU TALK BIG IDEALS.
YOU'LL BE ABLE TO WHIP THE MOB INTO A FURY, BUT YOU'LL NEVER HAVE THE DEVOTION SHE INSPIRED.
BUT YOU'VE NEVER SAVED A LIVING THING.
NO BODIES. THAT'S GOOD. I HAD...
...NIGHT-MARES...
YOU MUST HAVE KNOWN YOUR PRECIOUS DEAD BITCH WINTERMUTE COLLECTED THE DEAD IN THE DAYS AFTER THE WAKE.
THEIR FLESH IN A FREEZER DOWN BELOW, ALLOTTED OUT TO THE INDIGENT AND STARVING.
EVEN THE ANTS CAME FOR THE BLOOD. THERE IS PROTEIN, AMINO ACIDS, GLUCOSE, AND SO ON, EVEN IN THAT.
ALL THE MEDICINE AND MACHINES STRIPPED OUT AND HAULED INTO THE CITY, TO GIVE YOU A LOCALIZED PLACE TO OPERATE.
WINTERMUTE COMMANDEERED THE OTHER VETERINARIANS IN THE CITY INTO TEACHING, ALMOST EXCLUSIVELY--
--FELT THEY WERE MORE VALUABLE IN CREATING MORE DOCTORS AND HEALERS, RATHER THAN DOING THE DOCTORING THEMSELVES.
SHE LIKED YOU IN THE ROLE OF A HEALER.
YOU WERE ONE OF THE FEW SHE LEFT IN HIS VOCATION.
SHE LIKED ME FOR MY LOYALTY.
THAT'S ALL
BUT YOU...

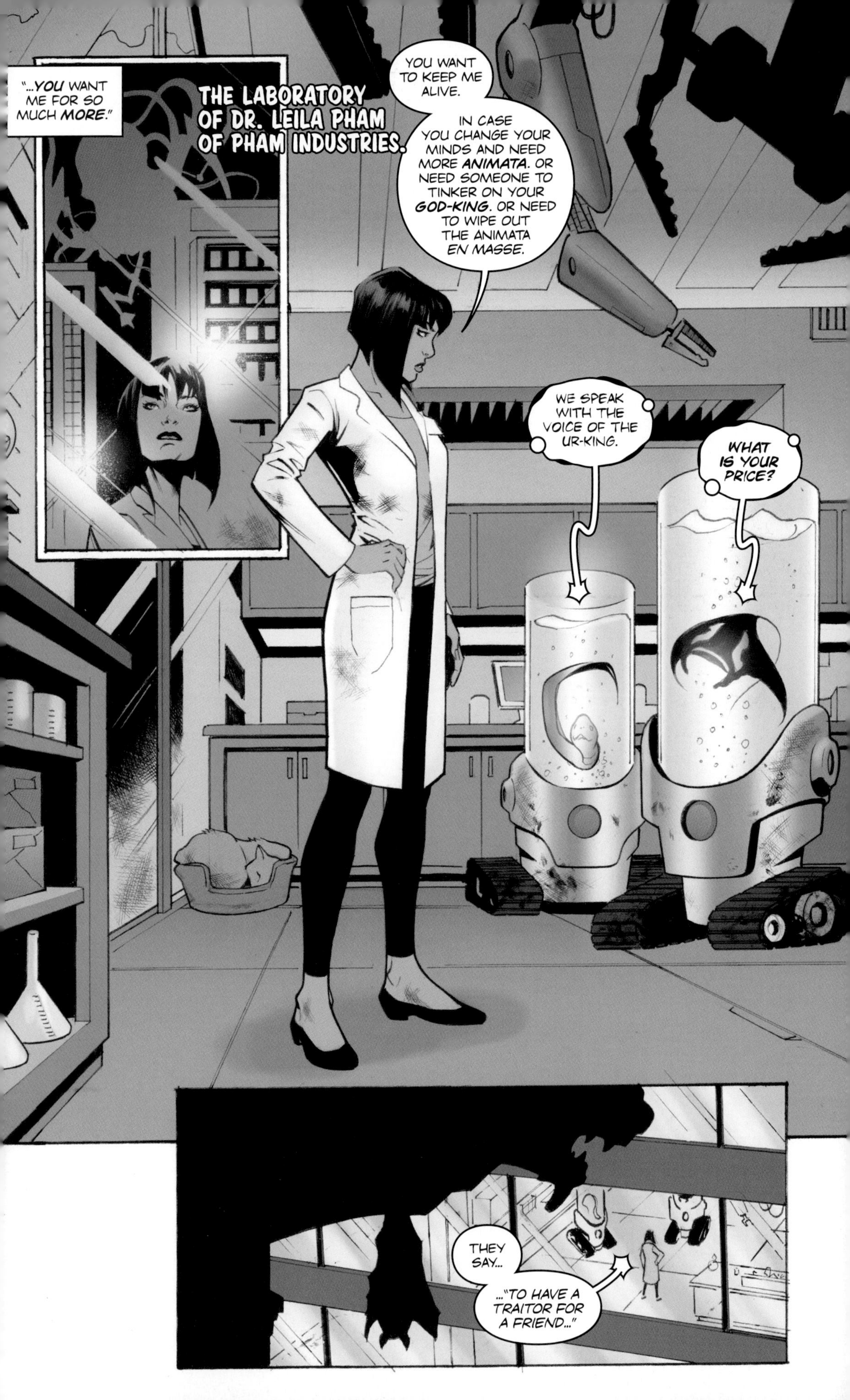
"...*YOU* WANT ME FOR SO MUCH *MORE*."
THE LABORATORY OF DR. LEILA PHAM OF PHAM INDUSTRIES.
YOU WANT TO KEEP ME ALIVE.
IN CASE YOU CHANGE YOUR MINDS AND NEED MORE *ANIMATA*. OR NEED SOMEONE TO TINKER ON YOUR *GOD-KING*. OR NEED TO WIPE OUT THE ANIMATA *EN MASSE*.
WE SPEAK WITH THE VOICE OF THE UR-KING.
WHAT IS YOUR PRICE?
THEY SAY...
..."TO HAVE A TRAITOR FOR A FRIEND..."

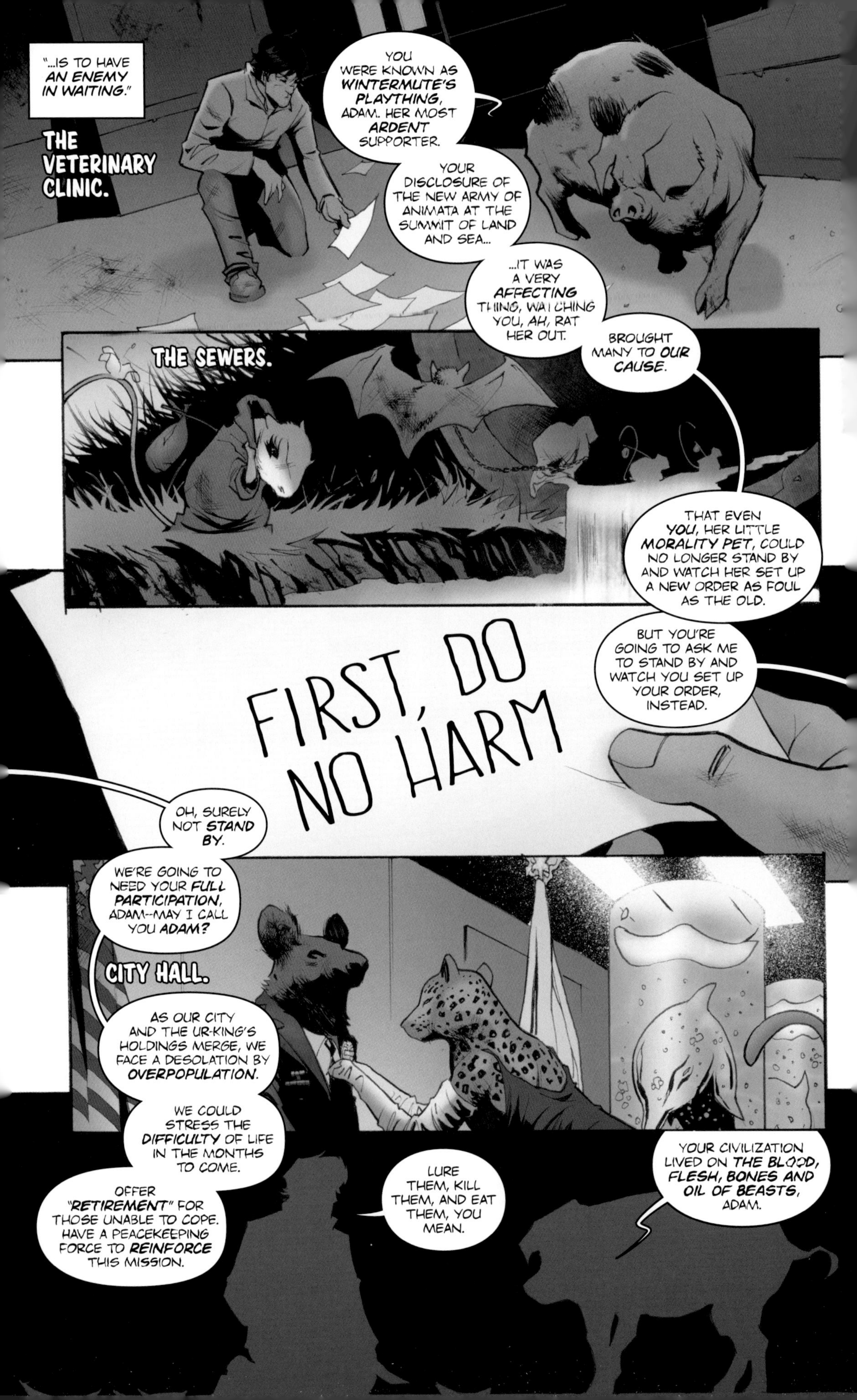
"...IS TO HAVE AN ENEMY IN WAITING."
THE VETERINARY CLINIC.
YOU WERE KNOWN AS WINTERMUTE'S PLAYTHING, ADAM. HER MOST ARDENT SUPPORTER.
YOUR DISCLOSURE OF THE NEW ARMY OF ANIMATA AT THE SUMMIT OF LAND AND SEA...
...IT WAS A VERY AFFECTING THING, WATCHING YOU, AH, RAT HER OUT.
THE SEWERS.
BROUGHT MANY TO OUR CAUSE.
THAT EVEN YOU, HER LITTLE MORALITY PET, COULD NO LONGER STAND BY AND WATCH HER SET UP A NEW ORDER AS FOUL AS THE OLD.
FIRST, DO NO HARM
BUT YOU'RE GOING TO ASK ME TO STAND BY AND WATCH YOU SET UP YOUR ORDER, INSTEAD.
OH, SURELY NOT STAND BY.
WE'RE GOING TO NEED YOUR FULL PARTICIPATION, ADAM--MAY I CALL YOU ADAM?
CITY HALL.
AS OUR CITY AND THE UR-KING'S HOLDINGS MERGE, WE FACE A DESOLATION BY OVERPOPULATION.
WE COULD STRESS THE DIFFICULTY OF LIFE IN THE MONTHS TO COME.
OFFER "RETIREMENT" FOR THOSE UNABLE TO COPE. HAVE A PEACEKEEPING FORCE TO REINFORCE THIS MISSION.
LURE THEM, KILL THEM, AND EAT THEM, YOU MEAN.
YOUR CIVILIZATION LIVED ON THE BLOOD, FLESH, BONES AND OIL OF BEASTS, ADAM.

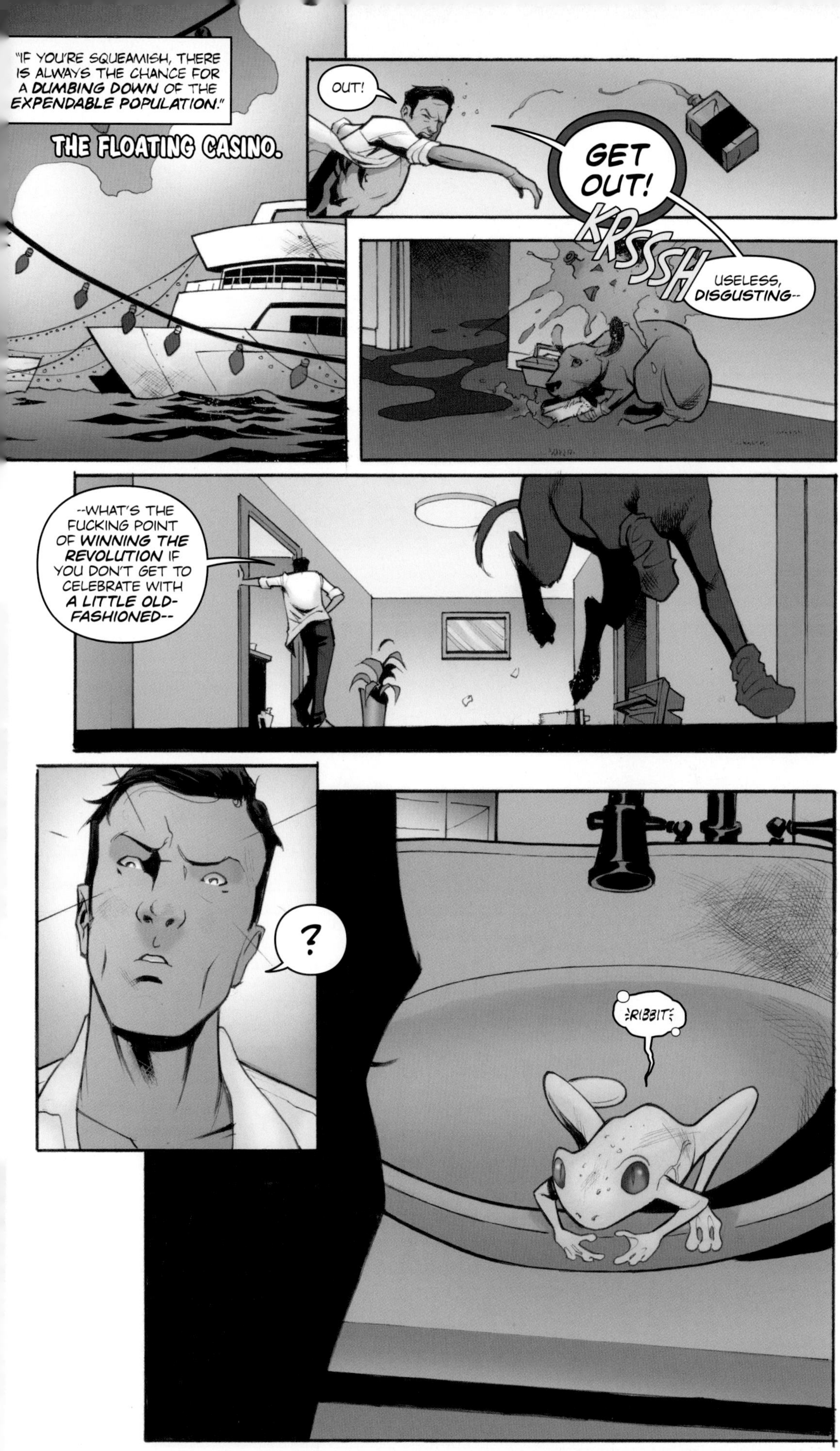
"IF YOU'RE SQUEAMISH, THERE IS ALWAYS THE CHANCE FOR A DUMBING DOWN OF THE EXPENDABLE POPULATION."
THE FLOATING CASINO.
OUT!
GET OUT!
KRSSSH
USELESS, DISGUSTING--
--WHAT'S THE FUCKING POINT OF WINNING THE REVOLUTION IF YOU DON'T GET TO CELEBRATE WITH A LITTLE OLD-FASHIONED--
?
RIBBIT

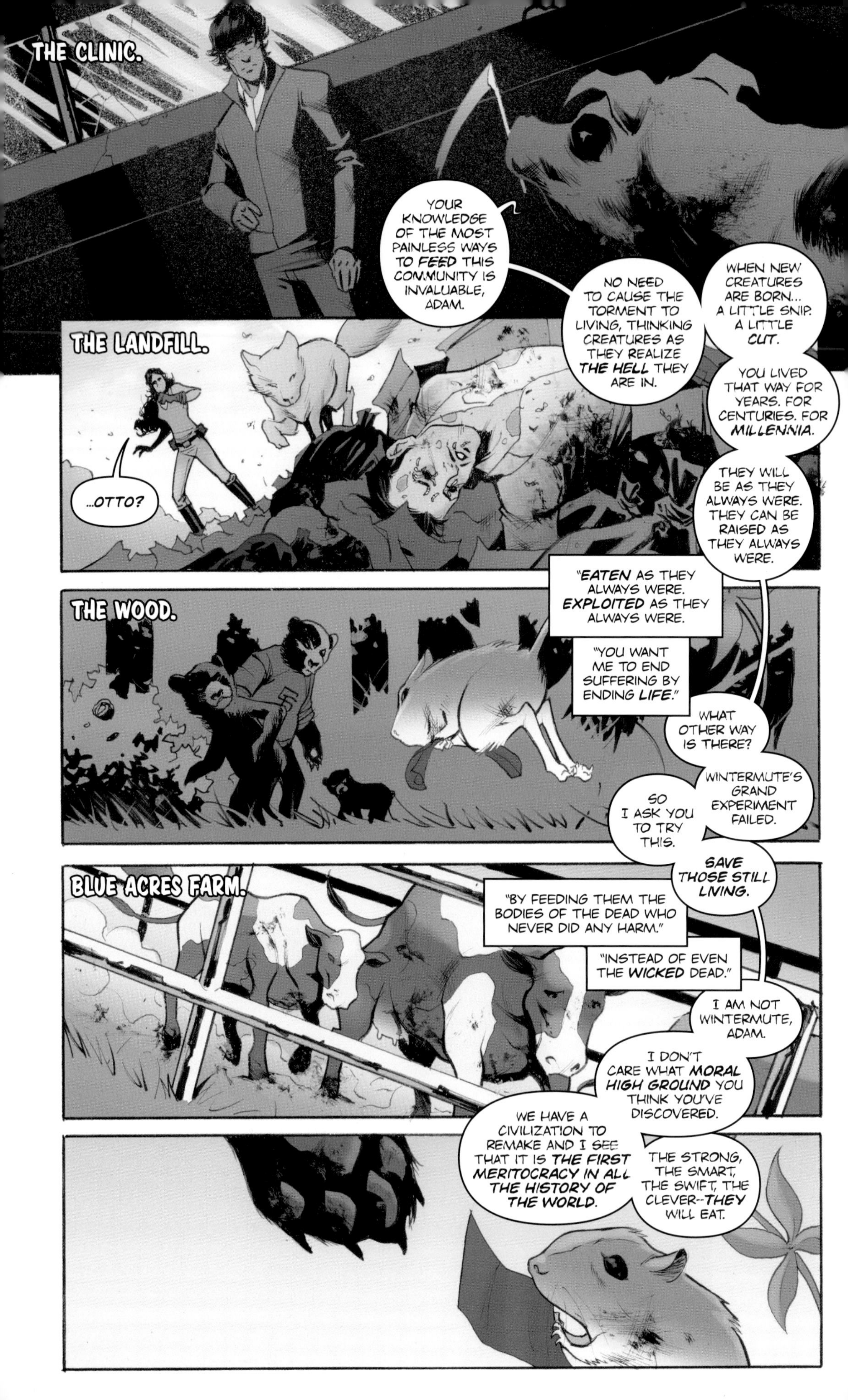
THE CLINIC.
YOUR KNOWLEDGE OF THE MOST PAINLESS WAYS TO FEED THIS COMMUNITY IS INVALUABLE, ADAM.
NO NEED TO CAUSE THE TORMENT TO LIVING, THINKING CREATURES AS THEY REALIZE THE HELL THEY ARE IN.
WHEN NEW CREATURES ARE BORN... A LITTLE SNIP. A LITTLE CUT.
THE LANDFILL.
YOU LIVED THAT WAY FOR YEARS. FOR CENTURIES. FOR MILLENNIA.
...OTTO?
THEY WILL BE AS THEY ALWAYS WERE. THEY CAN BE RAISED AS THEY ALWAYS WERE.
THE WOOD.
"EATEN AS THEY ALWAYS WERE. EXPLOITED AS THEY ALWAYS WERE.
"YOU WANT ME TO END SUFFERING BY ENDING LIFE."
WHAT OTHER WAY IS THERE?
WINTERMUTE'S GRAND EXPERIMENT FAILED.
SO I ASK YOU TO TRY THIS.
BLUE ACRES FARM.
SAVE THOSE STILL LIVING.
"BY FEEDING THEM THE BODIES OF THE DEAD WHO NEVER DID ANY HARM."
"INSTEAD OF EVEN THE WICKED DEAD."
I AM NOT WINTERMUTE, ADAM.
I DON'T CARE WHAT MORAL HIGH GROUND YOU THINK YOU'VE DISCOVERED.
WE HAVE A CIVILIZATION TO REMAKE AND I SEE THAT IT IS THE FIRST MERITOCRACY IN ALL THE HISTORY OF THE WORLD.
THE STRONG, THE SMART, THE SWIFT, THE CLEVER--THEY WILL EAT.

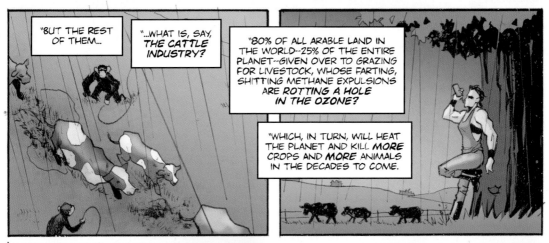

"BUT THE REST OF THEM...

"...WHAT IS, SAY, *THE CATTLE INDUSTRY?*

"80% OF ALL ARABLE LAND IN THE WORLD--25% OF THE ENTIRE PLANET--GIVEN OVER TO GRAZING FOR LIVESTOCK, WHOSE FARTING, SHITTING METHANE EXPULSIONS ARE *ROTTING A HOLE IN THE OZONE?*

"WHICH, IN TURN, WILL HEAT THE PLANET AND KILL *MORE* CROPS AND *MORE* ANIMALS IN THE DECADES TO COME.

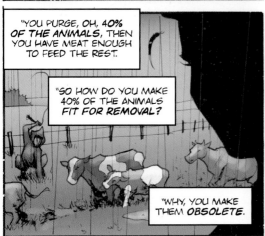

"YOU PURGE, OH, 40% *OF THE ANIMALS*, THEN YOU HAVE MEAT ENOUGH TO FEED THE REST.

"SO HOW DO YOU MAKE 40% OF THE ANIMALS *FIT FOR REMOVAL?*

"WHY, YOU MAKE THEM *OBSOLETE.*

"DO WE *REALLY* NEED HORSES AND PIGS? I MEAN THAT SINCERELY.

"EVEN DEAR, DEFIANT GWENDOLYN YI DOESN'T NEED A HORSE--SHE SIMPLY ENJOYS THE *THEATRICALITY.*

"AND I CANNOT IMAGINE ANY HUMAN TRULY *GRIEVES* AN ANIMAL THE WAY SHE GOES ON AND ON, MOURNING FOR POOR DEAD GOLIATH.

"HOW COULD A HUMAN SEE THE DEATHS OF BILLIONS OF COWS, CHICKENS, AND SHEEP, BUT CRY OVER *A SINGLE PET?*

"I PERSONALLY THINK GWENDOLYN DOES IT TO PROMOTE THE IDEA THAT WE'RE ALL IN THIS TOGETHER, HUMAN AND ANIMAL ALIKE--

"--AND WE'RE NOT."

"SO YOUR SOLUTION TO SAVING THE ANIMALS...IS..."

"YES, ADAM."

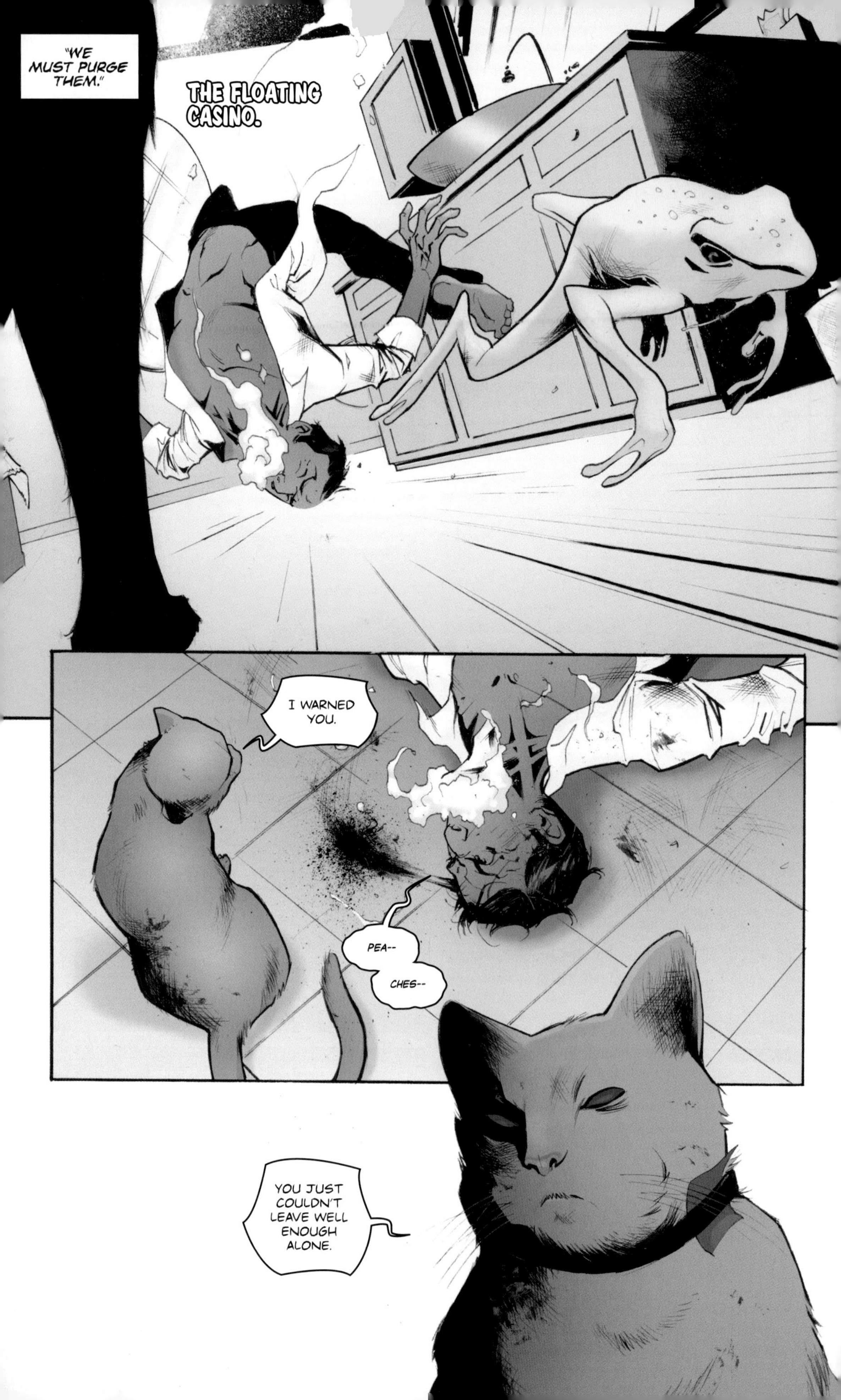
"WE MUST PURGE THEM."
THE FLOATING CASINO.
I WARNED YOU.
PEA--
CHES--
YOU JUST COULDN'T LEAVE WELL ENOUGH ALONE.

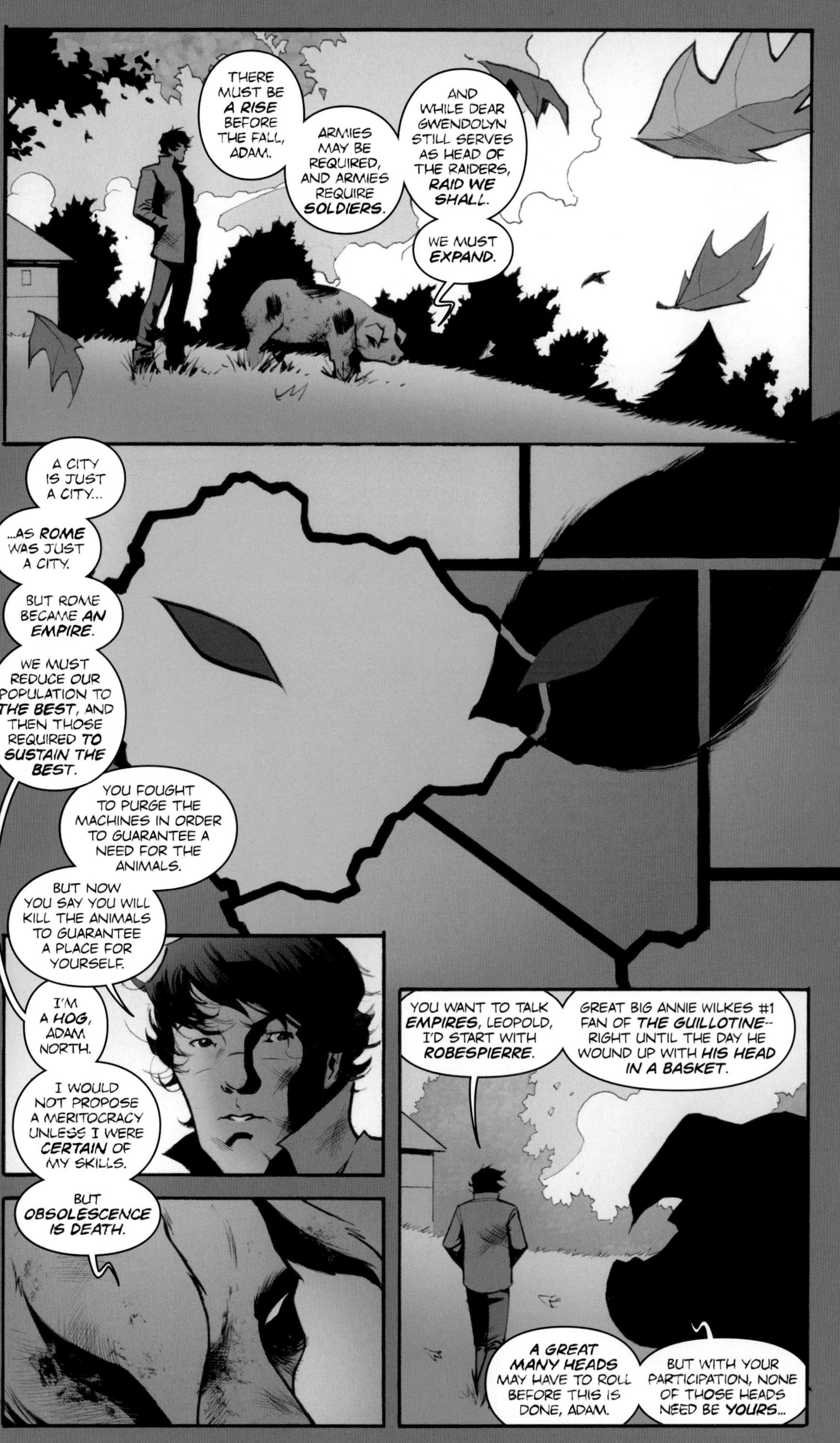

THERE MUST BE A RISE BEFORE THE FALL, ADAM.
ARMIES MAY BE REQUIRED, AND ARMIES REQUIRE SOLDIERS.
AND WHILE DEAR GWENDOLYN STILL SERVES AS HEAD OF THE RAIDERS, RAID WE SHALL.
WE MUST EXPAND.
A CITY IS JUST A CITY...
...AS ROME WAS JUST A CITY.
BUT ROME BECAME AN EMPIRE.
WE MUST REDUCE OUR POPULATION TO THE BEST, AND THEN THOSE REQUIRED TO SUSTAIN THE BEST.
YOU FOUGHT TO PURGE THE MACHINES IN ORDER TO GUARANTEE A NEED FOR THE ANIMALS.
BUT NOW YOU SAY YOU WILL KILL THE ANIMALS TO GUARANTEE A PLACE FOR YOURSELF.
I'M A HOG, ADAM NORTH.
I WOULD NOT PROPOSE A MERITOCRACY UNLESS I WERE CERTAIN OF MY SKILLS.
BUT OBSOLESCENCE IS DEATH.
YOU WANT TO TALK EMPIRES, LEOPOLD, I'D START WITH ROBESPIERRE.
GREAT BIG ANNIE WILKES #1 FAN OF THE GUILLOTINE-- RIGHT UNTIL THE DAY HE WOUND UP WITH HIS HEAD IN A BASKET.
A GREAT MANY HEADS MAY HAVE TO ROLL BEFORE THIS IS DONE, ADAM.
BUT WITH YOUR PARTICIPATION, NONE OF THOSE HEADS NEED BE YOURS...

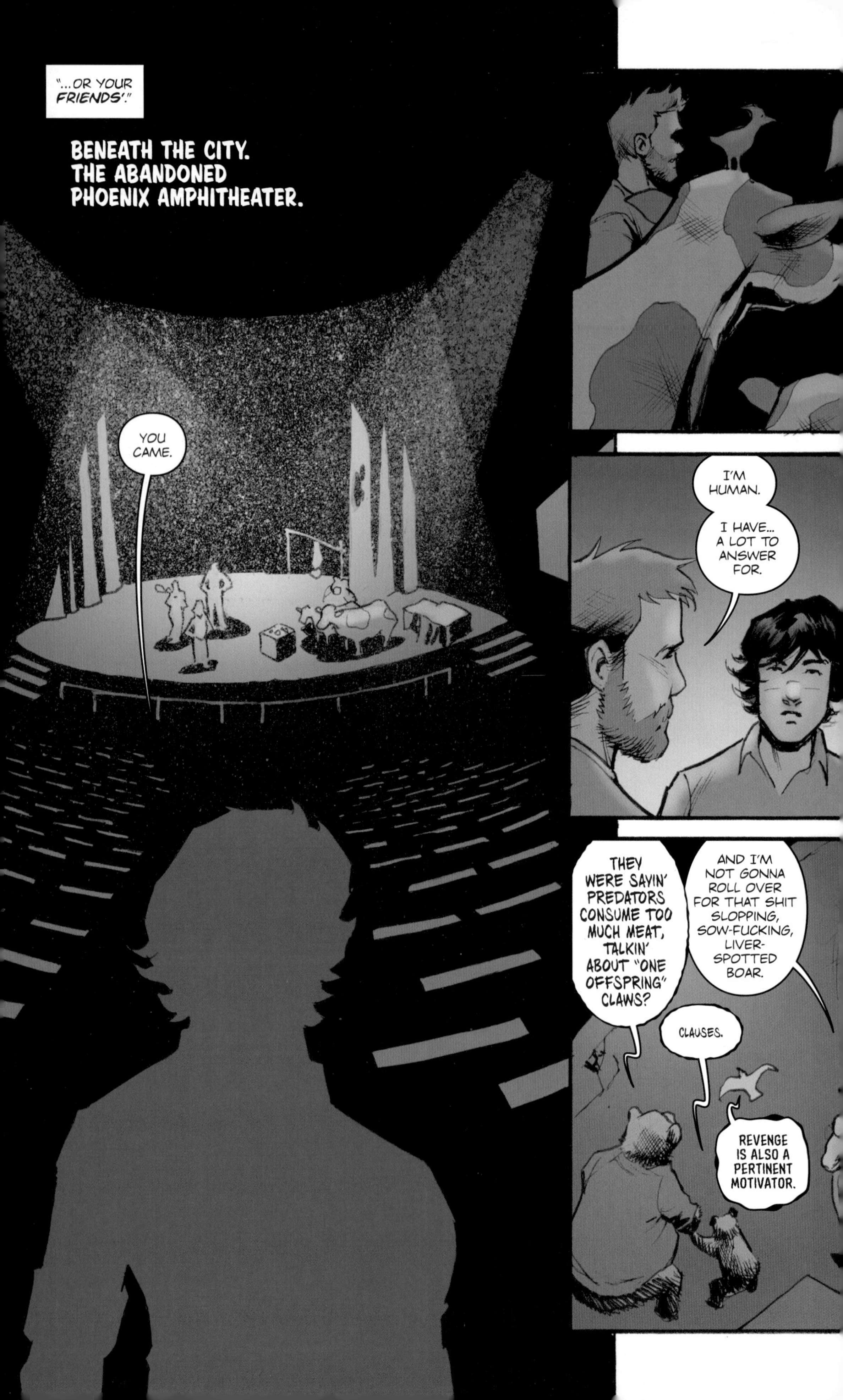
"...OR YOUR FRIENDS'."
BENEATH THE CITY. THE ABANDONED PHOENIX AMPHITHEATER.
YOU CAME.
I'M HUMAN.
I HAVE... A LOT TO ANSWER FOR.
THEY WERE SAYIN' PREDATORS CONSUME TOO MUCH MEAT, TALKIN' ABOUT "ONE OFFSPRING" CLAWS?
AND I'M NOT GONNA ROLL OVER FOR THAT SHIT SLOPPING, SOW-FUCKING, LIVER-SPOTTED BOAR.
CLAUSES.
REVENGE IS ALSO A PERTINENT MOTIVATOR.

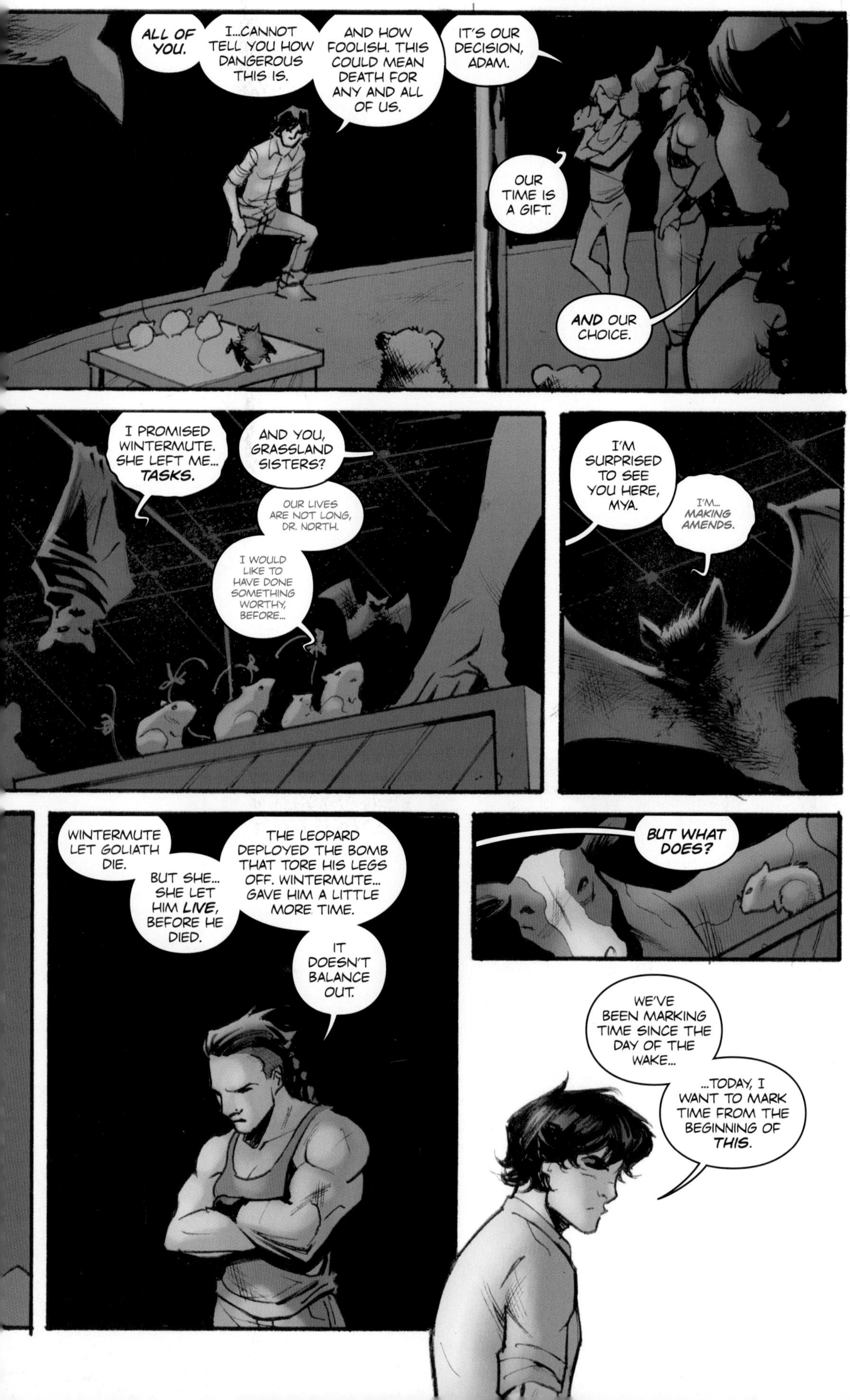
ALL OF YOU.
I...CANNOT TELL YOU HOW DANGEROUS THIS IS.
AND HOW FOOLISH. THIS COULD MEAN DEATH FOR ANY AND ALL OF US.
IT'S OUR DECISION, ADAM.
OUR TIME IS A GIFT.
AND OUR CHOICE.
I PROMISED WINTERMUTE. SHE LEFT ME... TASKS.
AND YOU, GRASSLAND SISTERS?
OUR LIVES ARE NOT LONG, DR. NORTH.
I WOULD LIKE TO HAVE DONE SOMETHING WORTHY, BEFORE...
I'M SURPRISED TO SEE YOU HERE, MYA.
I'M... MAKING AMENDS.
WINTERMUTE LET GOLIATH DIE.
BUT SHE... SHE LET HIM LIVE, BEFORE HE DIED.
THE LEOPARD DEPLOYED THE BOMB THAT TORE HIS LEGS OFF. WINTERMUTE... GAVE HIM A LITTLE MORE TIME.
IT DOESN'T BALANCE OUT.
BUT WHAT DOES?
WE'VE BEEN MARKING TIME SINCE THE DAY OF THE WAKE...
...TODAY, I WANT TO MARK TIME FROM THE BEGINNING OF THIS.

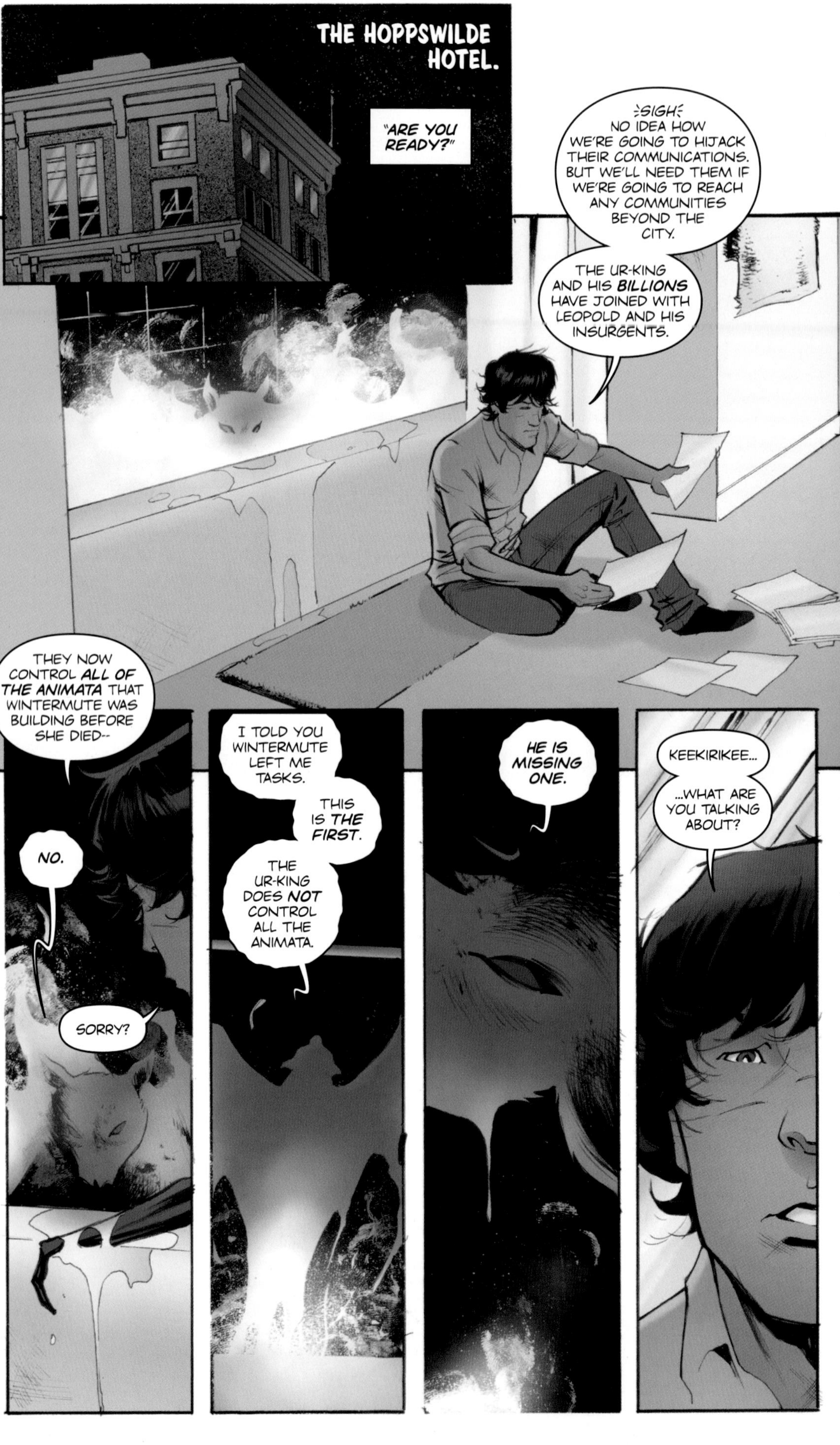
THE HOPPSWILDE HOTEL.
"ARE YOU READY?"
≶SIGH≷ NO IDEA HOW WE'RE GOING TO HIJACK THEIR COMMUNICATIONS. BUT WE'LL NEED THEM IF WE'RE GOING TO REACH ANY COMMUNITIES BEYOND THE CITY.
THE UR-KING AND HIS BILLIONS HAVE JOINED WITH LEOPOLD AND HIS INSURGENTS.
THEY NOW CONTROL ALL OF THE ANIMATA THAT WINTERMUTE WAS BUILDING BEFORE SHE DIED--
NO.
SORRY?
I TOLD YOU WINTERMUTE LEFT ME TASKS.
THIS IS THE FIRST.
THE UR-KING DOES NOT CONTROL ALL THE ANIMATA.
HE IS MISSING ONE.
KEEKIRIKEE...
...WHAT ARE YOU TALKING ABOUT?

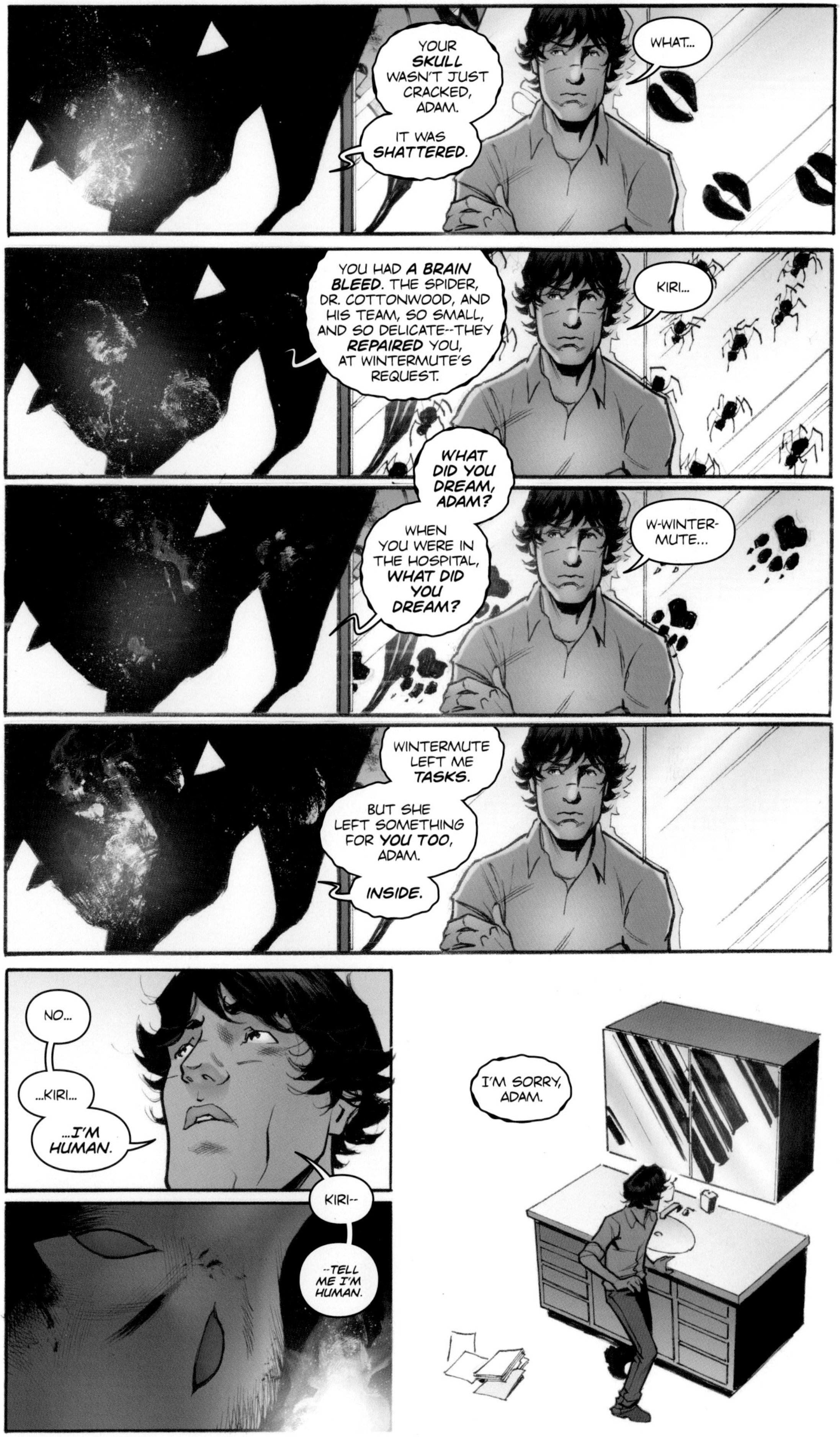

YOUR SKULL WASN'T JUST CRACKED, ADAM.
IT WAS SHATTERED.
WHAT...
YOU HAD A BRAIN BLEED. THE SPIDER, DR. COTTONWOOD, AND HIS TEAM, SO SMALL, AND SO DELICATE--THEY REPAIRED YOU, AT WINTERMUTE'S REQUEST.
KIRI...
WHAT DID YOU DREAM, ADAM?
WHEN YOU WERE IN THE HOSPITAL, WHAT DID YOU DREAM?
W-WINTER-MUTE...
WINTERMUTE LEFT ME TASKS.
BUT SHE LEFT SOMETHING FOR YOU TOO, ADAM.
INSIDE.
NO...
...KIRI...
...I'M HUMAN.
KIRI--
--TELL ME I'M HUMAN.
I'M SORRY, ADAM.

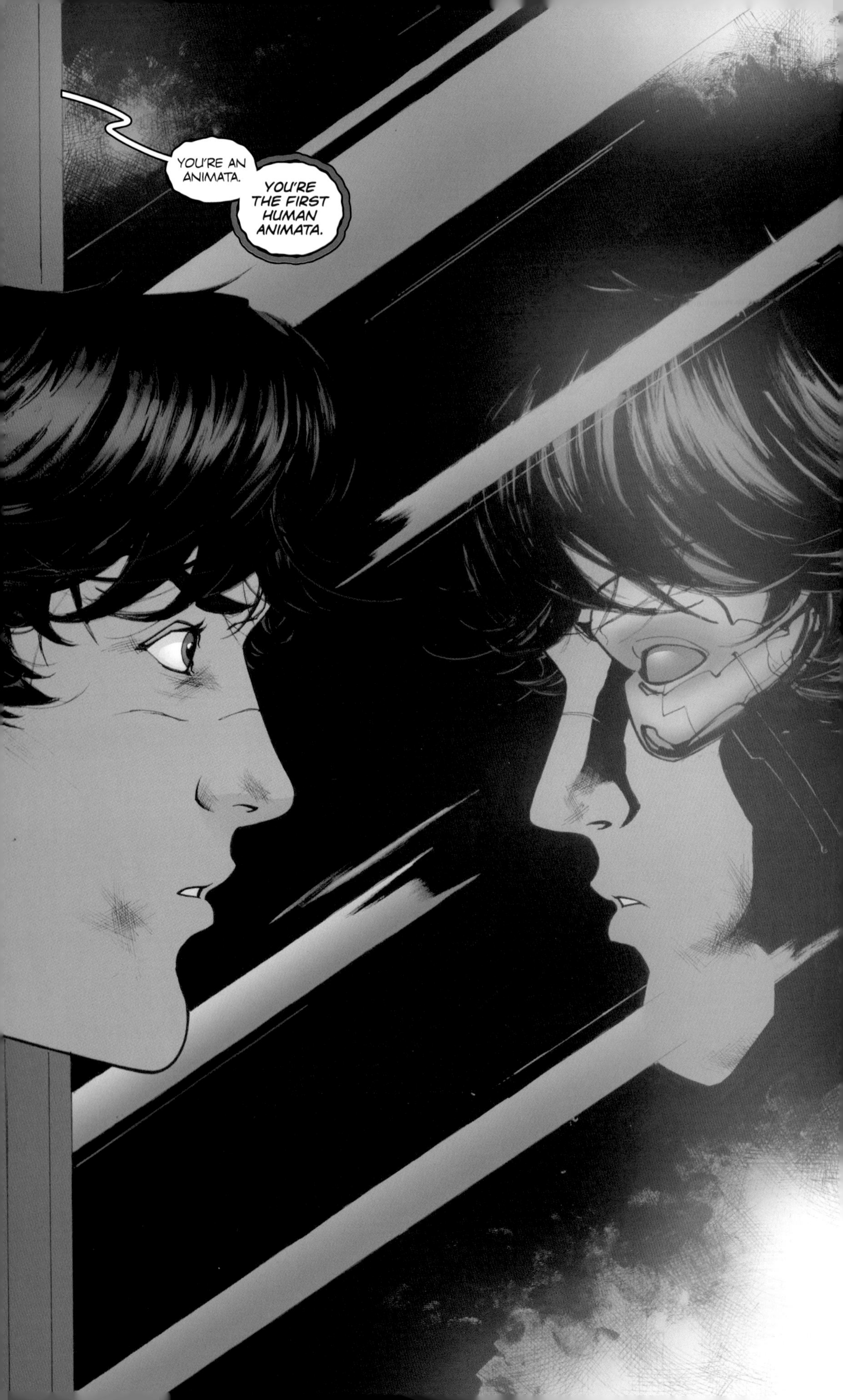
YOU'RE AN ANIMATA.
YOU'RE THE FIRST HUMAN ANIMATA.

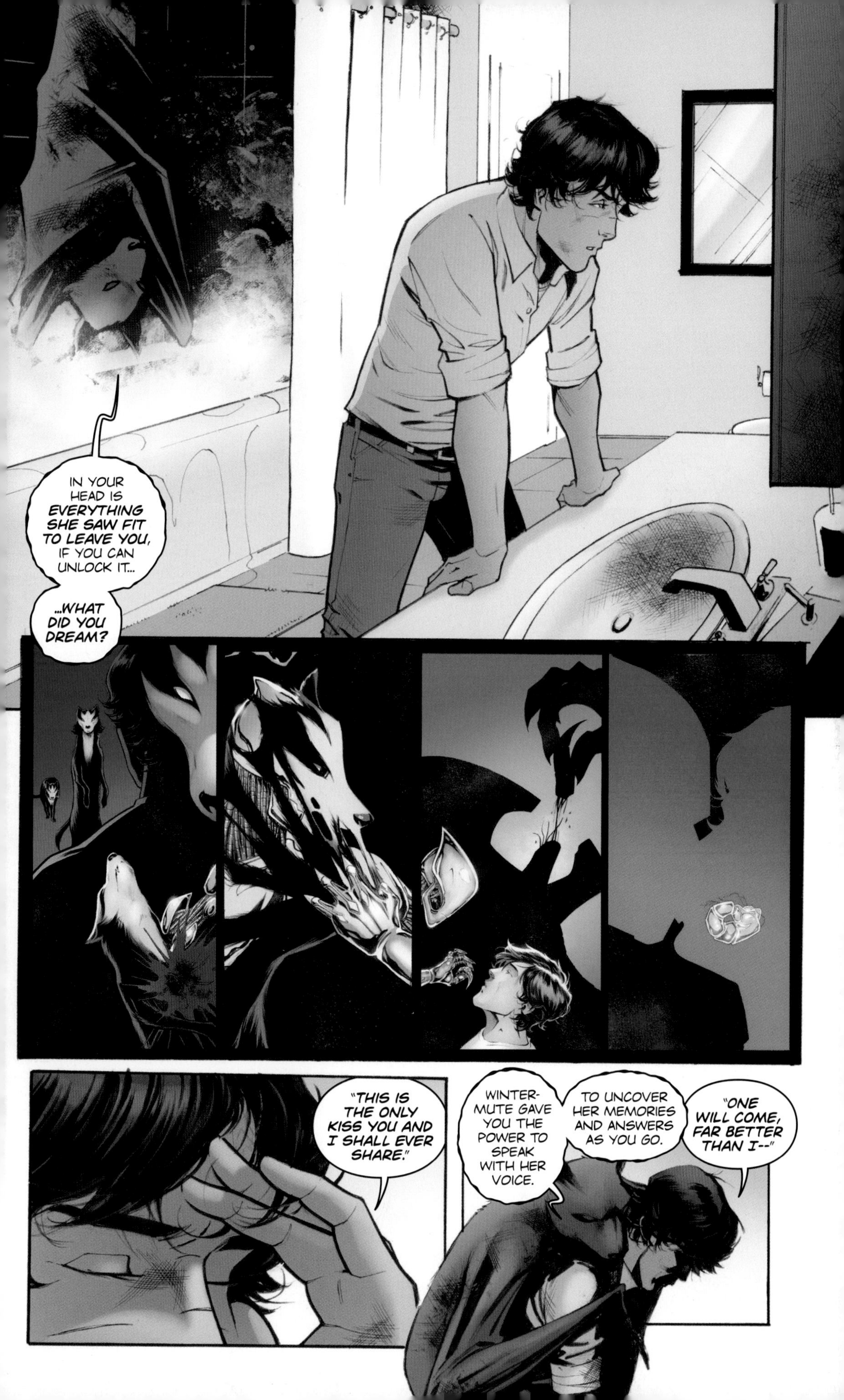
IN YOUR HEAD IS EVERYTHING SHE SAW FIT TO LEAVE YOU, IF YOU CAN UNLOCK IT...
...WHAT DID YOU DREAM?
"THIS IS THE ONLY KISS YOU AND I SHALL EVER SHARE."
WINTER-MUTE GAVE YOU THE POWER TO SPEAK WITH HER VOICE.
TO UNCOVER HER MEMORIES AND ANSWERS AS YOU GO.
"ONE WILL COME, FAR BETTER THAN I--"

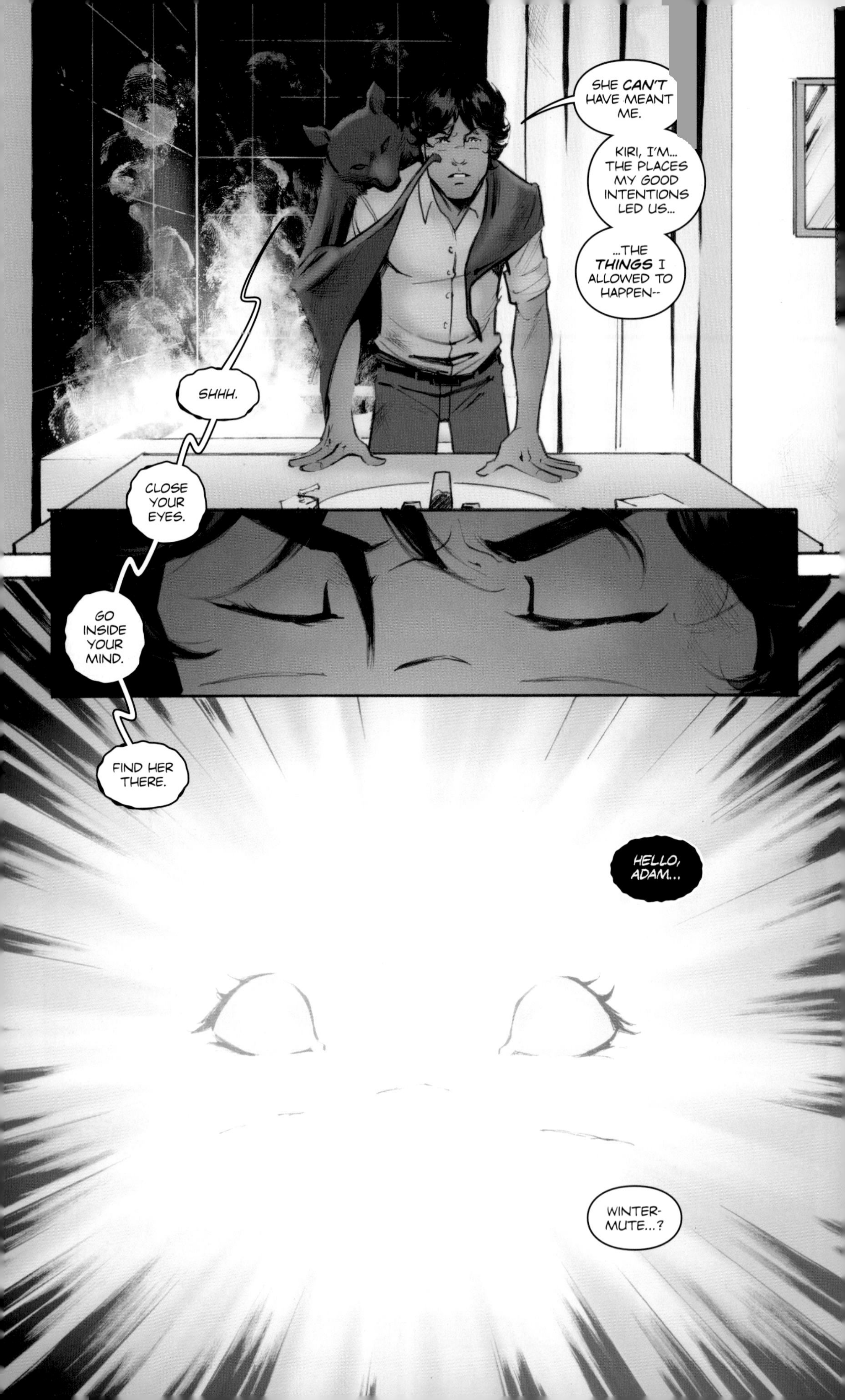
SHE *CAN'T* HAVE MEANT ME.
KIRI, I'M... THE PLACES MY GOOD INTENTIONS LED US...
...THE *THINGS* I ALLOWED TO HAPPEN--
SHHH.
CLOSE YOUR EYES.
GO INSIDE YOUR MIND.
FIND HER THERE.
HELLO, ADAM...
WINTER-MUTE...?

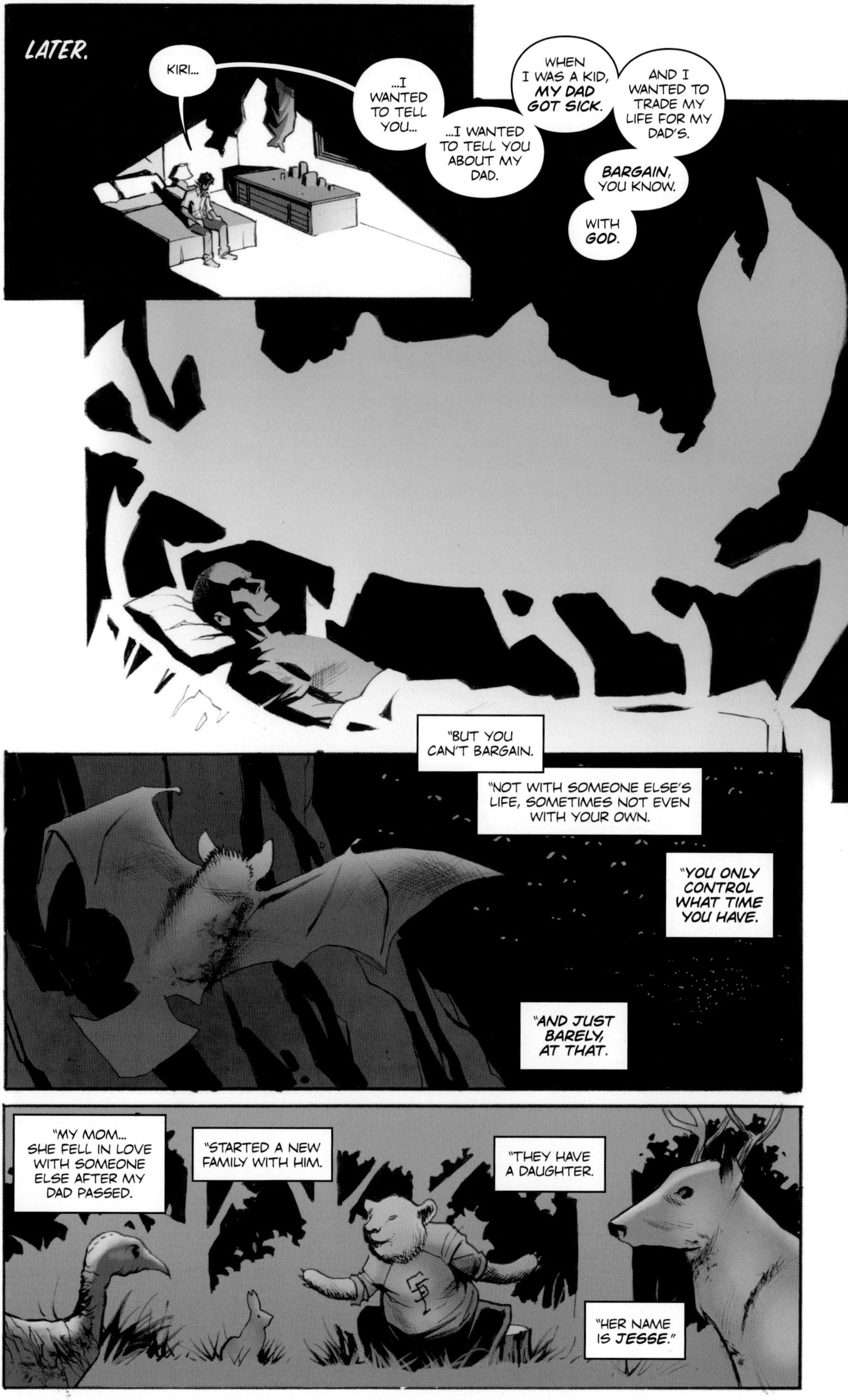
LATER.
KIRI...
...I WANTED TO TELL YOU...
...I WANTED TO TELL YOU ABOUT MY DAD.
WHEN I WAS A KID, MY DAD GOT SICK.
AND I WANTED TO TRADE MY LIFE FOR MY DAD'S.
BARGAIN, YOU KNOW.
WITH GOD.
"BUT YOU CAN'T BARGAIN.
"NOT WITH SOMEONE ELSE'S LIFE, SOMETIMES NOT EVEN WITH YOUR OWN.
"YOU ONLY CONTROL WHAT TIME YOU HAVE.
"AND JUST BARELY, AT THAT.
"MY MOM... SHE FELL IN LOVE WITH SOMEONE ELSE AFTER MY DAD PASSED.
"STARTED A NEW FAMILY WITH HIM.
"THEY HAVE A DAUGHTER.
"HER NAME IS JESSE."

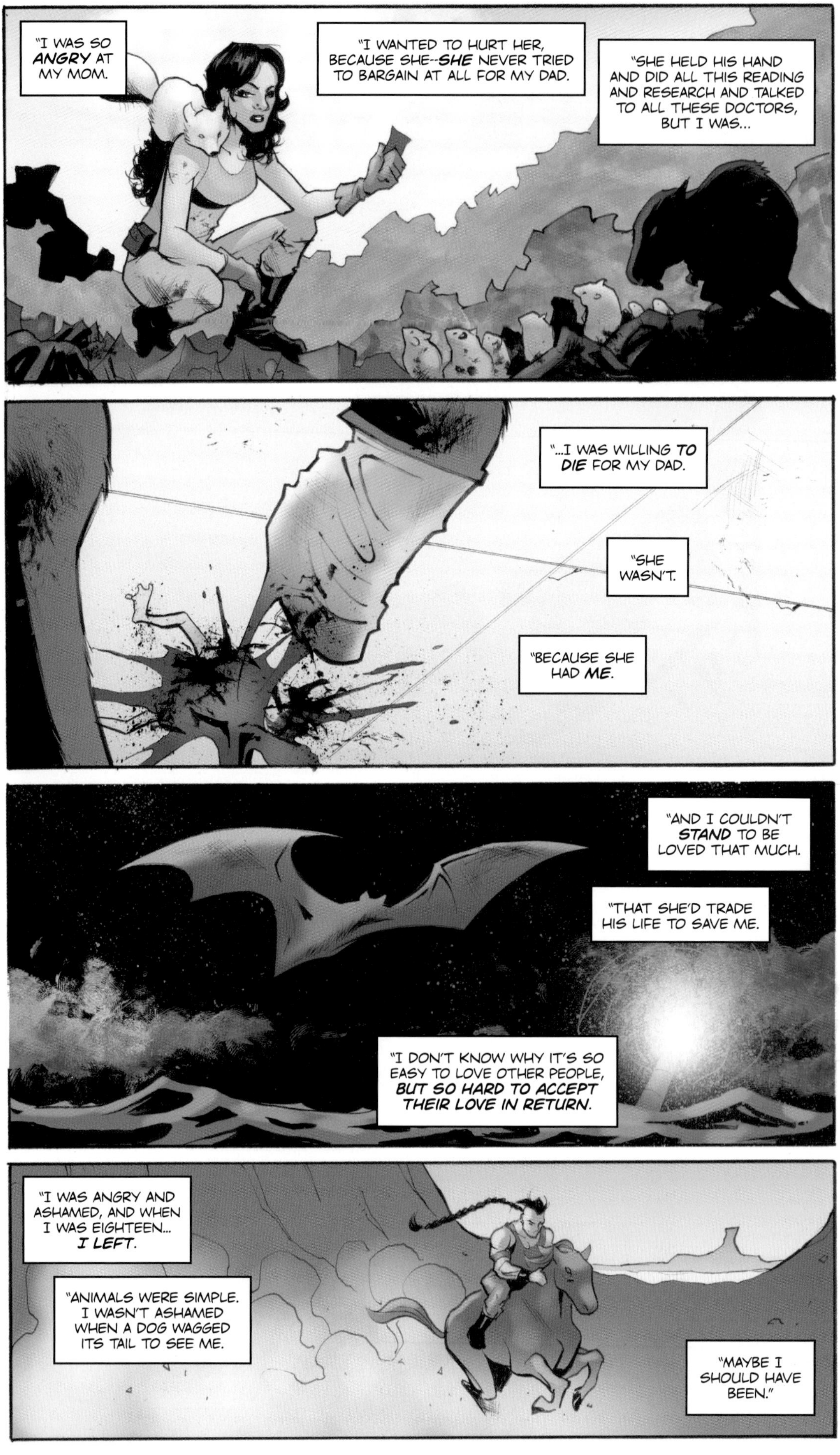
"I WAS SO ANGRY AT MY MOM.
"I WANTED TO HURT HER, BECAUSE SHE--SHE NEVER TRIED TO BARGAIN AT ALL FOR MY DAD.
"SHE HELD HIS HAND AND DID ALL THIS READING AND RESEARCH AND TALKED TO ALL THESE DOCTORS, BUT I WAS...
"...I WAS WILLING TO DIE FOR MY DAD.
"SHE WASN'T.
"BECAUSE SHE HAD ME.
"AND I COULDN'T STAND TO BE LOVED THAT MUCH.
"THAT SHE'D TRADE HIS LIFE TO SAVE ME.
"I DON'T KNOW WHY IT'S SO EASY TO LOVE OTHER PEOPLE, BUT SO HARD TO ACCEPT THEIR LOVE IN RETURN.
"I WAS ANGRY AND ASHAMED, AND WHEN I WAS EIGHTEEN... I LEFT.
"ANIMALS WERE SIMPLE. I WASN'T ASHAMED WHEN A DOG WAGGED ITS TAIL TO SEE ME.
"MAYBE I SHOULD HAVE BEEN."

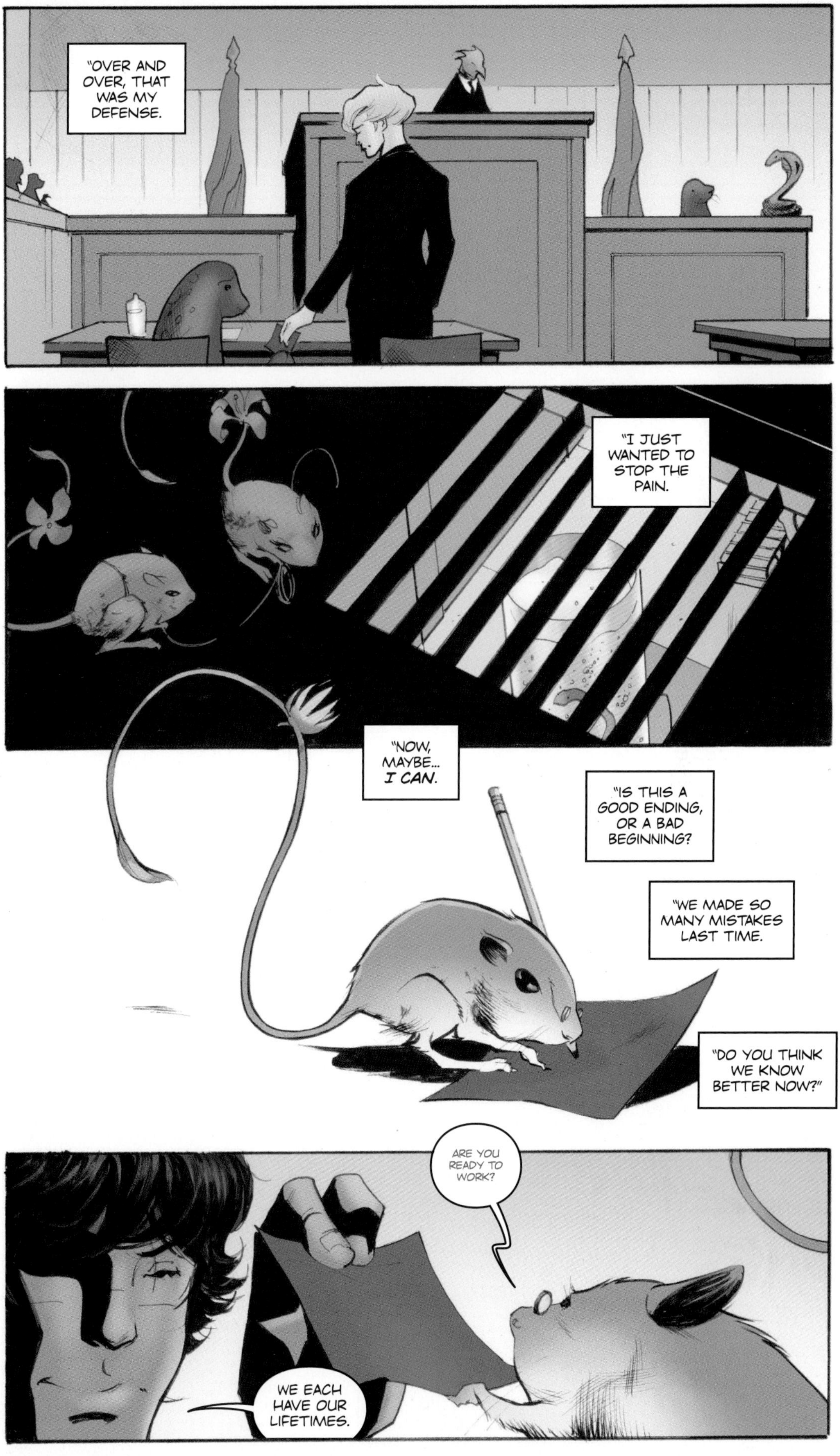
"OVER AND OVER, THAT WAS MY DEFENSE.
"I JUST WANTED TO STOP THE PAIN.
"NOW, MAYBE... *I CAN*.
"IS THIS A GOOD ENDING, OR A BAD BEGINNING?
"WE MADE SO MANY MISTAKES LAST TIME.
"DO YOU THINK WE KNOW BETTER NOW?"
ARE YOU READY TO WORK?
WE EACH HAVE OUR LIFETIMES.

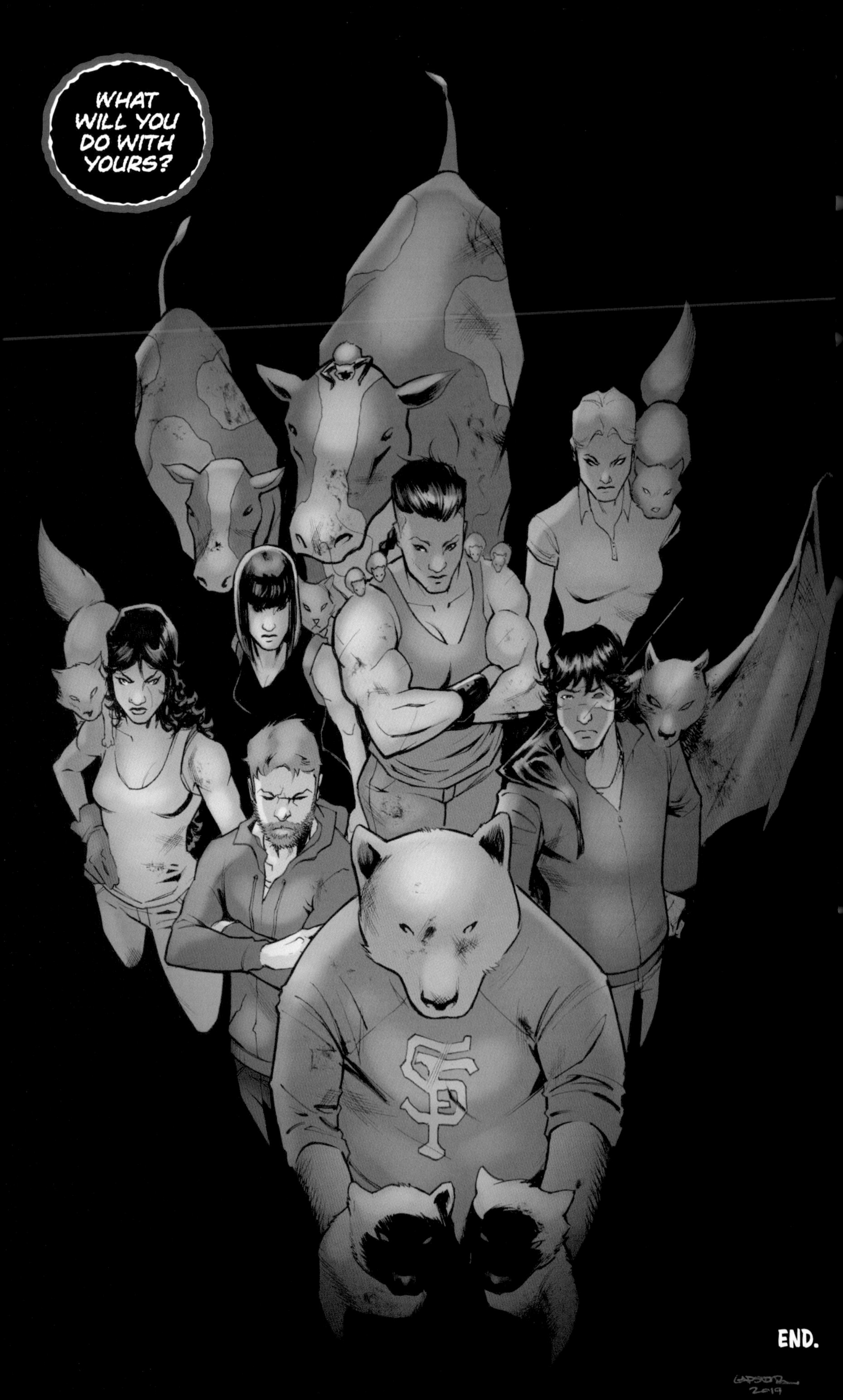
WHAT WILL YOU DO WITH YOURS?
END.

ANIMOSITY: EVOLUTION ™

BEHIND THE SCENES

#7

PAGES
2-3
PROCESS

ANIMOSITY: EVOLUTION #7
PAGE TWO – THREE (1 Panel)

Massive more-than-splash.
ADAM is in a murky dead space beyond that looks crazy and feverish—bizarre colors, inverted inks, Jen Bartel neons in a cosmos. We are in Adam's fever dream. Balls to the wall craziness. A blended forest and cityscape, filled with weirdo imagery—forest trees between buildings, tiny windows (as if from skyscrapers) inside the trunks of the trees, animal skulls hanging from the branches, ANIMALS in human clothing, a huge banner painted with the words "Because they can't tell us where it hurts," and a massive CRAB that crouches above everything, big as a mountain (perhaps too big to fit everything).

1 ADAM CAPTION: The holy books tell different tales about the sons of Abraham.
2 ADAM CAPTION: The Hebrew Bible says that Isaac was chosen, and went all unknowing to his death.

3 STYLIZED CAPTION: "Behold the fire and the wood: but where is the lamb for a burnt offering?" (Genesis 22:7)

4 ADAM CAPTION: The Qu'ran says that Ishmael was chosen, and readied his heart.

5 STYLIZED CAPTION: "O my father, do as you are commanded. You will find me, if Allah wills, among the steadfast." (QS 37: 102)

6 ADAM CAPTION: I only wanted to be a good son, for my mother, for my father.
7 ADAM CAPTION: And here is what I learned in my attempt:

8 ADAM CAPTION: *You can't bribe God.*

9 ADAM CAPTION: God doesn't care about pain.
10 ADAM CAPTION: So I decided that *I* had to care.

11 ADAM CAPTION: I never gave a damn about *good* or *evil* or *any of it.*
12 ADAM CAPTION: I only cared about *pain*, and *how to make it stop.*

13 ADAM CAPTION: But nothing has worked.
14 ADAM CAPTION: Every day, I help a tyrant rule a city of huddled masses, starving and laboring for a dream they won't survive to see.
15 ADAM CAPTION: I can't live and be good.
16 ADAM CAPTION: I can't die and be good.
17 ADAM CAPTION: I thought that if I protected Wintermute, she might be able to save them all.

18 ADAM CAPTION: We both just want an end to pain.
19 ADAM CAPTION: How do we do that, in a world that seems to need pain to survive?
20 ADAM CAPTION: What is the answer?
21 ADAM CAPTION: *What deal can I make?*

script by
MARGUERITE BENNETT

art by
ERIC GAPSTUR

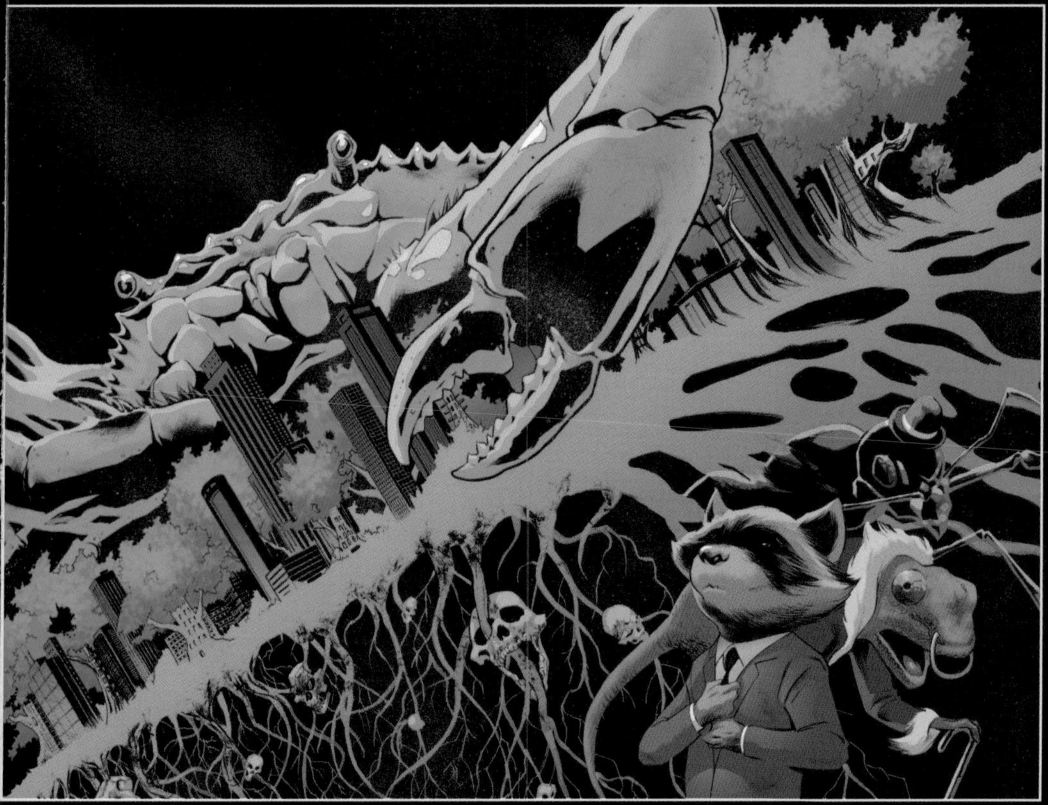

colors by
ROB SCHWAGER

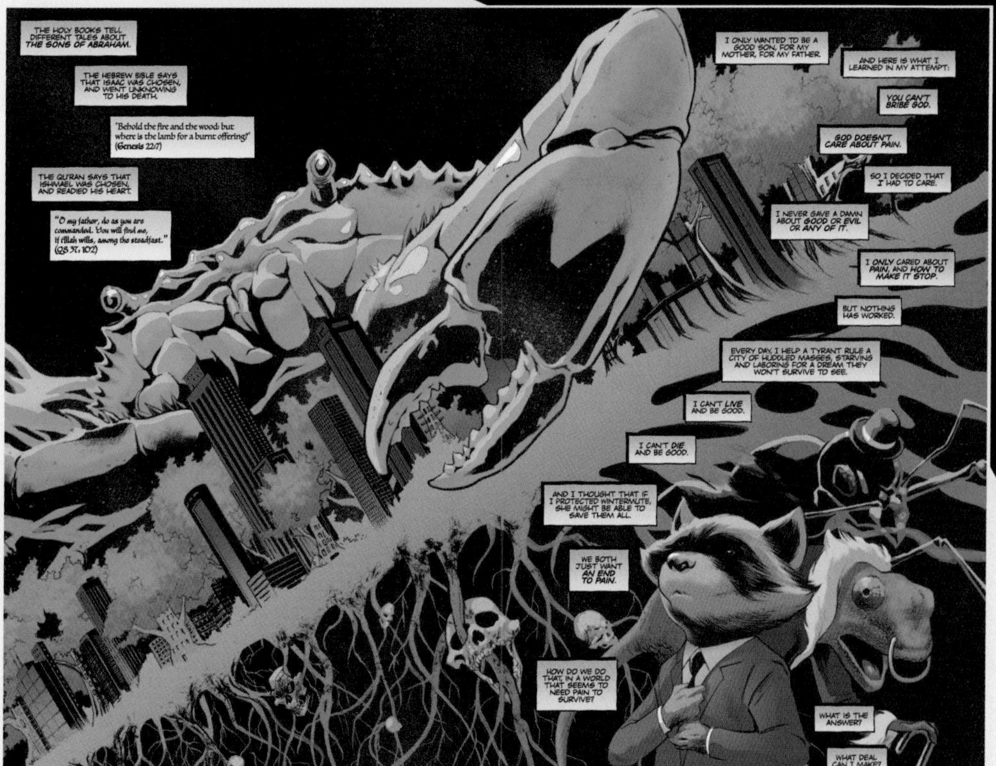
THE HOLY BOOKS TELL DIFFERENT TALES ABOUT THE SONS OF ABRAHAM.
THE HEBREW BIBLE SAYS THAT ISAAC WAS CHOSEN, AND WENT UNKNOWING TO HIS DEATH.
"Behold the fire and the wood: but where is the lamb for a burnt offering?" (Genesis 22:7)
THE QU'RAN SAYS THAT ISHMAEL WAS CHOSEN, AND READIED HIS HEART.
"O my father, do as you are commanded. You will find me, if Allah wills, among the steadfast." (QS 37:102)
I ONLY WANTED TO BE A GOOD SON, FOR MY MOTHER, FOR MY FATHER.
AND HERE IS WHAT I LEARNED IN MY ATTEMPT:
YOU CAN'T BRIBE GOD.
GOD DOESN'T CARE ABOUT PAIN.
SO I DECIDED THAT I HAD TO CARE.
I NEVER GAVE A DAMN ABOUT GOOD OR EVIL OR ANY OF IT.
I ONLY CARED ABOUT PAIN, AND HOW TO MAKE IT STOP.
BUT NOTHING HAS WORKED.
EVERY DAY, I HELP A TYRANT RULE A CITY OF HUDDLED MASSES, STARVING AND LABORING FOR A DREAM THEY WON'T SURVIVE TO SEE.
I CAN'T LIVE AND BE GOOD.
I CAN'T DIE AND BE GOOD.
AND I THOUGHT THAT IF I PROTECTED WINTERMUTE, SHE MIGHT BE ABLE TO SAVE THEM ALL.
WE BOTH JUST WANT AN END TO PAIN.
HOW DO WE DO THAT, IN A WORLD THAT SEEMS TO NEED PAIN TO SURVIVE?
WHAT IS THE ANSWER?
WHAT DEAL CAN I MAKE?

lettering by
MARSHALL DILLON

EV(O)LUTION™

ANIMOSITY:

#10

ANIMOSITY: EVOLUTION #10
PAGE TWENTY (1 Panel)

Final splash page.

ADAM stands amid the humans and Animals, as these strange allies who will begin a true rebellion against the Ur-King and everything Leopold has brought above. A call to action. We see them from slightly above, and their positions create WINTERMUTE'S FACE, with ADAM as her red eye. His own eye is blazing red.

ADAM, KIRI, OCTAVIA AND HER SISTERS, MYA, IRENE, MAKALA, CHARLIE, SARAH, THE MOTHER BEAR AND HER CUBS, PENNY, OLLIE, DOMNALL, SALIX, GWENDOLYN, etc, filled out with any new recruits you so desire.

1 WINTERMUTE (VO, red circle):

What will you do with yours?

script by
MARGUERITE BENNETT

PAGE
20
PROCESS

art by
ERIC GAPSTUR

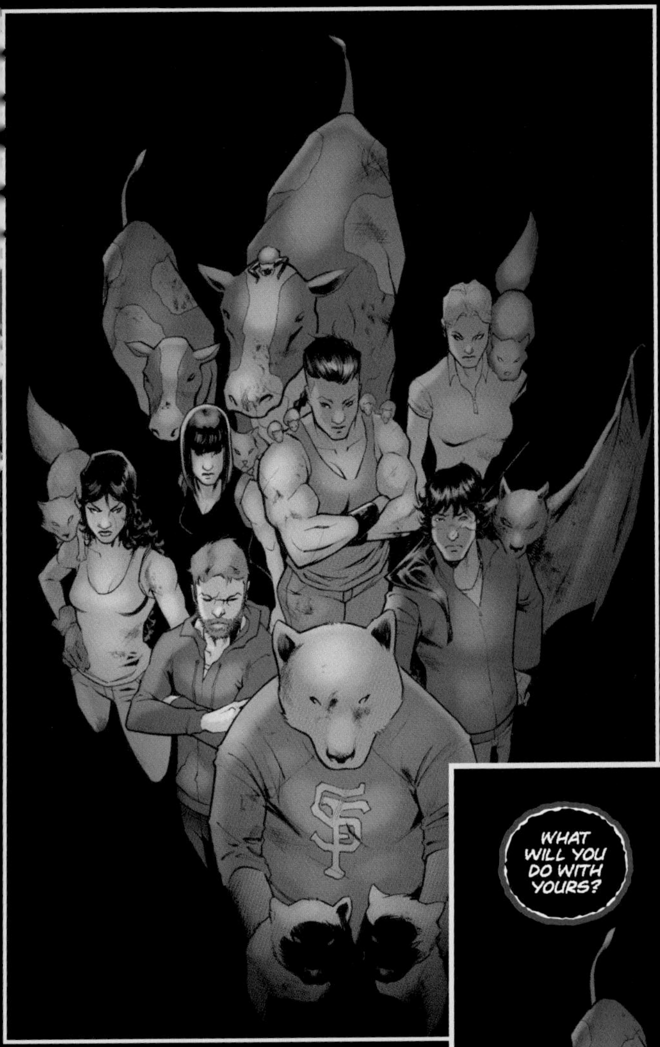

colors by
ROB SCHWAGER

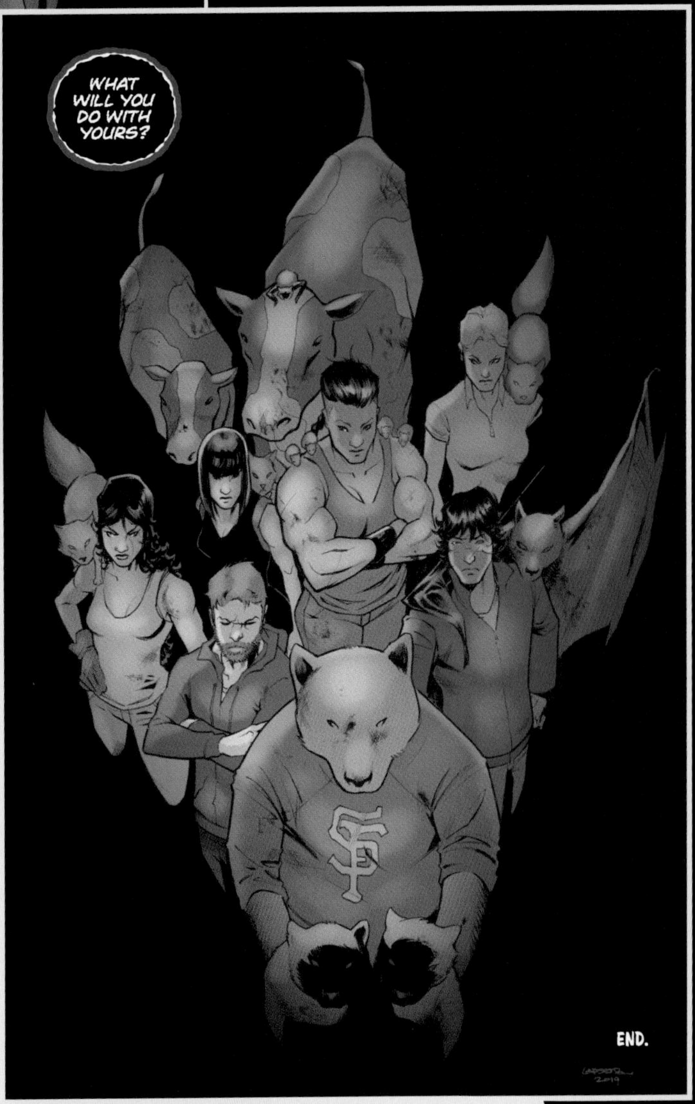

WHAT WILL YOU DO WITH YOURS?
END.

lettering by
MARSHALL DILLON

ABOUT THE CREATORS OF

ANIMOSITY: EVOLUTION™

MARGUERITE BENNETT writer

@EvilMarguerite

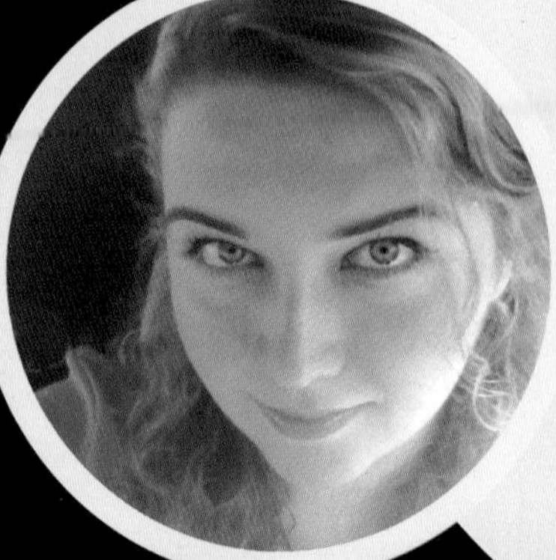

Marguerite Bennett is a comic book writer from Richmond, Virginia, who currently splits her time between Los Angeles and New York City. She received her MFA in Creative Writing from Sarah Lawrence College in 2013 and quickly went on to work for DC Comics, Marvel, BOOM! Studios, Dynamite, and IDW on projects ranging from *Batman*, *Bombshells*, and *A-Force* to *Angela: Asgard's Assassin*, *Red Sonja*, and FOX TV's *Sleepy Hollow*.

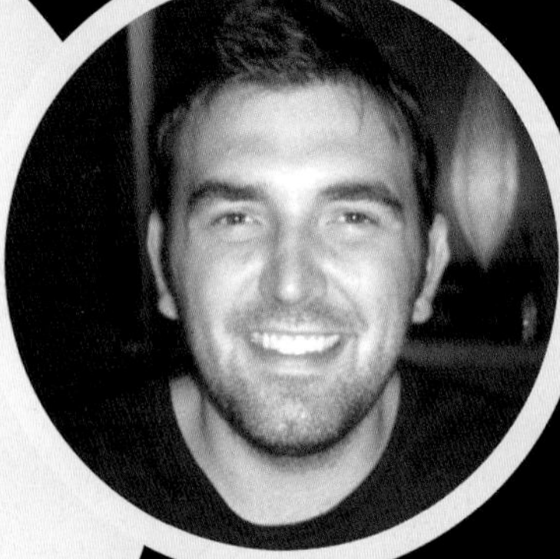

ERIC GAPSTUR artist

@EricGapstur

Eric has been creating comics professionally since 2011, most notably inking Phil Hester on such titles as *Legends of the Dark Knight*, *Adventures of Superman* and *Batman Beyond 2.0*. Additionally, Eric is pencilling *Flash: Season Zero*. He lives in Eastern Iowa with his wife, Michelle, and son, Liam.

ROB SCHWAGER colorist

@RobSchwager

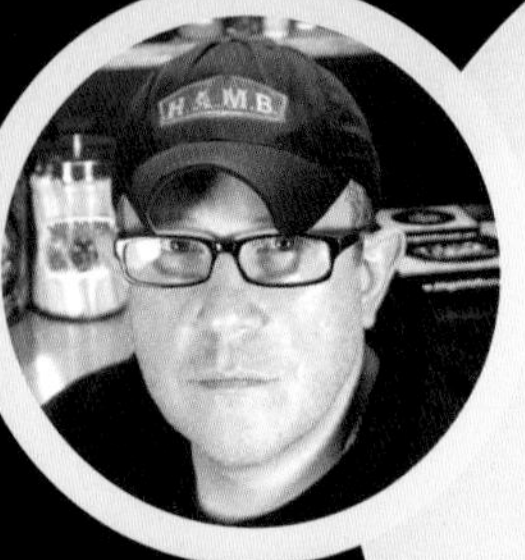

Rob Schwager is a self taught artist with over twenty-five years experience as a colorist in the comic book industry. He's worked on such iconic titles as *Batman*, *Superman*, *Green Lantern*, *Jonah Hex*, *Ghost Rider*, *Deadpool*, *Spider-Man*, *X-Men* and many others. He currently resides in the Tampa Bay area with his wife and three children and is extremely excited to be part of the AfterShock family of creators.

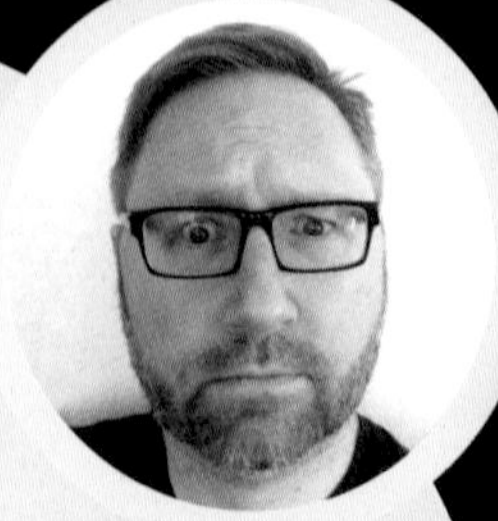

MARSHALL DILLON letterer

@MarshallDillon

A comic book industry veteran, Marshall got his start in 1994, in the midst of the indie comic boom. Over the years, he's been everything from an independent self-published writer to an associate publisher working on properties like *G.I. Joe*, *Voltron*, and *Street Fighter*. He's done just about everything except draw a comic book, and worked for just about every publisher except the "big two." Primarily a father and letterer these days, he also dabbles in old-school paper and dice RPG game design. You can catch up with Marshall at firstdraftpress.net.